The Seamanship Examiner

For STCW Certification Examinations

Other Works Published by D.J. House

Seamanship Techniques, 3rd Edition, 2004, Elsevier Butterworth-Heinemann, ISBN 0750663154

Seamanship Techniques, Volume III 'The Command Companion', 2000, Elsevier Butterworth-Heinemann, ISBN 0750644435

Marine Survival and Rescue Systems, 2nd Edition, 1997, Witherby, ISBN 1856091279

Navigation for Masters, 3rd Edition, 2005, Witherby, ISBN 1856092712

An Introduction to Helicopter Operations at Sea – A Guide for Industry, 2nd Edition, 1998, ISBN 1856091686

Cargo Work, 7th Edition, 2005, Elsevier Butterworth-Heinemann, ISBN 0750665556

Anchor Practice – A Guide for Industry, 2001, Witherby, ISBN 1856092127

Marine Ferry Transports – An Operators Guide, 2002, Witherby, ISBN 1856092313

Dry Docking and Shipboard Maintenance, 2003, Witherby, ISBN 1856092453

Heavy Lift and Rigging, 2005, Brown Son and Ferguson, ISBN 0851747205

Website www.djhouseonline.com

The Seamanship Examiner

For STCW Certification Examinations

D.J. House

With Interactive CD (Rules of the Road & Buoyage) by *Farhan Saeed*

ELSEVIER
BUTTERWORTH
HEINEMANN

AMSTERDAM • BOSTON • HEIDELBERG • LONDON • NEW YORK • OXFORD
PARIS • SAN DIEGO • SAN FRANCISCO • SINGAPORE • SYDNEY • TOKYO

Elsevier Butterworth-Heinemann
Linacre House, Jordan Hill, Oxford OX2 8DP
30 Corporate Road, Burlington, MA 01803

First Edition 2005

British Library Cataloguing in Publication Data
A catalogue record for this book is available from the British Library

Library of Congress Control Number: 2005924354

ISBN 0 7506 6701 X

For information on all Elsevier Butterworth-Heinemann
publications visit our website at www.books.elsevier.com

Typeset by Charon Tec Pvt. Ltd, Chennai, India
website: http://www.charontec.com
Printed and bound in Great Britain

Working together to grow
libraries in developing countries

www.elsevier.com | www.bookaid.org | www.sabre.org

ELSEVIER   BOOK AID International   Sabre Foundation

Contents

About the Authors

D.J. House

David House became interested in a sea-going career between the ages of 12 and 15 during a period with the 'Sea Cadet Corps'. He then spent nearly 15 years in a variety of ships and trades after leaving his pre-sea days at the Fleetwood Nautical College. Since his sea-going period, he started to lecture in his main disciplines of Navigation and Seamanship and also started to write in 1979.

His first books, *Seamanship Techniques*, Volumes I and II, were published by Heinemann in 1988. Subsequent works have followed in the related topics of 'Navigation for Masters', 'Helicopter Operations at Sea', 'Marine Survival and Rescue Systems', 'The Command Companion', 'Cargo Work', 'Anchors and Anchor Practice', 'Marine Ferry Transports', 'Dry Docking and Shipboard Maintenance' and his latest work on 'Heavy Lift'.

His books continue to be widely read throughout the maritime nations of the world. Twelve books, all well illustrated, have been written to positively meet the needs of marine students and a demanding Marine Industry. This latest work is designed as a preparatory book for Mercantile Marine Officers expecting to take up a 'Certificate of Competency' (Deck). It was initially devised to provide students with an awareness of potential questions that may or may not arise at the Seamanship Oral Examination. However, it was abundantly clear during writing, that the formulated text was probably one of the better learning techniques for current and future mariners.

It is hoped that the work will benefit those whose chosen path is that of a seafarer.

Farhan Saeed

Farhan Saeed joined the Merchant Navy in 1988 and was engaged in worldwide trading as a deck officer on General Cargo ships, Container vessels, and Passenger vessels with the Pakistan National Shipping Corporation. His working career has been influenced by a variety of trades and cargoes inclusive of bulk loads, heavy lifts and unitised parcels. His marine experiences encompass derricks, cranes, gantries, as well as specialised lifting gear.

His marine studies, leading to a Master Mariners qualification, have been undertaken both in the Australian Maritime College and at the Fleetwood Nautical Campus in the UK. He became interested in the Information Technology explosion and developed himself in computing skills to obtain an MSc in 2001 from the University of Sunderland.

He is currently engaged as a Lecturer in Maritime Studies at the Fleetwood Campus where his computing skills and maritime background have contributed to his first published work and positive movement into anticipated research projects for the future.

As the co-author of the Seamanship Examiner, his contribution with the inclusion of the Interactive Compact Disc should hopefully provide the user with an insight into an enjoyable, marine learning programme.

Acknowledgements

Ankar Advies Bureau b.v.
C.M. Hammar AB, Sweden
Dubia Dry Docks U.A.E.
Henry Brown and Sons Ltd.
I.C. Brindle and Co.
Lloyds Beal Ltd.
Maritime Coastguard Agency
Smit International
United States Coastguard
Viking A/S Nordisk Gummibadsfabri
Viking Life Saving Equipment

ADDITIONAL PHOTOGRAPHY

Mr. K.B. Millar, Master Mariner, Lecturer Nautical Studies
Mr. N. Lovick, 3rd Officer (MN)
Mr. J. Leyland, Lecturer Maritime Safety and Security

I.T. Assistant Mr. C.D. House
Additional Assistance Mr. Amir Hameed

List of Maritime Abbreviations

AB — Able Seaman
ABS — American Bureau of Shipping
AC — (i) Admiralty Class (Cast)
    (ii) Alternating Current
ACV — Air Cushion Vessel
AHV — Anchor Handling Vessel
AIS — Automatic Identification Systems
ALRS — Admiralty List of Radio Signals
AMD — Advanced Multi-Hull Design
AMVER — Automated Mutual Vessel Reporting system
APP — Aft Perpendicular
ARCS — Admiralty Raster Chart Service
ARPA — Automatic Radar Plotting Aids
ATT — Admiralty Tide Tables
AUSREP — Australian Ship Reporting system
Aux — Auxiliary

B — Position of the Centre of Buoyancy
B/A — Breathing Apparatus
B/L — Bill of Lading
BP — (i) Between Perpendiculars
    (ii) British Petroleum
BS — (i) British Standards
    (ii) Breaking Strain
BST — British Summer Time
BT — Ballast Tank
BV — Bureau Veritas

cc — Corrosion Control (LR – notation)
CCTV — Closed-Circuit Television

CD   (i) Chart Datum
             (ii) Compact Disc
CDP   Controlled Depletion Polymers
CES   Coast Earth Station
CG   Coast Guard
CIE   International Commission on Illumination
CL   Centre Line
cm   Centimetres
CMG   Course Made Good
CML   Centre of Maritime Leadership (USA)
CNIS   Channel Navigation Information Service
CO   (alt. Ch. Off) Chief Officer
CO_2 Carbon Dioxide
COG   Course over Ground
C of B   Centre of Buoyancy
C of G   Centre of Gravity
COI   Certificate of Inspection (as issued by USCG)
ColRegs   The Regulations for the Prevention of Collisions at Sea
COW   Crude Oil Washing
C/P   Charter Party
CPA   Closest Point of Approach
CPP   Controllable Pitch Propeller
CPR   Cardiac Pulmonary Resuscitation
CRS   Coast Radio Station
CSH   Continuous Survey Hull
CSM   Continuous Survey Machinery
CSP   Commencement Search Pattern
CSS   (code) IMO code of Safe Practice for Cargo
            Stowage and Securing
CSWP   Code of Safe Working Practice
CW   Continuous Wave
cwt   Hundred weights

Da   Draugh Aft
DAT   Double Acting Tanker
dB   Decibels
DB   Double Bottom
DC   Direct Current
DD   Dry Dock
Df   Draught Forward
DGN   Dangerous Goods Note
DGPS   Differential Global Positioning System

Disp	Displacement
Dm	Midships Draught
DNV	Det Norske Veritas
DOC(Alt.DoC)	Document of Compliance
DP	Dynamic Position
DPA	Designated Person Ashore
DR	Dead Reckoning
DSC	(i) Digital Selective Calling
	(ii) Dynamically Supported Craft
DSV	Diving Support Vessel
DW	Dock Water
DWA	Dock Water Allowance
d.w.t. (dwt)	Deadweight Tonnage
E	East
EBM	(EBI) Electronic Bearing Marker
EC	European Community
ECDIS	Electronic Chart Display and Information System
ECR	Engine Control Room
EEBDs	Emergency Escape Breathing Device (IMO shipping by July 2002)
EFSWR	Extra Flexible Steel Wire Rope
ENC	Electronic Navigation Chart
EPIRB	Emergency Position Indicating Radio Beacon
ETA	Estimated Time of Arrival
ETD	Estimated Time of Departure
ETV	Emergency Towing Vessel
EU	European Union
FFA	Fire-Fighting Appliances
FLIR	Forward Looking Infra Red
FMECA	Failure Mode Effective Critical Analysis
FO	Fuel Oil
foap	Forward of Aft Perpendicular
F.Pk.	Fore Peak Tank
FPSOs	Floating Production Storage Offloading system
FPV	Fisheries Protection Vessel
FRC	Fast Rescue Craft
FRD (Fwd)	Forward
FSE	Free Surface Effect
FSMs	Free Surface Moments
FSU	Floating Storage Unit

FSW	Friction Stir Welding
FSWR	Flexible Steel Wire Rope
FW	Fresh Water
FWA	Fresh Water Allowance
FWE	Finished With Engines
G	Ships centre of gravity
gals	Gallons
GG_1	The distance measured from the ships original C of G, to a new position of the ships C of G
GHz	gigahertz
GL	Germanischer Lloyd
GM	Metacentric Height
GMDSS	Global Maritime Distress and Safety System
GMT (z)	Greenwich Mean Time
GPS	Global Positioning System
GRB	Garbage Record Book
GRP	Glass Reinforced Plastic
grt (GT)	Gross Registered Tonnage
GZ	Ships Righting Lever
HDOP	Horizontal Dilution of Precision
HEX	Hexagonal
HFO	Heavy Fuel Oil
H/L	Heavy Lift
HLO	Helicopter Landing Officer
HMS	Her Majesty's Ship
HMAS	Her Majesty's Australian Ship
HP	(i) Horse Power
	(ii) High Pressure
HPFWW	High Pressure Fresh Water Wash
HRN	House Recovery Net
HRU	Hydrostatic Release Unit
HSC	High Speed Craft
HSE	Health and Safety Executive
HSSC	Harmonised System of Survey and Certification
I	Intensity
IACS	International Association of Classification Societies
IALA	International Association of Lighthouse Authorities
IAMSAR	International Aeronautical and Marine Search & Rescue manual

ICS   International Chamber of Shipping
IE   Index Error
IFR   Instrument Flying Rating
IG   Inert Gas
IGS   Inert Gas System
IHO   International Hydrographic Office
IIP   International Ice Patrol
ILO   International Labour Organisation
IMDG   International Maritime Dangerous Goods (code)
IMO   International Maritime Organisation
INS   Integrated Navigation System
IOPPC   International Oil Pollution Prevention Certificate
IPS   Integrated Power System (Controllable 'Podded' propulsion)
IRF   Incident Report Form
ISM   International Safety Management (code)
ISO   International Organisation of Standardisation
ITP   Intercept Terminal Point
IWS   In Water Survey

K   Representative of the position of the ships keel
KG   The distance measured from the Keel to the Ships C of G
kg   Kilogram
KM   The distance measured from the keel to the Metacentre 'M'
kN   Kilo Newtons
kts   Knots
kW   Kilowatt

Lat   Latitude
LBP   Length Between Perpendiculars
lbs   Pounds
LCD   Liquid Crystal Display
LCG   Longitudinal Centre of Gravity
LCV   Landing Craft vessel
LFL   Lower Flammable Limit
LMC   Lloyds Machinery Certificate
LNG   Liquid Natural Gas
LOA   Length Overall
LOF   Lloyds Open Form (salvage)
Lo-Lo   Load on, Load off
LL   Long Longitude
LP   Low Pressure
LPG   Liquid Petroleum Gas

LR	Lloyds Register
LSA	Life Saving Appliances
LUT	Land User Terminal
M	Metacentre
m	meters
MAIB	Marine Accident Investigation Branch
MARPOL	Marine Pollution (convention)
MCA	Maritime and Coastguard Agency
MEC	Marine Evacuation Chute
Medivac	Medical Evacuation
MEPC	Marine Environment Protection Committee
MES	Marine Evacuation System
MEWP	Mobile Elevator Work Platform (Cherry Picker)
MF	Medium Frequency (300 kHz to 3 MHz)
MFAG	Medical First Aid Guide (for use with accidents involving dangerous goods)
MGN	Marine Guidance Notice
MHR	Mean Hull Roughness
MHz	Megahertz
MIN	Marine Information Notice
MMSI	Maritime Mobile Service Identity Number
MN	Mercantile Marine (Merchant Navy)
MNTB	Merchant Navy Training Board
MoB	Man over Board
MODU	Mobile Offshore Drilling Unit
MOT	Ministry of Transport
MPCU	Marine Pollution Control Unit
Mrad	Metre Radians
MRCC	Marine Rescue Co-ordination Centre
MSC	Maritime Safety Committee (of IMO)
MSI	Marine Safety Information
MSN	Merchant Shipping Notice
MTC	Moment to Change Trim 1 centimetre
MV	Motor Vessel
MW	Mega Watt
N	North
NE	North East
nm	Nautical Miles
NOE	Notice of Eligibility
NUC	Not Under Command

NVE	Night Vision Equipment
NVQ	National Vocational Qualification
NW	North West
O/A	Overall
OBO	Oil, Bulk, Ore (Carrier)
OiC	Officer in Charge
OIM	Offshore Installation Manager
OLB	Official Log Book
OMBO	One Man Bridge Operation
OOW	Officer of the Watch
OPIC	Oil Pollution Insurance Certificate
ORB	Oil Record Book
O/S	Offshore
OSC	(i) On Scene Commander
	(ii) On Scene Co-ordinator
OSV	Offshore Standby Vessel
P	Port
P/A	Public Address System
P&I (club)	Protection and Indemnity
PEC	Pilot Exemption Certificate
PHA	Preliminary Hazard Analysis
P/L	Position Line
PPI	Plan Position Indicator
ppm	Parts per million
PRS	Polish Register of Shipping
PSC	Port State Control
psi	Pounds per square inch
pts	pints
RAF	Royal Air Force
RBD	Return of Births and Deaths
RCDS	Raster Chart Display System
RCC	Rescue Co-ordination Centre
RD	Relative Density
RGSS	Register General of Shipping and Seaman
RINA	Registro Italiano Navale (Classification Society – Italy)
RMC	Refrigerated Machinery Certificate
RMS	Royal Mail Ship
RN	Royal Navy
Ro-Pax	Roll On–Roll Off Passenger Vessel
Ro-Ro	Roll On–Roll Off

RoT   Rate of Turn
ROV   Remotely Operated Vehicle
rpm   revolutions per minute
RS   Reflected Sun
RT   Radio Telephone
Rx   Receiver

S   South
S (stbd)   Starboard
SAR   Search and Rescue
SART   Search and Rescue Transponder
SATCOM   Satellite Communications
SBE   Stand By Engines
SBM   Single Buoy Mooring
SCBA   Self-Contained Breathing Apparatus
SE   South East
SEP   Ships Emergency Plans
SES   Ship Earth Station
SF   Stowage Factor
SFP   Structural Fire Protection
sg   Specific Gravity
shp   Shaft Horse Power
SI   Statutory Instrument
SMC   Safety Management Certificate
SMG   Speed Made Good
SMS   Safety Management System
SOG   Speed Over Ground
SOLAS   Safety of Life at Sea (Convention)
SOPEP   Ships Oil Pollution Emergency Plan
SPC   Self Polishing Copolymer (Anti-Fouling Paint)
SPM   Single Point Mooring
SQU (sq)   Square
SS   Steam Ship
SSA   Ship Building and Ship Repair Association
STCW   Standards of Training, Certification and Watchkeeping
SW   Salt Water
SWATH   Small Waterplane Area Twin Hull
SWL   Safe Working Load
SWR   Steel Wire Rope

TBT   Tributyltin
TCPA   Time of Closest Point of Approach

TEMPSC	Totally Enclosed Motor Propelled Survival Craft
TEU	Twenty foot Equivalent Unit
Tk	Tank
TLV	Threshold Limit Value
TMC	Transmitting Magnetic Compass
TMCP	Thermo-mechanically controlled processed
TPA	Thermal Protective Aid
TPC	Tons per Centimetre
TRC	Type Rating Certificate
TRS	Tropical Revolving Storm
TS	True Sun
TSS	Traffic Separation Scheme
TWI	The Welding Institute
Tx	Transmitter
UAE	United Arab Emirates
UHP	Ultra High Pressure
UK	United Kingdom
UKC	Under Keel Clearance
UKOOA	United Kingdom Offshore Operators Association
UKOPP	United Kingdom Oil Pollution Prevention (cert)
ULCC	Ultra Large Crude Carrier
UMS	Unmanned Machinery Space
UNECE	United Nations Economic Commission for Europe
USA	United States of America
USCG	United States Coast Guard
UV	Ultra Violet
VCG	Vertical Centre of Gravity
VDR	Voyage Data Recorder
VDU	Visual Display Unit
VFI	Vertical Force Instrument
VHF	Very High Frequency
VLCC	Very Large Crude Carrier
VLGC	Very Large Gas Carrier
VTIS	Vessel Traffic Information Service
VTMS	Vessel Traffic Management System
VTS	Vessel Traffic Services
W	(i) West
	(ii) Representative of Ships Displacement
	(iii) Watts

WAT	Wing Assisted Trimaran
WBT	Water Ballast Tank
WIG	Wing in Ground-effect
W/L	Water Line
WPC	Wave Piercing Catamaran
wps	Wires per strand
W/T	Walkie Talkie Radio
z	Greenwich Mean Time (GMT)

Conversion and Measurement Table

IMPERIAL/METRIC MEASUREMENT

1 in. $= 2.5400$ cm	1 cm $= 0.3937$ in.
1 ft $= 0.3048$ m	1 m $= 3.2808$ ft

1 in.$^2 = 6.4516$ cm^2	1 cm$^2 = 0.1550$ in.^{2}
1 ft$^2 = 0.09293$ m^2	1 m$^2 = 10.7639$ ft^2

1 in.$^3 = 16.3871$ cm^3	1 cm$^3 = 0.0610$ m^3
1 ft$^3 = 0.02832$ m^3	1 m$^3 = 35.3146$ ft^2

Metres to feet

Centimetres	Feet	Metres	Feet	Metres	Feet	Metres	Feet
1	0.03	1	3.28	19	62.34	100	328.08
2	0.06	2	6.56	20	65.62	200	656.17
3	0.09	3	9.84	21	68.90	300	984.25
4	0.13	4	13.12	22	72.18	400	1312.33
5	0.16	5	16.40	23	75.46	500	1640.42
6	0.19	6	19.69	24	78.74	600	1968.50
7	0.22	7	22.97	25	82.02	700	2296.58
8	0.26	8	26.25	26	85.30	800	2624.66
9	0.30	9	29.53	27	88.58	900	2952.74
10	0.33	10	32.81	28	91.86	1000	3280.83
20	0.66	11	36.09	29	95.15		
30	0.98	12	39.37	30	98.43		
40	1.31	13	42.65	40	131.23		
50	1.64	14	45.93	50	164.04		
60	1.97	15	49.21	60	196.85		
70	2.30	16	52.49	70	229.66		
80	2.62	17	55.77	80	262.47		
90	2.95	18	59.06	90	295.28		

(*contd.*)

Feet to Metres

Inches	Metres	Feet	Metres	Feet	Metres	Feet	Metres
1	0.03	1	0.30	80	24.38	800	243.84
2	0.05	2	0.61	90	27.43	850	259.08
3	0.08	3	0.91	100	30.48	900	274.32
4	0.10	4	1.22	150	45.72	950	289.56
5	0.13	5	1.52	200	60.96	1000	304.80
6	0.15	6	1.83	250	76.20	1100	335.28
7	0.18	7	2.13	300	91.44	1200	365.76
8	0.20	8	2.44	350	106.68	1300	396.24
9	0.23	9	2.74	400	121.92	1400	426.72
10	0.25	10	3.05	450	137.16	1500	457.20
11	0.28	20	6.10	500	152.40	2000	609.60
12	0.30	30	9.14	550	167.64		
		40	12.19	600	182.88	3000	914.40
		50	15.24	650	198.12		
		60	18.29	700	213.36	4000	1219.20
		70	21.34	750	228.60	5000	1524.00

TONNAGE AND FLUID MEASUREMENT (MULTIPLICATION FACTORS)

	US gallons	Imperial gallons	Capacity cubic feet
1 gallon (imperial)	× 1.2	× 1	× 0.1604
1 gallon (US)	× 1.0	× 0.8333	× 0. 1337
1 cubic foot	× 7.48	× 0.2344	× 1.0
1 litre	× 0.2642	× 0.22	× 0.0353
1 ton fresh water	× 269	× 224	× 35.84
1 ton salt water	× 262.418	× 218.536	× 35

Weight	Short ton	Long ton	Metric ton
Long ton (imperial)	× 1.12	× 1.0	× 1.01605
Short ton (US)	× 1.0	× 0.89286	× 0.90718
Metric ton	× 1.10231	× 0.98421	× 1.0

Grain	Bushel (imperial)	Bushel (US)	Cubic feet
1 bushel (imperial)	× 1.0	× 1.0316	× 1.2837
1 bushel (US)	× 0.9694	× 1.0	× 1.2445
1 cubic foot	× 0.789	× 0.8035	× 1.0

MISCELLANEOUS

Pounds 1 lb = 0.45359 kg   1 kg = 2.20462 lb
1 ft^3/ton   = 0.16 imperial Gallons per ton
1 tonne/m^3 = 0.02787 ton/ft^3
1 m^3/tonne = 35.8816 ft^3/ton

Guide and References to This Book

The questions and answers contained within this text are generally directly related to the following International Conventions and Respected Authorities:

- BCH, Code for the Construction and Equipment of Ships Carrying Dangerous Chemicals in Bulk
- CGS, Carriage of Goods at Sea Act
- CSC, International Convention for Safe Containers
- CSWP, Code of Safe Working Practice for Merchant Seaman
- HSC, High Speed Craft Code
- IAMSAR, International Aeronautical and Maritime Search and Rescue manual
- IMDG, The International Maritime Dangerous Goods code
- IMO, International Code for the safe Carriage of Grain in bulk (Grain Regulations)
- Interco, International Code of Signals
- IRPCS, International Regulations for Preventing Collisions at Sea 1972 (Amended)
- ISM, The International Safety Management code
- ISPS, The International Ship and Port Security code
- LOF 2000, Lloyds Standard Form of Salvage Agreement
- MARPOL, the International Convention for the Prevention of Pollution by Ships
- SOLAS, Safety of Life at Sea Convention
- STCW'95 Convention: Seafarers' Training, Certification and Watchkeeping Code

Code of Safe Working Practice for:

- Ships carrying Deck Cargoes
- Ships carrying Timber Deck Cargoes
- The safe loading and unloading of Bulk Carriers

Preface

Marine Examiners can ask many thousands of questions to many potential candidates who hope to acquire a Deck Certificate of Competency. The following pages contain only a few examples of questions and answers of the more popular items of the respective syllabi. The book is not aimed at any maritime nation's examination procedure, but is meant as a learning method on the vast topic of what we generally assume to be collective seamanship.

The Australian method of assessment differs to the British system, while the Panamanian and Greek systems are different again. The theme that unites all the assessors, the world over, is to ensure that our young mariners are first and foremost, seamen and seawomen.

It is they that will drive our ships over the oceans of the world. They will meet every other nationality on the high seas and it is in all our interests that each man or woman conning each ship, is of a similar competence and standing, whatever his or her nationality.

The book is based on the British model of oral assessment, and the appendice carries the respective syllabi for the UK Deck Certificates of Competency. All qualifications, however, carry testing elements regarding the topic of Rule of the Road and to this end a copy of the regulations for the Prevention of Collisions at Sea is included in the appendix.

This work is designed to be a learning tool and as such is illustrated throughout. The diagrams and photographs being included to ensure that the potential officer will understand better the road to becoming a Master Mariner. Merchant Navy Officers must be capable of thinking for themselves and it would be wrong for individuals to accept every answer contained within as verbatim. Neither the modern text nor the modern industry are not looking for repeating parrots. Candidates must realise from the onset that assessors are looking to be convinced that a level of understanding of the topic is present. Be advised that Marine Examiners can easily spot a performing parrot.

It is the hope that this book will be a steady and continual influence on young potential officers and that the Compact Disc version will work alongside the different environments that the student may find himself or herself in, when at sea.

Finally, when using the book, the potential candidate should be aware that Marine Examiners are at liberty to ask questions from lower grade certificate syllabi, especially so if weakness in a topic is detected during the course of the assessment.

David House

1 Questions for the Rank of Officer of the Watch

INTRODUCTION

The sequence of questions and answers in this chapter are directed towards Junior Officers of the Mercantile Marine who are studying or who intend to study for the Standards of Training, Certification and Watchkeeping (STCW) Seamanship Oral Examination, conducted by the Marine Authorities around the world. The Junior Officer should familiarise himself or herself with the topics of the respective syllabus prior to entering for the examination. It should be realised from the onset that General Seamanship is a vast subject and covers many topics often with numerous variants. In order to be successful in the examination candidates need to portray a confident attitude as being first and foremost, a competent seaman.

The Marine Examiners do not expect candidates for the qualification of Officer of the Watch (OOW) to be superhuman. However, they do expect candidates to present themselves in a smart manner and show an in-depth knowledge of the art of good seamanship. This does not mean individuals will be expected to know everything about everything, this is clearly an impossible task. Certain areas of questioning must be considered as essential to the conduct of the examination, like 'rules of the road' questions. If these were answered incorrectly, the examiner would be unlikely to issue the candidate with a licence to be in charge of a navigation bridge. For further information, extracts from Marine Guidance Notice (MGN) 69 (Conduct of Candidates) is given in Appendix A.

It should be remembered that this is the first of several rungs of the ladder towards the successful attainment of becoming a Master Mariner and it is not a qualification to be taken lightly. It will allow the candidate to take charge of a navigational watch at sea and on deck,

1

when the vessel is in port. Once the licence is issued, the candidate will be called upon to act as the Master's representative in many and varied situations. This responsibility is known by the examiner and the candidate should ensure that when presenting himself for examination he should be well prepared with regard to all the related subjects for that rank.

BRIDGE PROCEDURES (OOW)

Question 1.   After completing the 8–12 night watch at sea and handing over to the 2nd Officer, what would be your actions?

Answer: Having handed over the watch, I would complete writing up the Deck Log Book, and sign the book as a true record of events. I would proceed below decks and carry out 'ships rounds' and security checks, inspecting all accommodation alleyways, storage and domestic spaces.

Question 2.   What specific items/topics would you include, when handing over the navigation watch to another relief Officer?

Answer: I would expect to follow any company policy and include the following:

(a) Appraise the relieving Officer of the ship's course, gyro and magnetic headings, highlighting any compass or gyro errors.
(b) Provide the relieving Officer with the current updated position of the vessel and indicate the position respective to the chart.
(c) Draw attention to any visible shipping traffic and provide details as to the current actions and intentions effecting relevant targets.
(d) Appraise the watch Officer of the current weather patterns and advise on the past and present state of visibility, passing on the latest weather report.
(e) The watch Officer would be appraised of any night orders left by the Master.
(f) If it is relevant, I would draw attention to the next 'way point' and any expected alteration of course.
(g) If making a landfall or in coastal regions the under keel clearance would be noted and attention drawn to the least oncoming areas of depth.
(h) Any potential navigational hazards or possible security incursions would be discussed in conjunction with the 'passage plan'.

(i) Should any defects have occurred these would be brought to the attention of the OOW (as well as the Master, as they occur).
(j) The OOW would be appraised of all the operational instruments as to their performance. Radar specifics such as range and presentation would also be positively discussed.
(k) It would also be normal practice to discuss events and activities over the previous watch period that may or may not affect the overall performance of the vessel.

Note: As the outgoing OOW it would be my duty to ascertain the state and condition of the relieving Officer. Having let the incoming Officer adjust his eyes to the light and visibility conditions I would note any adverse feelings, that may be affecting the relieving Officer which may have been caused by sickness, over-tiredness, drugs or alcohol. (In such an event where an officer felt that the relieving Officer was not in a fit state to carry out normal watchkeeping duties he would be expected to inform the Master of his doubts.)

Question 3. While acting as OOW, you encounter deterioration in the condition of visibility. What action would you take?

Answer: As OOW I would take the following actions:

(a) Place the ship's main engines on 'stand-by' and reduce the vessels speed.
(b) Advise the Master of the change in visibility conditions.
(c) Commence sounding fog signals.
(d) Switch on the navigation lights.
(e) Close all watertight doors in the vessel.
(f) Commence systematic plotting of any targets on the radar.
(g) Place a current position on the chart.
(h) Post additional lookouts.
(i) Stop all noisy work on deck.
(j) Enter a statement of my actions into the ship's Deck Log Book.

Question 4. When would you consider it necessary, as OOW, to call the Master?

Answer: The OOW should call the Master in any of the following circumstances:

(a) In the event of visibility dropping below 4 miles (company policy may be more or less than this figure).
(b) If traffic was causing concern effecting the safe passage of the vessel.
(c) In the event of failure of any of the ship's navigational equipment.

(d) If failing to sight a landfall when expecting to.

(e) If sighting a landfall when it is unexpected.

(f) If soundings are shelving when unexpected.

(g) In the event that difficulty is experienced in maintaining the course.

(h) If a scheduled position is unattainable or suspect.

(i) In the event that the man management of watch keepers becomes untenable.

(j) In the event of heavy weather or on receipt of a bad weather forecast.

(k) On sighting ice, or receiving an ice warning of ice being reported on or near the vessels track.

(l) If sighting oil on the surface.

(m) On any issue of security or shipboard alert.

(n) In any other emergency, such as fire or flooding, imminent contact or contact with a submerged object.

Question 5. When on watch at night, the alarm for the non-function of navigation lights is activated, what action would you take as OOW?

Answer:

- I would immediately inspect the navigation light sentinel to ascertain which navigation light had malfunctioned and caused the alarm to be triggered.
- I would make a note of the defective light and switch the backup light on in its place and cancel the alarm.
- In the event the light circuit had failed I would activate the secondary circuit and cancel the alarm.
- During the hours of darkness it may not be prudent, following a risk assessment, to repair the light or circuit, before daylight hours. Provided navigation lights remain operational on one or other circuits. In any event the Master would be informed and repairs instigated during daylight hours.

Question 6. When approaching a pilot station, to take the Marine Pilot, you are sent down below to meet the pilot on deck at the ladder position. What actions would you take when at the ladder position?

Answer:

- As a responsible Officer, I would inspect the rigging of the ladder, especially the deck securing hitches of the ladders rope tails.

- I would further ensure that the stanchions and manropes were correctly rigged.
- The pilot station would expect to have a heaving line and a lifebuoy readily available and I would check that these are on hand.
- It must be anticipated that the stand-by man would also be on station and the immediate deck area was safe and clear of obstructions.
- If all was in order I would report to the bridge (by two-way radio) my presence at the ladder station and that all was ready to receive the pilot on board.
- I would report again to the bridge that the pilot was on the ladder and when he had attained the deck position.

Note: Pilot entry may be obtained via a shell door in some cases and access procedures may be changed to suit the opening and closing of the door.

Question 7. As the OOW, how often would you be expected to take an azimuth/amplitude in order to obtain a compass error?

Answer: Most certainly every watch, and on every alteration of course, within the watch period (exception under pilotage where transits maybe a possible alternative). Also in the event that I was concerned about the reliability of the 'gyro' or 'magnetic compass' (i.e. concern may be caused by magnetic anomalies).

Note: Some shipping companies policies may differ from this procedure.

Question 8. When the vessel is at anchor, what would you consider as the main functions of the OOW?

Answer: When conducting an 'anchor watch' the ship is still considered as being at sea. As such the prime duty of the OOW is to maintain an effective lookout, by all available means, including visual, audible and radar.

Neither would I allow the vessel to stand into danger and would check the position at regular intervals to ensure that the ship was not 'dragging her anchor'.

Position monitoring while at anchor would entail checking by primary and secondary position fixing methods, i.e. checking Visual Anchor Bearings, Radar Range and Bearings, Global Positioning System (GPS) and optional transit marks if obtainable.

While at anchor the OOW would monitor the state of visibility, the state of the weather, especially wind and tide changes, and traffic movement in and out of the anchorage. Navigation signals should be checked continuously that they are visible and lights are correctly functioning. Access to the ship would also be of concern and The International Ship and Port Security (ISPS) Code controls would be implemented.

The very high frequency (VHF) radio would be monitored throughout for communication traffic. Log Books would be maintained, and the Master kept informed of anything untoward.

Question 9.   When approaching a pilotage station, when you require a pilot, describe the actions and duties of the OOW.

Answer: As OOW, and when approximately 1 hour from the pilot station, I would comply with the International Safety Management (ISM) checklist and anticipate the following actions:

(a) Advise the Master of the expected estimated time of arrival (ETA) to the pilot boat rendezvous.
(b) Establish communications with the pilot station and advise the pilot of the ship's name and ETA. It would be normal practice to ascertain the pilot ladder details (e.g. side for ladder and height above water). Also the local weather conditions at the rendezvous position would be established to enable the Master to provide a 'lee' for the launch.
(c) Continuous position monitoring should be ongoing throughout the approach.
(d) Under keel clearance would be monitored through out, on approach, by use of the echo sounder.
(e) An effective lookout would be maintained throughout the approach period.
(f) The bridge team would be established to include changing from auto to manual steering and the positioning of extra lookouts.
(g) Log Book entries would be made throughout.
(h) All correct signals would be indicated, prior to approach.
(i) Engines would be placed on 'stand-by' in ample time and astern propulsion tested.
(j) The ETA would be updated with the pilotage authority and the speed of engagement with the launch, clarified.
(k) Radar reduced to 6 mile range on approach, and a sharp lookout maintained for small traffic and through traffic, affecting the area.
(l) Master would take the 'conn'.

Question 10. When instructed to inspect, check and test the bridge navigation equipment, prior to sailing, what actions would you take?

Answer: I would follow the company 'checklist' with regard to checking the bridge equipment. This would necessitate the duty engineer monitoring the rudder and steering gear inside the 'steering flat', as the steering gear systems are tested from amidships to hard over to each side.

Rudder movement would be monitored by the movement of the 'rudder indicator' on the bridge.

Radars would be switched on and performance tested, and left in the 'stand-by' mode, not switched off. All navigation lights and domestic lights would be tested, together with all instrument lights.

Checks would be made on the echo sounder, communication equipment, signalling apparatus, inclusive of ship's whistles and the engine room telegraph synchronisation.

An entry would be made into the Deck Log Book, that all equipment was found satisfactory and in good order.

The Master would be informed that the bridge equipment had been checked and no defects found.

Question 11. How would you maintain and correct the ship's navigational charts?

Answer: The navigation charts would be maintained under a Chart Management System and corrected in accord with the 'Weekly Notices to Mariners'. All chart corrections being noted in the 'Chart Correction Log'.

Question 12. What is ITP and what would you do with it?

Answer: The ITP stands for the Intercept Terminal Point and is in celestial navigation practice. It is that point through which to draw the obtained position line (P/L) (see figure on next page).

Question 13. Having obtained a morning sight of the sun, the weather changes and becomes partially cloudy around the time of noon, prior to obtaining the latitude by meridian altitude. What would you do?

Answer: I would anticipate the cloudy weather and calculate the limits of working an ex-meridian altitude. In the event that cloud persisted

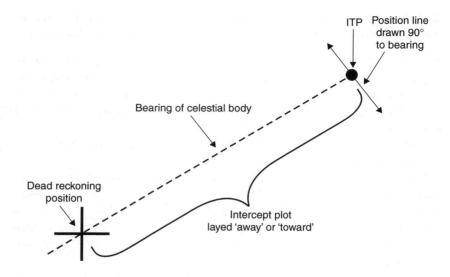

ITP Position line
     drawn 90°
     to bearing

Bearing of celestial body

Dead reckoning
position

Intercept plot
layed 'away' or 'toward'

and an ex-meridian was not obtained I would try to obtain a double altitude as soon as the sun became visible, later in the day.

Question 14.   While at sea, during your bridge watch, a man is lost overboard from an amidships position. What would be your immediate actions as OOW?

Answer: I would immediately raise the alarm, place the engines on stand-by, release the MoB bridge wing lifebuoy, and alter the helm towards the side that the man has been seen to fall.

  The above four actions should be carried out as near simultaneously as possible. The helm movement would be an attempt to clear the propellers away from the man in the water and move the vessel towards a Williamson Turn operation.

Question 15.   Following a man overboard incident the OOW has carried out the immediate required actions of raising the alarm, SBE, MoB lifebuoy release and altered course. What subsequent actions should be carried out by the Officer?

Answer: Additional actions by the OOW, should include the following:

(a) Post lookouts high up and on the foc'stle head.
(b) Activate the GPS immediate position indicator.

(c) Inform the Master, as soon as practical.
(d) Reduce ship's speed.
(e) Adjust the vessels helm to complete the Williamson Turn manoeuvre.
(f) Sound 'O' on the ship's whistle.
(g) Hoist 'O' Flag during the hours of daylight.
(h) Change to manual steering.
(i) Order the rescue boat to be turned out and crew to stand-by.
(j) Order the hospital and medical team to a state of readiness.
(k) Obtain up-to-date weather forecast.
(l) Enter a statement into the Log Book of sequential events when practical.

In the event that the Williamson Turn is complete and that the man in the water is no longer visible, the Master is legally obliged to carry out a surface search. This would mean that a 'sector search' would in all probability be conducted and the OOW would be expected to plot this pattern onto the chart.

Note: With any incident of this nature, a 'bridge team' would be immediately placed in situation to handle support activities, inclusive of communications.
Alternative manoeuvres to the Williamson Turn are available for use.

Question 16. When engaged in coastal navigation, would you use the Admiralty List of Lights and Fog Signals? And if so, how would you use it?

Answer: Yes, I would use the light list in conjunction with the navigation chart. The lights are listed 'geographically' and it would act as an additional checking operation to match the coastal light order as presented by the chart.

The light list also contains more information about individual lights, than is normally contained on the chart, and this fact would further enhance the safe navigation practice of the vessel.

Question 17. While holding the watch at anchor, you see another vessel at anchor display the 'Y' Flag. What would you assume from this?

Answer: That the vessel displaying the 'Y' Flag is dragging her anchor.

Question 18. What three types of notices, promulgate marine information to ships and seafarers?

Answer:
- The Merchant Shipping Notices (MSNs)
- The Marine Guidance Notices (MGNs)
- The Marine Information Notices (MINs).

Question 19. What are the duties of the OOW when in pilotage waters, with a pilot on board?

Answer: The OOW remains the Master's representative in the absence of the Master, despite the presence of a pilot (exception Panama Canal). During any pilotage period he would be expected to maintain an effective lookout at all times. In addition, he would continually monitor the ship's position by primary and secondary means and ensure that the under keel clearance is adequate throughout.

His duties will also include the management of the bridge personnel and he would ensure that the pilot's instructions are executed in a correct manner by the members of the 'bridge team'. He would further ensure that the pilot is made familiar with the bridge instrumentation and advised of compass errors and any defects which may affect the safe navigation of the vessel.

OOW and pilot, maintaining lookout duties aboard a vessel with integrated bridge features. Radar and Electronic Chart Display and Information System (ECDIS) positioned either side of the control consul.

Question 20.   While on watch during a coastal passage, you sight a vessel aground, on a bearing of approximately one (1) point off the port bow. What action would you take?

Answer: As the OOW, I would place the engines on 'stand-by' and the situation may make it necessary to take all way off my own ship.
   My subsequent actions would include:

(a) Advising the Master of the situation of the vessel aground.
(b) Carrying out a 'chart assessment' to include my own ship's position and the position of the vessel aground.
(c) Switch on the echo sounder and note the Under keel Clearance.
(d) Position lookouts and turn from auto pilot to manual steering.
(e) Communicate with the vessel aground, with station identification, obtaining the draught of the aground vessel and the time of grounding.
(f) Carry out an assessment of the extent of the shoal that the vessel has run aground on.

Note: Once the Master was present on the bridge it would be normal practice for him to take the 'conn' but he would equally expect a detailed report from the OOW.

Question 21.   When involved in making up a 'passage plan', what principles would you employ in its construction?

Answer: I would base any passage plan on the four fundamental principles:

• Appraisal
• Planning
• Execution
• Monitoring.

I would construct the plan to operate from 'berth to berth' bearing in mind that any plan is meant to be flexible and carry with it relevant contingency plans to cater for exceptional circumstances.

Question 22.   When on watch at sea, specific signs indicate the possible presence of a tropical revolving storm in the area. What positive evidence would you take into account to show this is so in the absence of radio information?

Answer: Assuming that the vessels position was between 5° and 35° latitudes N/S of the equator and that it was the seasonal period for tropical revolving storm (TRS), I would look for the following indications:

(a) A swell may be experienced at a distance of up to 1000 miles from the storm.
(b) A decrease in the diurnal range, showing on the barograph.
(c) A change of direction in the 'trade wind'.
(d) An ugly threatening sky with black Cumulonimbus or Nimbostratus cloud formation.

Question 23.   What is contained in the '*Weekly Notices to Mariners*' and what would you use the information for?

Answer: The Weekly Notice contains six (6) sections, which include the corrections to Admiralty List of Radio Signals and the Admiralty List of Lights/Fog Signals. It also contains an index and chart correction index in the front of the notice, followed by the respective, individual chart corrections. Additional notices for the correction of sailing directions and publications is also included.

Question 24.   How would you ascertain the reliability of the navigation chart?

Answer: The navigation chart is probably the best aid to navigation available to the OOW. However, it is not infallible and should be used with caution at all times. Its reliability can be judged from the date of the charts printing, found in the border at the bottom of the chart. It can further be assessed by inspection of the 'source data block' which provides the date/year of survey and the authority which carried out the survey.

If the chart is corrected up to date this should be indicated by the last 'small correction' being inserted in the left-hand corner of the chart by the ship's navigator. The correction should also be noted in the chart correction log.

Question 25.   How often would you expect to carry out an 'emergency steering drill'?

Answer: Emergency steering gear drills are conducted at least once every three (3) months.

Question 26. When on watch at night, how would you know that the visibility was deteriorating?

Answer: By observing the back scattering light of the navigation lights. This misting effect could be visibly seen. The visible range being established from radar observation of a target as and when it becomes visible to the naked eye.

Question 27. What is a ship reporting system and what is its function?

Answer: Ship reporting systems are organisations like Automated Mutual Vessel Reporting (AMVER), Australian Ship Reporting system (AUSREP), INSPIRES, JASREP, etc.

They can be voluntary position reporting schemes like AMVER or compulsory reporting schemes like AUSREP, for vessels entering Australian waters.

It allows the organisation to monitor ship's positions during the ocean voyages and provides mutual assistance in the event of a marine emergency.

Question 28. While on watch at sea in the North Atlantic you receive an iceberg warning from the International Ice Patrol providing iceberg positions. What would you do?

Answer: The positions of the icebergs would be plotted onto the navigation chart along with the ship's current position. The ship's Master would be informed of the report and made aware of the proximity of the danger to the ship's position.

Question 29. When involved in a coastal passage, in clear weather, how would you ascertain the vessels position to ensure that the ship is maintaining her course?

Answer: It would be normal practice to obtain the vessels position at regular intervals by both a primary and secondary position fixing methods to ensure that the ship is proceeding on its intended track by using a primary and secondary system (each method becomes a self-checking procedure).

Question 30. What is expected of you as the designated prime lookout when acting as OOW?

Answer: Every vessel shall at all times maintain a proper lookout by sight and hearing as well as by all available means appropriate to the prevailing circumstances and conditions so as to make a full appraisal of the situation and of the risk of collision.

MARINE INSTRUMENTS

Question 1. What is a 'Mason's hygrometer' and what is it used for?

Answer: It is the name given to dry and wet bulb thermometers, usually contained in the Stevenson's screen often found on the ship's bridge wing. It is used for measuring the 'humidity'.

Question 2. For what would you use a hydrometer when aboard ship?

Answer: A hydrometer is used to obtain the density of dock water. The obtained value is then used in conjunction with the Fresh Water Allowance (FWA) to obtain the Dock Water Allowance, i.e. the amount that the vessel may submerge her load line mark, in any water other than sea water.

Question 3. When reading the precision aneroid barometer, what corrections would you make to the reading?

Answer: The barometer is supplied with a calibration correction card which allows for a correction to be added to the reading to adjust to mean sea level (table of height in metres × air temperature in °C).

Question 4. How would you check that the azimuth bearing circle, of the compass was correct?

Answer: By taking a bearing of a terrestrial object, e.g. a lighthouse, with the arrow indication uppermost. Take a second bearing of the same object, with the arrow in the downward position.
   Both readings should be the same and the bearing circle can be used with confidence.

Question 5. What is the liquid found inside a magnetic compass bowl?

Answer: The older design of liquid magnetic compass contained a mixture of one part alcohol to two parts distilled water. The more modern magnetic compass would be filled with a clear oily fluid, derived from 'Bayol'.

Question 6. The purpose of the alcohol in the liquid compass was to prevent the fluid from freezing in cold, high latitudes. What was the purpose of the distilled water in the mixture?

Answer: Distilled water was included in the fluid mixture to prevent the alcohol evaporating in warm latitudes.

Question 7. How would you check the performance of the radar on the navigation bridge?

Answer: I would operate the 'performance monitor' (if fitted) on the instrumentation panel. Once activated the range of the 'plume' could be compared with the *Radar Specification Manual* details.

Note: New radars are usually fitted with a self-test control to meet instrument specifications.

Question 8. When taking a visual three-point position fix, you find the charted plot produces a 'cocked hat'. What would you do?

Answer: I would consider the position as unreliable and take another set of bearings. It would be prudent to also obtain a secondary fix by an alternative method, e.g. radar or GPS.

Question 9. How would you test the steering gear prior to the vessel departing from a port?

Answer: Having ascertained that the rudder and propeller area is clear of obstructions, I would turn the ship's wheel, hard over each way to port and starboard. When in the hard over positions I would note the 'Helm Indicator' and the 'rudder indicator' are both shown in the hard over positions.

The auto-pilot would also be tested to port and starboard, together with the tiller control. The rudder indicator should be noted to reach the hard over position on each occasion.

Question 10. What information can you obtain from a barograph?

Answer: The barometric tendency measured over the last three (3) hours.

Question 11.   When joining a ship for the first time, how would you ascertain if the vessel had any 'Blind Sectors' affecting the radar(s)?

Answer: It is common practice to display a diagram on a bulkhead, in close proximity to the radar, if its operation is hampered by Blind Sectors. Alternatively, the *Radar Specification Manual* could be consulted and any Blind Sectors would be indicated in the manual.

Question 12.   When ascertaining risk of collision with another vessel, it is normal practice to take a series of 'compass bearings' as per the COLREGS (Reference Rule 7(d)(i), see Appendix B). Why would you use 'compass bearings'?

Answer: The compass card is a fixed reference and eliminates the 'Yaw' of the ship's head when taking the bearings.

Question 13.   What are the three correctable errors that exist on a marine sextant?

Answer: The first adjustment is for any error of perpendicularity, the second adjustment is for any side error, and the third adjustment is for any Index Error.

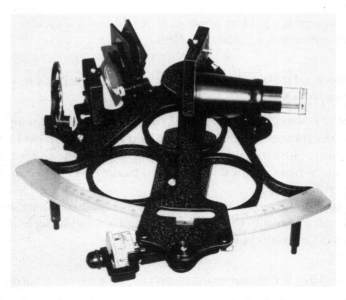

Example of a marine micrometer sextant seen with the index arm set in the middle of the arc.

Question 14. Where would you find the instrument error for a marine sextant?

Answer: The instrument error of the sextant is found on the certificate, inside the lid of the sextant's box.

Question 15. What is Collimation, with reference to the marine sextant?

Answer: Collimation is an error on the sextant caused by the axis of the telescope not being parallel to the plane of the instrument. With modern sextants the collar holding the telescope is permanently fixed and no adjustment is possible.

Question 16. What are the non-correctable errors that are found with the marine sextant?

Answer: Non-adjustable (or non-correctable) errors of the sextant, include:

(i)   shade error,
(ii) prismatic error,
(iii) graduation error.

Question 17. Where would you find the 'lubber line'?

Answer: The lubber line is found on the inside of the magnetic compass bowl, in line with the fore and aft line of the vessel. It is used to reference the ship's head on to a compass heading.

Question 18. While on watch you notice that the magnetic compass card is shuddering, what do you think might be wrong with the instrument?

Answer: Unusual movement of the compass card in this manner could be a reflection of dirty bearings or a lack of lubrication on the gimbals.

Question 19. When obtaining the density of the dock water using a sample bucket of water obtained from the dock, how would you ensure accuracy of your hydrometer reading?

Answer: When obtaining the water sample I would ensure that the bucket is allowed to sink below the surface and draw a sample that would be uncontaminated with surface debris.

When using the hydrometer, I would spin the instrument to break any surface tension against the scale bar and so obtain an accurate reading.

Question 20. How would you find the Index Error, of the marine sextant, by use of the sun?

Answer: When checking the errors of the sextant, the third adjustment for Index Error, using the sun is found by:

- setting the arm of the sextant at approximately 32′on the arc and bringing the true sun above the reflected sun. Adjust the two images until they are 'limb upon limb', then note the reading (say 28′on the arc);
- re-set the arm at approximately 32′off the arc and bring the images again Limb upon Limb, and read the sextant again (say 37′off the arc).

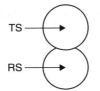

Reading = 28′ on the arc

Reading = 37′ off the arc

Take the difference of the two readings and divide by '2' to give the Index Error, and call it the higher of the two.

Example

$$37' - 28' = 9'$$

$$\frac{9}{2} = 4.5' \text{ off the arc (Index Error)}$$

Question 21. How would you check that the Index Error so obtained, is correct?

Answer: Add the two readings together and divide by 4. The result should equal the sun's semi-diameter of the day in question. This can subsequently be compared with the Nautical Almanac to see if correct.

Example

$$37' + 28' = 65'$$

$$\frac{65}{4} = 16.1' \text{ (16.1 should equal the sun's semi-diameter of the day).}$$

Question 22.   When engaged in manual radar plotting operations, an OAW triangular plotting format is established. What do OA, WA and OW represent?

Answer: Manual radar plotting techniques employ a minimum of three timed plots on any one target.

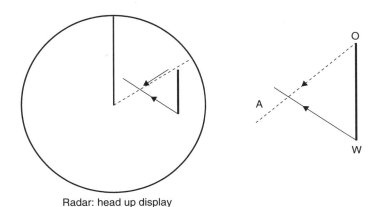

Radar: head up display

OA represents the apparent motion of the target
WA represents the true course and speed of the target
OW represents own ship's motion (course and speed)

Question 23.   When taking a position fix by use of the azimuth bearing circle, the charted position shows an enlarged 'cocked hat'. What would you do?

Answer: Any 'cocked hat' of size would probably indicate that one or more of the bearings and respective position line(s) was incorrect.

I would therefore consider that the position was unreliable and would look to take another position. It is expected that primary and secondary position fixing methods are employed wherever and whenever possible. Having confirmed the position by an alternative system, I would inspect the azimuth mirror for defect and check its use by carrying out another sequence of bearings. Any fault detected would be reported to the Master.

Question 24.   How often do you test and check the ship's steering gear?

Answer: The regulations state that the steering gear must be tested by the ship's crew, twelve (12) hours before departure. In reality the steering gear is thoroughly checked out alongside the navigation equipment 1 to 2 hours before leaving any port. An entry is made into the Deck Log Book and the Master would be advised that the operational features were effective and free of defects (ships will have an ISM checklist for such procedures).

Question 25.   How are the ship's chronometers maintained?

Answer: Most vessels are now equipped with 'quartz chronometers' and as such they do not have to be wound at regular intervals like the 2- and 8-day mechanical chronometers.

Most ships will keep the chronometer(s) in a robust wood box with the instrument slung on a gimbal arrangement. This box will in turn be mounted in an insulated cabinet with a glass, see through, dust protective cover.

It is normal practice to rate the chronometer daily by comparison with a radio 'time check signal'.

Question 26.   Is the Automatic Identification System (AIS) being fitted to all ships?

Answer: No. Vessels less than 500 grt are not required to have AIS.

Question 27.   What is the compass error and when do you apply it?

Answer: The compass error is obtained by taking an azimuth or amplitude or by making a comparison on the chart with a known bearing. The error is made up of the algebraic sum of Variation and Deviation and is used to convert 'compass' bearings and courses to 'true' directions, and vice versa, true to compass.

Question 28.   While on watch the 'off course alarm' is activated. What actions would you take as the Officer of the Watch?

Answer: The off course alarm is an audible signal and I would cancel this and investigate the cause of activation.

As the OOW I would ensure that the steering motor(s) is on and functioning correctly and immediately check the comparison course on the magnetic compass with the gyro heading and the auto pilot heading.

The weather and/or sea state could have affected the course temporarily. If the cause cannot be ascertained and rectified, I would engage manual steering by the magnetic compass and inform the ship's master of the defect. A statement would be entered into the deck log book to this effect.

Question 29.   On a Roll On–Roll Off (Ro-Ro) vessel you are on stations on the bridge prior to sailing. The cargo load has just completed. How would you know that the stern ramp, and bow door/visor are locked down and secured ready for sea?

Answer: It is a requirement that Ro-Ro vessels have closed-circuit television (CCTV) monitoring all access points into the vessel. It would be necessary to check the visual display monitor to see the watertight integrity of the ship is intact. This would additionally be checked by a red/green light tell tale, sensor-activated display showing all green lights. Each station operator or Deck Officer would also verbally confirm by radio that the respective aperture is closed and locked.

Question 30.   Men are assigned to clean and paint the radar scanner tower. What precautions would you take as OOW? (Assume that the vessel is in open water and clear visibility.)

Answer: It would be expected to draw the fuses from the circuit box and place a notice on the Plan Position Indicator (PPI) screen to the

Example radar mast. Typical mast arrangement accommodating two radar scanners, signal and navigation lights, flag halyards and communication aerials.

effect that maintenance was ongoing on the scanner to prevent accidental switch on. The Master would also be informed.

LIFE SAVING APPLIANCES AND REGULATIONS

Question 1.   How many immersion suits must be provided to each lifeboat?

Answer: Three per boat (assuming totally enclosed boats) if the boat is a designated rescue boat.

Note: New legislation (2006) will require immersion suits for all the ship's complement.

Question 2.   How many lifejackets must be carried aboard a passenger carrying vessels over 500 grt?

Answer: One for every person on board plus an additional 5% and enough child lifejackets equal to 10% of the total number of persons on board to ensure one lifejacket for every child on board.

Question 3.   What pyrotechnics are carried in survival craft?

Answer: Six hand flares, four rocket parachute flares and two orange smoke floats.

Question 4.   How many lifebuoys must be carried aboard your ship?

Answer: The number of lifebuoys carried will be dependent on the ship's length:

Length of ship in metres	Minimum number of lifebuoys
Less than 100	8
100 or more but less than 150	10
150 but less than 200	12
200 or more	14

Question 5.   What additional equipment, over and above standard lifeboat equipment, would you expect to be carried by a designated 'rescue boat'?

Answer:

- A buoyant towing line of 50 m length.
- Two rescue lines and quoits each of 30 m in length.
- A waterproof first aid kit.
- A search light.
- An effective radar reflector.
- Thermal Protective Aids (TPAs) sufficient for 10% of the number of persons that the boat is certified to carry, or two, whichever is the greater.
- Walkie-talkie communications if from a non-passenger vessel.
- A painter system with a quick release operational method.

A typical example 'rescue boat' employed with offshore 'stand-by' vessels, passenger ferries, and vessels fitted with 'free-fall lifeboats'.

- A whistle or sound signalling apparatus.
- A waterproof electric torch.

Question 6.   What is the length of the painter fitted to a manually launched, inflatable liferaft?

Answer: The Safety of Life at Sea (Convention) (SOLAS) Regulations require the liferaft painter to be 15 m in length. However, it should be noted that manufacturers supply liferafts with a standard painter length of 25 m.

Question 7.   Why are 'davit launched liferafts' supplied with two (2) painters?

Answer: Davit launched liferafts have a short painter for causing inflation in the davit launched mode. The liferafts employed with a davit launching system must be capable of being launched by the throw over inflatable method, in the event that the davit system becomes inoperable. If such conditions arise there must be a long painter to allow launching in the manual, throw over, inflatable manner, hence a second painter.

Question 8.   What markings do you expect to see on the outside of the liferaft canister?

Answer: The canister will be marked by the following:

(a)   The manufacture's name and/or logo.
(b)   The instructions for launching in diagram and text format.
(c)   The capacity (manning) that the raft is designed for.
(d)   Whether it is equipped with a survival pack and type of pack (A or B).
(e)   The length of painter fitted to the survival craft.
(f)   The date of last service.
(g)   The next date of service due.
(h)   The symbol 'do not roll' sign.

Question 9.   What is the period of validity of the HAMMAR disposable Hydrostatic Release Unit?

Answer: Two (2) years.

HAMMAR®

H20 FOR LIFERAFTS

ONE, TWO, THREE AND YOU'RE SAFE AT SEA

A typical liferaft securing arrangement.

Question 10. What are the two functions of the 'rescue boat'?

Answer: A rescue boat should be capable of recovery of person or persons from the water. It must also be capable of marshalling survival craft together.

Question 11. At what depth would you expect a liferaft's Hydrostatic Release Unit, to activate?

Answer: Between 2 and 6 m.

Question 12. Are all ships liferafts fitted with Hydrostatic Release Units (HRUs)?

Answer: No. Some large vessels over 100 m in length with accommodation either all forward, or all aft, will be required to be fitted with a 6-man liferaft. This 6-man liferaft is not required to be fitted with an HRU.

Question 13. What is the breaking strength of the 'weak link' fitted with the HRU?

Answer: 2.1 kN ± 45 kg.

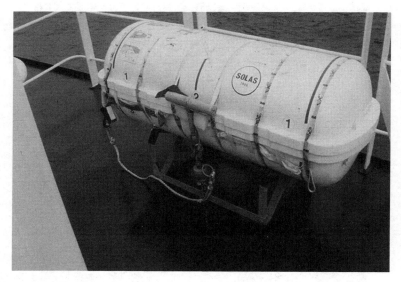

Inflatable liferaft canister, situated on exposed deck in a secured frame. It is fitted with securing retaining straps, manual release 'senhouse' slip arrangement and a Hydrostatic Release Unit.

Question 14.   How often is the Liferaft and Hydrostatic Release Unit serviced, and can this period be extended?

Answer: The raft and the HRU are both serviced at 12 monthly intervals.

Note: Exception is a disposable HRU = 2 years period and then replaced.

The service period can be extended by 5 months for both HRU and liferaft.

Question 15.   What type of distress signals could you make from a survival craft?

Answer: Use of pyrotechnics:

- Rocket parachute flare throwing red star.
- Volume of orange-coloured smoke (smoke float).
- Red hand flares (six per survival craft).

Also:

- Raising and lowering of the arms.
- Burning bucket of oily rags.
- Whistle – continuous sounding (any fog signal apparatus).
- Square flag having above or below it a ball (improvised shapes).
- Explosive signal (improvised axe bang on metal bucket).
- Activation of Emergency Position Indicating Radio Beacon (EPIRB) if carried in survival craft.
- SART operation.
- SOS transmitted by any means, use of flashing torch.
- Spoken word 'MAYDAY' by means of walkie-talkie radios (carried under Global Maritime Distress and Safety System (GMDSS) Regulations).

Question 16.   Describe how you would take a ship's boat away from the vessels side when the parent vessel is underway and making way through the water at four (4) knots.

Answer: Ensure that the boats painter is secured well forward on the parent vessel. Lower the boat to the surface with the crew wearing suitable clothing and lifejackets. Have the boats engine operational, but in neutral gear and have bowman and crew standing by to slip and clear the falls. Once at the surface and the falls are clear, the coxswain should use the tiller (wheel/rudder angle) to sheer the boat away from

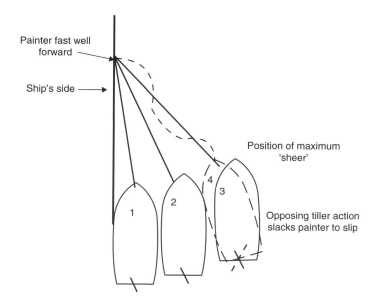

the ship's side. Once at the point of maximum sheer, slack painter to permit slipping by movement of rudder/bow angle.

Question 17. Totally enclosed lifeboats are equipped with a compressed 'breathing air' bottle. What is the purpose of this and how long will the air last for?

Answer: The air in the bottle of the TEMSC is to allow the boat to clear the immediate area in a battened down condition so as to be free from toxics or harmful gases. Provided the boat is correctly battened down and sealed the air will last for a period of 10 minutes and will tend to pressurise the inside of the craft. This is expected to provide enough time for the boat to head upwind into a clean atmosphere.

Question 18. How many self-contained rocket line throwing apparatus are carried aboard a Class VII vessel, and what are the specifications of this equipment?

Answer: Class VII vessels carry at least four (4) rocket line throwing apparatus.

Specification of self-contained line throwing apparatus: the rocket line must have the capability to stretch the line 235 m, in order to achieve this most manufactures include approximately 275 m of line. Size of line is 4 mm diameter.

When operated it is expected that 10% of the flight distance is an expected deflection allowance.

Question 19. When firing a self-contained rocket line in an area of a strong cross wind, would you aim the rocket: (a) upwind, (b) downwind or (c) directly at the target?

Answer: The answer is (b) downwind – because the wind acts on the stretched line, not on the small rocket. This causes the line to 'bow outward' and allows the rocket to turn in towards the target area.

Question 20. What is the period of validity of ship's pyrotechnics?

Answer: Three (3) years.

Note: Out-of-date pyrotechnics should be handed over for disposal to the police or coastguard authorities.

Question 21. What is the construction of the wire falls lowering the ship's lifeboats?

Answer: Lifeboat falls are constructed in Extra Flexible Steel Wire Rope (EFSWR) of 6 × 36 w.p.s. Alternatives, include stainless steel manufactured falls, or a 'wirex' lay which has a multi-plat construction which has anti-rotational properties.

Question 22. Are the bowsing tackles for use with open boats rigged to advantage or disadvantage?

Answer: Disadvantage.

Question 23. What is the purpose of 'tricing pendants' fitted to lifeboats?

Answer: To bring the lifeboat alongside the ship during launching, when the parent vessel has an adverse list.

Question 24. Assuming you are in charge, how would you attempt to beach a liferaft?

Answer:
- I would order all persons to secure their lifejackets, and cause the floor of the liferaft to be inflated.
- I would prefer to carry out the operation in daylight onto a beach area which is rock free and without surf.
- I would deploy the sea anchor and man the two paddles on approaching the shore line, attempting to fend off any rock obstructions.

Question 25. What is the emergency muster signal aboard your last ship?

Answer: Seven or more short blasts, followed by one long blast on the ship's whistle.

Question 26. In an emergency situation if time is available prior to launching survival craft, what additional items would you place into the survival craft?

Answer: Several items would be useful if they are readily available and time permits. Any of the following are suggested:

(a) Extra blankets.
(b) Torch and extra batteries.
(c) Additional food and water.
(d) Hand held radios, EPIRBs or similar communication equipment.
(e) Cigarettes (lifeboats only, not liferafts).
(f) Notebook and pencil.
(g) A pack of playing cards.

Question 27.   What three methods are employed to allow a free-fall lifeboat to become water borne?

A 'free-fall lifeboat' seen in the stowed position at the aft end of the vessel 'Scandia Spirit'. The recovery crane is seen prominently in the upright position. The davit launched liferaft station is also seen in the quarter deck position on the starboard quarter.

Answer: The boat can be launched in the free-fall manner, or launched by lift off methods using the derrick or davit recovery system or alternatively allowed to float free.

Question 28.   How are lifeboat painters secured when the vessel is at sea?

Answer: Inside the lifeboat fall and outside all other projections and made fast as far forward as is practical.

Question 29.   What symptoms would you look for when suspecting hypothermia is affecting a person?

Answer: The casualty would experience discolouration of the skin, to a whiter pale shade. The lips could also turn bluish. When questioned the person may be incoherent. In acute hypothermia, loss of memory could be expected, pupil dilation and loss of consciousness could all follow.

Note: Shivering would probably have ceased.

Question 30.   What treatment would you provide to a hypothermic victim if inside a liferaft?

Answer: Remove any wet clothing from the person and replace by dry clothing if available.

Note: Damp clothing is better than no clothing at all.

- Place the person in a Thermal Protective Aid (TPA) if available.
- Huddle other people around the chilled person to generate body warmth.
- Ensure that the entrances to the survival craft are battened down in order to raise the internal temperature of the raft.

FIRE-FIGHTING APPLIANCES AND REGULATIONS

Question 1.   What is contained in the ship's fireman's outfits?

Answer: A fireman's suit with boots and gloves; a Self-Contained Breathing Apparatus (SCBA); harness and safety line; a protective helmet; safety lamp; and a fireman's hand axe with insulated handle.

Question 2.   What is the construction of the fireman's 'safety line' and why is so constructed?

Answer: The safety line is a woven flax line constructed about a steel core. The purpose of this construction is that the steel core would not be burned through, even if the flax caught alight.

Question 3.   When kitting a man up with the SCBA, what safety checks would you make?

Answer: I would check the condition of all the web straps that they are not worn and that they are secure about the body. Inspect the air content gauge and ensure that the bottle is full. When turning on the air valve I would listen for the 'whistle' alarm signal.

When placing the mask over the face an even tension must be applied to the mask straps in order to create an airtight/smoke seal. This would be subsequently checked by shutting the air valve so that the wearer would experience the mask 'crushing' onto the face, so creating a partial vacuum. This denotes that the wearer is not drawing air from around the sealed mask, and is therefore providing an effective smoke seal. I would then open up the valve to allow the wearer to breath on demand.

Finally, communication with the wearer and the control position would be checked to ensure a safe entry.

Note: Breathing apparatus use is covered by a checklist and permit to work system. Whenever donning B/A, these would be adhered to and completed.

Question 4.   What is the capacity of the 'emergency fire pump'?

Answer: The emergency fire pump must be capable of delivering the required two jets of water to any part of the vessel and also be able to produce a pressure of 2.1 bar on a third additional hydrant.

Question 5.   What length are the fire hoses on your ship?

Answer: Minimum of 18 m and a maximum of 27 m, as per the regulations.

Question 6.   How many hoses would you expect a Class VII vessel to carry?

Answer: A Class VII vessel could expect to carry a minimum of five (5) hoses, plus one (1) spare. When they are joined together the overall length must equal 60% of the ship's length.

Question 7. Where would you expect to find the International Shore Connection?

Answer: It is usually kept readily available and found often at the top of the gangway, or on the bridge or alternatively in the Chief Officer's office.

Question 8. What maintenance would you regularly carry out on 'dry powder' fire extinguishers?

Answer: It is customary to shake dry powder extinguishers in order to prevent the powder from congealing in the event it may become, damp. They are also serviced at regular intervals under the Chief Officer's 'planned maintenance schedule'. Where any extinguisher is test fired, it would be recharged under supervision and date labelled.

Note: Some company policies send extinguishers ashore for regular checks and maintenance inspections.

Question 9. In the event of fire on board, what signal would you expect to hear?

Answer: Continuous ringing of the ship's fire alarm bells.

Question 10. How much air time is contained in the 'Self-Contained Breathing Apparatus' bottles, assuming that the wearer is working at a steady rate?

Answer: Normal working conditions for a person wearing breathing apparatus, would expect to provide approximately, twenty-five (25) minutes of air. After this the low air alarm whistle should sound.

Note: In order to conserve air and make it last longer the wearer should sit down and rest. Heavy work demands more oxygen, and the air bottles would be consumed faster.

Question 11. It is now a requirement that Ro-Ro passenger vessels are equipped with an 'emergency equipment locker'. Where would you expect this locker to be located?

Answer: This type of locker should be clearly marked and stowed on an upper deck, near the ship's side.

Example of an emergency equipment locker established on Ro-Ro passenger vessels.

Question 12. What equipment is contained in the emergency equipment locker, as required for RoPax vessels, as stated above?

Answer:
(a) A long-handled fire axe.
(b) A short-handled fire axe.

(c) A 7 lb pin maul.
(d) A crowbar.
(e) Four torches or lamps.
(f) A lightweight collapsible ladder (of at least 3 m).
(g) A lightweight rope ladder (10 m length).
(h) A first aid kit.
(i) Six sealed thermal blankets or alternatively six TPAs.
(j) Four sets of waterproof clothing.
(k) Five-padded lifting strops for adults.
(l) Two-padded lifting strops for children.
(m) Three hand powered lifting devices.

Question 13. Where are the extinguishers in the main engine room?

Answer: Extinguishers must be strategically positioned so that a person walking in any direction of ten (10) metres will come upon a fire extinguisher.

Note: Appropriate types of extinguishers are placed to reflect the type of fire that maybe anticipated, i.e. electric board … CO_2 extinguisher close by.

Question 14. When acting as OOW, the duty engineer telephones the navigation bridge and states that there is a small fire in the engine room store. What immediate action would you take?

Answer: Not having already heard any fire alarm, I would immediately sound the bridge fire alarm and carry out the following actions:

(a) Advise the Master as soon as possible.
(b) Place the ship's position on the Chart.
(c) Engage 'manual steering' with a quarter master.
(d) Close all watertight and fire doors.
(e) Place engines on 'stand-by' as soon as appropriate and reduce speed.
(f) Alter the ship's course to position the wind direction, directly astern (to reduce the draught and oxygen content within the vessel).[1]
(g) Proceed to my muster station, once relieved on the bridge.

Note: Depending on manning, the engineers could be initially fighting the fire and consequently the engines may not be brought to 'stand-by' as quickly

_____
[1] Draught may be required to clear smoke. Course alteration navigation permitting.

as the bridge personnel might require. As manpower increased in the engine room both to fight the fire and hold the watch, machinery response could expect to become more effective.

Question 15.   Following your watch at sea, you are carrying out 'rounds' of the vessel and you discover smoke is issuing from under a cabin door. What action would you take?

Answer: Following the discovery of smoke in the accommodation block I would immediately assume a fire has occurred and I would take the following actions:

(a) Raise the alarm and inform the navigation bridge.[2]
(b) Isolate live electrical circuits effecting the location of the fire.
(c) Close off all ventilation to the fire-affected area.
(d) Prepare to attack the fire on as many sides as possible.
(e) Rig a hose to the cabin entrance ready for the fire party.
(f) Once the alarm has been sounded, it must be anticipated that a fire party is being mustered and fitted out with breathing apparatus.
(g) I would order the fire party, when ready to tackle the fire immediately, by kicking in the 'crash panel' at the base of the cabin door. This would allow a 'jet hose' to be pushed into the cabin and directed towards the deck head. This action would deflect the jet of water, off the deck head and cool the interior of the cabin.
(h) The hose could then be extracted and turned to a spray to protect fire fighters as they make an entry into the cabin.
(i) The entry being made with two hoses one in spray for protection, the second in jet to kill the fire. It should be realised that hoses should not be employed until the electrical circuits have been isolated.

Note: The cabin door should not be opened until back-up fire fighters are in position, as this action would only allow an ingress of oxygen and probably cause a flash fire scenario.

---

[2] Once the navigation bridge has been informed it would be anticipated that the Master would take the 'conn' of the vessel alter course to put the wind astern and reduce speed. This action would reduce the oxygen content throughout the ship and tend to starve the fire of oxygen. It must also be assumed that the Chief Officer would manage the fire fighting operation and carry out a role call of all personnel (especially the cabin occupant). His duties would also include establishing boundary cooling and first aid parties being placed on stand-by.

Question 16.   How is the 'paint room' fire protected, on your last ship?

Answer: Depending on the age of the vessel, regulations make it necessary for paint rooms to be protected by a fixed 'sprinkler system'.

Question 17.   What colour is a CO_2 fire extinguisher, and what type of fire would you expect to use it on?

Answer: CO_2 extinguishers are black in colour and would generally be expected to be used on electrical fires.

Question 18.   Is CO_2 a smothering agent or an extinguishing agent?

Answer: CO_2 is a smothering agent.

Question 19.   What extinguisher requirements are expected on the vehicle decks of Ro-Ro vessels?

Answer: Ro-Ro vehicle decks are expected to have at least two (2) portable extinguishers suitable for oil fires, for every forty (40) metre length of deck space.

Question 20.   Means of stopping the main engines from a remote position outside of the engine room is a requirement of the regulations. What types of 'stops' are provided and what do they cut off?

Answer: The more modern vessel will be equipped with 'solenoid switches' which operate 'gate valves'. These close down the fuel supply, shut down fans, and boilers inside the machinery space.

Question 21.   If your vessel is fitted with a heli-landing deck, what fire-fighting and emergency equipment would you expect to find available?

Answer: Helicopter landing areas are expected to have a crash-box of emergency equipment adjacent to the landing area and additionally the following fire-fighting appliances:

(a) Dry powder extinguisher of 45 kg capacity.
(b) A foam application system.
(c) CO_2 extinguisher of 16 kg capacity.

Question 22. How would passengers aboard a passenger vessel, be informed of a fire on the ship and be advised to move to muster stations?

Answer: Passenger vessels must have a Public Address (P/A) system as part of the statutory fire-fighting appliances. If deemed necessary to muster passengers this P/A system would be operated to give instructions and warnings.

Question 23. How is the pump room of a tanker, fire protected?

Answer: Pump rooms on tankers are protected spaces and covered by a fixed fire extinguishing system, which is operated from outside of the compartment. (Usually a CO_2 operation. Note: Pump rooms are treated as enclosed spaces.) After July 2002, under SOLAS II-2 Regulations 4, 5.10.3/4, cargo pump rooms were required to be fitted with gas detection/bilge alarm systems.

Question 24. A modern vessel is fitted with an emergency control room. What items of equipment and operational features would you expect to find inside such a room?

Answer: Emergency control rooms are usually fitted with the activation equipment for the operation of: the emergency main engine stops, the CO_2 total flooding system, water fog application unit, fireman's outfits, emergency pumping/valve systems together with bulkhead mounted plans for emergency operations. Communications are also featured, usually linked to the navigation bridge from such a compartment.

Question 25. What is a 'water fog application unit'?

Answer: SOLAS requirements (1995) require that passenger vessels and Ro-Ro Ferries, over 500 grt, carrying over 36 passengers are required to carry two (2) water fog application units.

These are pressure units which deliver a water-mist extinguishing agent to designated spaces of high risk. These units are carried in addition to the total flood systems required by the regulations.

Question 26. A fire is discovered around the oil stoves in the galley. What type of extinguishers would you expect to employ?

Answer: Oil stoves would usually generate oil fires and as such attack by 'foam' extinguishers would normally be expected.

Question 27.   What are the three elements of the so-called 'fire triangle'?

Answer: Fuel, oxygen and heat.

Question 28.   A man fitted with Breathing Apparatus would be expected to wear a harness and have a lifeline fitted. What is the construction of the lifeline and why is it so constructed?

Answer: The lifeline is constructed with a steel wire core and an outer covering of flax. The purpose of the wire core is to prevent the wire from being burnt through.

Question 29.   What type of nozzles are fitted to the hoses aboard ships?

Answer: Ships must be fitted with dual-operation spray and jet nozzles.

Question 30.   Where would you anticipate hydrants would be found in a ship's engine room?

Answer: At least one would be positioned on either side of the engine room and one would be inside any shaft tunnel. In any event sufficient hydrants must be placed to bring two jets of water to bear to any point.

ANCHORWORK

Question 1.   What type of anchors are generally fitted to Class VII vessels?

Answer: Stockless anchors.

Question 2.   What are the parts of a 'stockless anchor'?

Answer: Anchor Crown 'D' shackle, shank, arms, fluke, pea or bill, crown, tripping palms. The lower part of the anchor attached to the shank is termed the 'head' of the anchor.

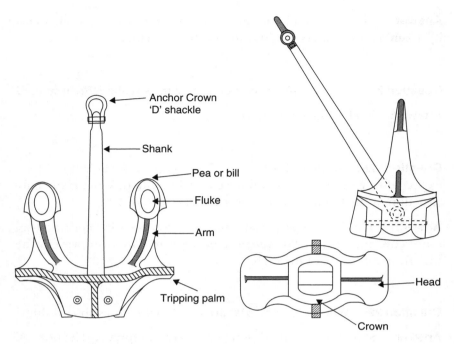

Example of a stockless anchor.

Question 3.   What is the length of a shackle of anchor cable?

Answer: A shackle length is 15 fathoms, or 27.5 m (90 ft).

Question 4.   How are shackle lengths joined together?

Answer: The most popular method of joining anchor cable shackles is by the use of 'Kenter Lugless joining shackles' alternatively 'D' lugged joining shackles may be used.

Question 5.   How would you secure the Stockless Anchor, when the vessel is about to proceed outward bound to sea?

Answer: Once the anchor is 'home' and stowed correctly into the 'hawse pipe' the windlass brake would be firmly applied. The hawse pipe cover would be set in position and the bow stopper would be secured.

A devils claw would be set and tensioned with the bottle screw and additional chain lashings may be passed through the Anchor Crown 'D' shackle and shackled on deck. Finally, the 'spurling pipes' would be sealed with either designated covers or by means of a stuffing pudding and cement.

Question 6. What is considered 'Good Holding Ground' for the anchor?

Answer: Mud or clay.

Question 7. What is considered 'Bad Holding' ground for the anchor?

Answer: Ooze, marsh, soft sand, rock, pebble.

Question 8. How does the anchor arrangement hold the ship tethered in one position?

Answer: It is the amount of chain cable that effectively keeps the vessel in the anchored position, not just the weight or size of the anchor itself.

When anchoring the vessel, the objective is to lay the chain cable in a line on the seabed and avoid the cable piling up.

This action is meant to provide a horizontal pull on the anchor to drive the 'flukes' into the holding ground.

Note: A short length of cable would have tendency to pull upwards and cause the anchor to 'break out'.

Question 9. What type of braking system, do you find on the ship's windlass?

Answer: There are several types of braking systems commercially available but probably the most widely used is the 'band brake'. Alternative system would be a 'disc brake'.

Question 10. How is the 'bitter end' of the anchor cable secured inside the chain locker?

Answer: The last link of the last shackle is usually an open link which is held in check by a through, draw bolt, in a bracket or clench, quick release arrangement.

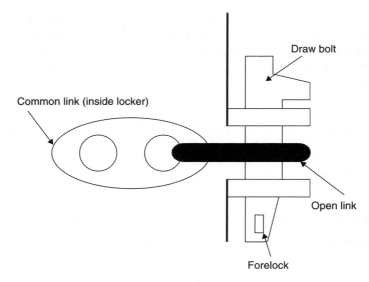

Securing the Bitter End. Current regulations require that the chain cable can be slipped from a position external to the cable locker. The bitter end attachment being achieved by an easily removed draw bolt system or similar arrangement.

Question 11.   How would you break a Kenter, Lugless joining shackle?

Answer: To break a Kenter joining shackle, 'punch and drift' the 'spile pin'. Movement of the spile pin will push out the 'lead pellet'. Once the spile pin is removed, knock out the centre stud then separate the two shackle halves by hammer blows to the side of the link.

Question 12.   What prevents the spile pin from accidentally falling out of the joining shackle with the vibration caused in the cable when operating anchors and cables?

Answer: Once the tapered spile pin has been inserted into the shackle, a lead mould pellet is forced into the 'dove tail chamber', a space above the top of the pin. This shaped cavity prevents the lead from dropping out, while at the same time retaining the spile pin.

Question 13.   Where would you find the 'ganger length' on an anchor cable?

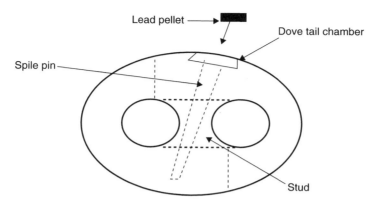

Kenter Lugless joining shackle.

Answer: The ganger length is the term given to the few additional links found between the Anchor Crown 'D' Shackle and the first (1st) joining shackle. The ganger length may or may not have a swivel piece within it.

Question 14. What and where is the 'snug' on a windlass?

Answer: The snug is the recess found on the gypsy of the windlass or cable holder – that holding position where the individual links drop into onto the gypsy.

Question 15. How do you know, after letting go the anchor, when the vessel is brought up?

Answer: By watching the cable after applying the brake once the required scope has been played out. If the cable rises up, to long stay and then bows, to form a 'catenary', then rises again.

This cable movement is an indication that the vessel is riding to her anchor not dragging her anchor. If the cable stays taught all the time it may be assumed that the anchor is dragging under the tension.

Question 16. How would you normally pump out the chain locker, aboard a general cargo vessel?

Answer: Normal practice would be to use a manual 'hand pump' operation. The reason for this is that the construction Regulations only allow the 'collision bulkhead' to be pieced once and this is usually

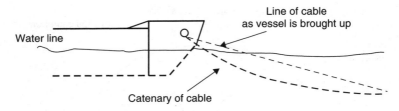

Cable brought up.

assigned to the fore peak tank because of its regular use, the chain locker being traditionally positioned forward of this bulkhead.

Note: Deep draughted vessels would usually employ an educator process.

Question 17.   What is the advantage of mooring using two anchors as opposed to a single anchor?

Answer: Use of two anchors is used where weather is causing problems and a second anchor is employed usually to prevent the vessel from dragging her single anchor.

   Where a designated moor is used, like a 'running moor' operation, two anchors are employed to reduce the 'circle of swing'.

Question 18.   How would you measure the size of anchor cable?

Answer: Measure the size of the bar that the link is manufactured from, by use of 'external callipers'.

Question 19.   How would you prepare an anchor for 'letting go' when coming in from sea?

Answer: Having received orders to prepare the anchor, I would obtain power on deck from the engineers and proceed to the foc'stle head with the stand-by man:

(a) Ensure that the windlass is out of gear, and turn the machinery over. The gears and moving parts would be oiled as the machinery is stopped.
(b) Place the anchor in gear.

(c) Remove the hawse pipe cover of the specified anchor.
(d) Remove the 'devils claw' and any additional chain lashings.
(e) Remove the bow stopper (guillotine or compressor type).
(f) Remove the brake on the windlass.
(g) If spurling pipe covers are employed these would be removed. (If cement and pudding has been used – walk back the anchor a small amount, approximately 0.2 m. This will be enough for the cement to crack and clear the mouth of the spurling pipe. Waste cement can then be cleared with ease.)
(h) Continue to walk back the anchor, until the anchor is clear of the hawse pipe and above the water surface.
(i) Place the brake on hard, and check that the brake is holding.
(j) Once the brake is seen to be effective, take the anchor out of gear.
(k) Report to the bridge that the anchor is ready for letting go.

Note: Not all ships 'let go' the anchor and it is common practice with the large and heavy anchor arrangements to walk the anchor back all the way to the seabed. This would also apply to 'deep water anchorages'.

Question 20.   How would you test the brake on the windlass?

Answer: Once the brake has been turned on, it can be tested by the following methods:

(a) Having walked the anchor clear, reverse the movement of the windlass and turn the gear plates back to provide a small space between them. Turn off the power and watch to see if the gear plates close up on themselves. If the gear plates remain stationary and the 'gap' does not close the brake is effective.
(b) Alternative method would be to put the brake on and provide a burst of power to the chain movement. Provided the anchor chain does not move forward, it will be observed that the windless bed shudders under the stationary weight. The brake can be considered as being effective. (This is not the best method as over time it could strain the securing of the windlass bed.)

Question 21.   When in Dry Dock, it is decided to 'end for end' the anchor cables. Once this operation is completed, what action must now be carried out before the cables are returned to the chain lockers?

Answer: Following end for ending, the cables would need to be re-marked.

Question 22. When weighing the anchor, when would you inform the bridge that the anchor is 'aweigh'?

Answer: The ship is still considered to be anchored all the while the anchor is in contact with the seabed. Once the anchor clears the bottom, the up and down chain will be seen to fall away, back to the ship and it can be assumed that this moment in time is when the anchor is termed 'aweigh'.

Note: The experienced Officer is generally not in any hurry to signal to the bridge, 'anchor aweigh'. He would much prefer to see the anchor hove up, to a position of being 'sighted and clear'. This avoids embarrassment later, in the event that the anchor has been fouled.

Question 23. What is the difference between 'short stay' and 'long stay'?

Answer: Short stay is a term used to express a short amount of visible cable at a steep angle from the hawse pipe to the water surface. Whereas long stay is a term which describes where the cable is in a more horizontal direction towards being parallel to the surface of the water. The cable is said to 'grow' from a shorter stay to a long stay aspect.

Question 24. What 'day signal' must a vessel display when lying to her anchor?

Answer: A vessel at anchor must display a 'black ball', in the fore part of the vessel, where it can best be seen. The ball shall be not less than 0.6 m in diameter.

Question 25. What is the fog signal for a vessel at anchor?

Answer: A vessel at anchor, in fog, will sound a rapid ringing of the ship's bell, in the forepart of the vessel for a period of about 5 seconds, at intervals of not more than 1 minute. If the vessel is more than 100 m in length, the bell signal would also be followed by the gong signal, in the aft part of the vessel.

Question 26.   Where would you expect to find a swivel link in the anchor cable?

Answer: If the cable contains a swivel piece this would normally be found next to the Anchor Crown 'D' shackle set into the ganger length before the first joining shackle of the cable.

Question 27.   What type of bow stoppers do you know?

Answer: There are two popular types of bow stopper employed in the Mercantile Marine. These are the 'Guillotine Bar' type and the 'Compressor' type.
The tanker and offshore vessels often employ an auto-kick down (AKD) type stopper, which is counter weighted to wedge against the links of the chain.

Two AKD stoppers engaged on the forward chain moorings of a shuttle tanker engaged in offloading oil from a Floating Storage Unit (FSU).

Question 28.   What is the range of the anchor lights of a vessel over 50 m in length?

Answer: Three (3) miles.

Question 29.   What is the difference between a 'fouled anchor' and a 'fouled hawse'?

Answer: The fouled anchor is the description given to when the anchor itself is fouled by some object like a cast off fishing wire, or even by its own cable turned around the fluke.

A fouled hawse occurs when the vessel has moored with two anchors and ship's anchor cables have become entwined, usually caused by a change in the wind direction, causing the vessel to swing in opposition to the lay of cables.

Question 30.   While acting as OOW aboard a vessel riding to a single anchor, you observe that the vessel is yawing excessively from side to side. What are the dangers of this and what action would be expected?

Answer: If excessive yawing is taking place there is a danger that the anchor will be broken out of the ground allowing the vessel to subsequently drag her anchor. The OOW would be expected to inform the master of the vessels movement and he would probably order more cable to be laid. The position and the weather conditions should be tightly monitored and the state of any tidal stream should be checked.

DUTIES OF OFFICERS OF THE DECK (TANKERS AND DRY CARGO) CARGO WORK

Question 1.   What do you understand by the term 'stowage factor'?

Answer: Stowage factor is the volume occupied by unit weight and expressed in either ft^3/ton, or m^3/ton. (No account is taken of broken stowage).

Question 2.   What is 'broken stowage'?

Answer: Unfilled spaces between cargo packages is termed 'broken stowage'. It tends to be the greatest amongst assorted sizes of large cases where the stow is at the turn of the bilge or where the vessel fines off, in the fore and aft regions.

Question 3.   What is 'Grain Space'?

Answer: This is the total internal volume of the cargo compartment measured from the internal side of the shell plating to the shell plating on the opposite side. Also measured from the 'tank tops' to the under deck. This measurement is used for any form of bulk cargo which could completely fill the space. An allowance being made for space occupied by beams and frames, etc.

Question 4.   What is 'bale space'?

Answer: Bale space is the internal volume measured from the underside of beams to the tank tops and from the inside edges of the spar ceiling and bulkhead stiffeners.

Question 5.   How could you separate similar cargoes but destined for different Ports of discharge?

Answer: Depending on the nature of the cargo parcels would depend on the type of separation that could be employed. Clearly the best form of separation is to stow cargoes in alternative compartments. In the event that the loading plan does not permit this, paint, paper, dye mark, dunnage, burlap or nets can be used on a variety of general cargoes.

Question 6.   If loading a cargo parcel of hazardous material, where would you obtain the details of such a cargo?

Answer: Dangerous and hazardous goods are detailed in the International Maritime Dangerous Goods (IMDG) Code (the International Maritime Organisation (IMO) publication: International Maritime Dangerous Goods Code).

Question 7.   How would you prepare a cargo hold for the carriage of 'Grain'?

Answer: I would ensure that the hold was thoroughly clean and dry. It should be seen to be free of rust and infestation. The hold should be free of any 'taint' from previous cargoes. I would test the hold bilge suctions and 'tween deck scuppers and ensure that the bilge bays are clean and dry. The bilges would then be covered with 'burlap' (sack clothing) to allow passage of water but not solid matter.

The vessel would be expected to comply with the 'Grain Regulations' and may need feeder construction or the rigging of shifting boards.

Prior to commencement of loading it would be anticipated that the hold may be inspected by a cargo surveyor to provide National Authority Approval, for the carriage of grain.

Note: Bulk carrier type vessels require a 'Document of Authorisation' and do not require the National Authority Approval.

Question 8.   How many classes of dangerous cargoes are covered by the IMDG Code?

Answer: There are nine (9) classes of dangerous cargoes + pollutants.

Question 9.   What is the purpose of 'dunnage'?

Answer: Dunnage is wood plank boards laid under cargoes to provide ventilation and in some cases assist drainage of moisture from cargoes. Some cargoes require 'double dunnage'. All dunnage must be clean and free of oil or grease contamination as this could spoil cargo quality.

Dunnage can be used as a separation mode between cargo parcels but its prime function is to separate cargo from the steel decks and avoid cargo sweat.

Question 10.   While engaged in loading a tanker, a malfunction occurs in the inert gas system (IGS). What should the Cargo Officer of the Deck do?

Answer: Any failure in operation of the IGS would immediately cause all loading operations to cease.

Question 11.   What are the main concerns for the Chief Officer if the vessel is scheduled to carry timber as deck cargo?

Answer: When carrying timber as deck cargo there are two main concerns:

(1) the securing of the timber cargo,
(2) the absorption factor of timber, effecting the stability of the vessel.

Question 12.   How would you load bags of 'Mail' and what precautions would you take aboard a general cargo vessel?

Answer: Mail bags are treated as a 'special cargo' and would be loaded by nets or in a container under the supervision of a Security Officer.[3] They would normally be tallied aboard, if loose and given 'lock up' stow.

Question 13.   If your vessel is fitted with 5 ton safe working load (SWL) derricks could you load a 4.5 ton weight?

Answer: Yes, the load could be lifted but not on the single whip, cargo runner. Normal practice would dictate that the derrick is fitted with a 24 mm FSWR cargo runner and the SWL of the wire would be exceeded.

In order to lift this weight the derrick would need to be doubled up, so providing a 'gun tackle' (two parts of wire in the purchase). This would effectively place 2.25 ton on each part of wire, each under the SWL.

Question 14.   Tanker vessels employ an IGS when engaged in loading. What prevents inert gas flowing backwards, towards the accommodation?

Answer: Inert gas is prevented from going into a reverse flow, because each system is fitted with a 'deck water seal' effectively a non-return valve.

Question 15.   What alarms would you expect to find on an IGS?

Answer: All IGSs must carry the following alarms:

(a) Low water rate/pressure in the scrubber.
(b) High water level rate inside the scrubber.
(c) High gas temperature.
(d) Failure of inert gas blower.
(e) High oxygen.
(f) Power supply failure on automatic control.
(g) Low water level in the deck water seal.
(h) Low gas pressure.
(i) High gas pressure.

---

[3] Not to be confused with the ship's ISPS Security Officer.

Question 16.   What precautions would you take when opening up a 'single pull', chain McGregor steel hatch cover?

Answer: Steel hatch covers of the single pull type are opened by:

(a) Rigging a 'bull wire' to the leading hatch section.
(b) Rigging a 'check wire' to oppose the direction of pull.
(c) Ensuring all the cleating side 'dogs' are released.
(d) Releasing any hatch top wedges and completing any work on the hatch top.
(e) Turning down the eccentric wheels by use of the jacks.
(f) Checking that the stowage bay and trackways are clear.
(g) Taking the weight on the bull wire.
(h) Manning the check wire.
(i) Removing the safety end locking bolts.
(j) Warning personnel to stand clear and sighting the safe position of personnel.
(k) If all is in order, heaving the sections to roll open.

Question 17.   How would you stow 500 drums of corrosive liquid as deck cargo?

Answer: It would be normal practice to check the product with the IMDG Code, to ensure that it was not incompatible with any other deck cargo being carried. This publication would also advise on any special stowage conditions.

Unless otherwise advised these drums would be stowed in small batches so as to allow access to any leaking drums whilst in transit. In the event of a leaking drum developing while at sea, it may become necessary to 'jettison' the effected drum(s).

Each batch of drums would be lashed and netted against movement, alongside protected bulwarks and/or ship's rails. Securings would be inspected daily and re-tensioned if found to be slack during the passage.

Question 18.   What ventilation would you expect to provide to a full bulk cargo of coal?

Answer: Coal gives off gas which rises through the cargo to the top surface and therefore must be given, 'surface ventilation' in order to clear gases. It is customary to lift hatch edges on old ships, when in good weather to clear coal gases. However, hatches should not be opened in adverse conditions that could in any way have a detrimental effect on the watertight integrity of the ship.

New ships must comply with the BC Code and be provided with permanent venting systems.

Question 19.   What is the 'ullage' in a cargo oil tank?

Answer: Ullage is defined as the amount of liquid that a tank requires in order to be full. The ullage measurement is often measured by means of a gauge or a calibrated ullage stick.

Question 20.   Can any vessel carry all classes of dangerous goods?

Answer: No, passenger vessels are not allowed to carry Class I (explosives) dangerous goods.

Question 21.   What type of slinging arrangement would be employed to lift steel 'H' girders on board?

Answer: Most steelwork, including 'H' girders would use chain slings. A spreader may also be employed depending on the overall length of the girders.

Question 22.   Cargo 'pump rooms' must be fitted with certain alarm systems. What are these alarms?

Answer: Since July 2002, cargo pump rooms must have a gas detection alarm and a bilge alarm system.

Question 23.   What do you understand by the term 'flashpoint'?

Answer: Flashpoint is described as the lowest temperature at which a liquid gives off sufficient vapour to form a flammable mixture with air, near the surface of the liquid.

Question 24.   What goods require a magazine stowage?

Answer: Class I and II, explosive goods require a specially constructed magazine stowage.

Question 25.   What is cargo sweat?

Answer: Cargo sweat occurs when the vessel is going from a cold climate to a hot climate and ventilating hatches at the wrong time. When the temperature of the hold and cargo is below the dew point of the incoming outside air cargo sweat can occur.

Contrast is made to 'ships sweat' which is caused by not ventilating the cargo spaces.

Question 26.   What is the function of a cargo plan?

Answer: The purpose of the cargo plan is to show the disposition of cargoes, showing the amount and type of cargo together with its port of discharge. It is a pictorial display which is meant to prevent cargo being over carried. It also allows the Chief Officer to order the necessary labour/equipment to facilitate the discharge at respective ports.

Question 27.   How would you stow 40 ft drop trailers in the vehicle deck of a Roll On–Roll Off Vessel?

Answer: Vehicle decks on Ro-Ro vessels are fitted with star/dome lashing points. Drop trailers would be stowed and lashed in accord with the Cargo Securing Manual which would provide examples of securing methods.

This size of trailer would normally be secured by a minimum of six (6) chain lashings each fitted with a tension load binding bar, the trailer being landed on a trestle at the front end while the rear is balanced by back wheels. A manual brake system would also be applied.

Question 28.   How is the maximum load on a vehicle ramp determined?

Answer: Permitted ramp loads are determined by axle weight, namely the weight of the load divided by the number of wheel axles.

Question 29.   What precautions would you take prior to loading chemicals?

Answer: I would be expected to check the IMDG Code with the correct name of the commodity and note any stowage recommendations. It would also be prudent to note the procedures to take in the event of spillage of the product, making any reference to the *Medical First Aid Guide*. Documentation of hazardous goods would be supported by emergency contact names and numbers for relevant shore side assistance. These would normally be held on the bridge for immediate use.

Question 30.   While working cargo in port the fire alarm is activated. What would you do as the Duty Cargo officer at the time?

Answer: It would be prudent to stop all cargo work operations and remove all unnecessary Personnel from the ship, e.g. stevedores. I would instruct the ship's foreman to check his men are clear of the vessel by head count and report back to the Chief Officer that his men are clear and in safety. It would then be expected that the Cargo Officer would report to his designated fire muster station.

RIGGING AND LIFTING GEAR

Question 1. What is the construction of the topping lift of a 5 or 10 ton derrick?

Answer: Topping lifts are usually a 24 mm EFSWR of 6×36 w.p.s.

Question 2. What is the safe working angle, between the two runners when derricks are rigged in union purchase rig?

Answer: Runner wires have a safe working angle of 90° but may carry out occasional lifts up to 120°.

Question 3. A 5 ton SWL derrick is marked at the heel with a 'U' = 1.6. What does this signify?

Answer: 'U' represents the union purchase, safe working load, in this case U = 1.6 ton.

Question 4. What is the difference between a 'hounds band' and a 'spider band'?

Answer: A hounds band is the lugged band found around a mast to support the shrouds and the supporting stays. A spider band is found around the head of a derrick, to secure the guys, topping lift and lifting purchase.

Question 5. What marking would you expect to find on the binding of a metal block?

Answer: The safe working load and the certificate number.

Question 6. What is the difference between a 'head block' and a 'heel block'?

Answer: Very little difference other than the head fitting on the head block is an oval becket, while the 'heel block' will be fitted with a 'duck bill' fitting to accommodate the gooseneck arrangement.

Question 7. As Officer of the Deck, when would you inspect the rigging of the derricks or cranes?

Answer: Every time they are used.

Question 8. What is the SWL of a 24 mm FSWR?

Answer: The breaking strength (BS) of the wire is found by the formula:

$$BS = \frac{20\,D^2}{500}$$

where D represents the diameter of the wire, and

$$SWL = \frac{BS}{6}$$
$$BS = \frac{20 \times 24 \times 24}{500}$$
$$= 23.04 \text{ ton}$$
$$SWL = 23.04 \div 6 = \textbf{3.84 ton}.$$

Question 9. When doubling up a derrick, what lifting tackle is made?

Answer: A gun tackle.

Question 10. What is the purpose of the heart inside a flexible steel wire rope?

Answer: The purpose of the heart to the wire, is to provide 'flexibility' and 'lubrication'.

Question 11. What is the construction of a crane wire?

Answer: Crane wires have a multi-plat construction known as 'Wirex' this type of lay having non-rotational properties.

Question 12. Where would you expect to find a 'Union Plate' on a derrick rig?

Answer: Union Plates are employed on derricks which operate with a single span 'topping lift' as opposed to a 'span tackle', topping lift.

The downhaul of the single span topping lift is shackled to the apex of the Union Plate, while the bull wire, and chain preventer are secured to the base of the plate. They are also employed to secure the runners and hook arrangement in a union purchase rig, where a triple swivel hook is not used.

Question 13. What is a 'schooner guy'?

Answer: A schooner guy is set to replace the crossed inboard guys of two derricks when rigged in union purchase rig.

Two derricks rigged in union purchase rig, with a 'schooner guy' stretched between the spider bands at the derrick heads.

The schooner is shackled between the spider bands of each derrick and acts to brace the two derricks within the rig.

Question 14.   What is the difference between 'standing rigging' and 'running rigging'?

Answer: Running rigging is any wire or cordage which passes through a 'block'. In the case of steel wire ropes, running rigging would be of flexible construction.

Standing rigging, is generally steel wire rope, which does not pass over the sheave of a block. Its construction is 6 × 6, or 6 × 7 and is employed for such items as stays or shrouds.

Question 15.   How would you normally secure a pilot ladder?

Answer: Modern day tonnage is usually constructed with a pilot boarding station and a designated gateway either side of the vessel. This station is generally fitted with twin deck 'pad-eyes'. The rope tails of the pilot ladder are secured to the pad-eyes, by means of round turns and two half hitches.

If the ship is fitted with bulwarks, the ladder is passed over the gunwale capping and the rope tails are passed through the 'freeing port' and turned and secured about the ladders side ropes.

Question 16.   What maintenance operations would you expect to carry out on the lifeboat falls?

Answer: Lifeboat falls are either Extra Flexible Steel Wire Rope (EFSWR) or wirex or manufactured in stainless steel. Under IMO Regulations they must be end for ended every 2½ years and renewed every 5 years or whenever considered necessary (some Marine Authorities do these checks at 2 and 4 years). Lifeboat falls are also inspected at each Boat Drill.

In between these periods regular lubrication coatings would be applied as required and/or as designated by the ship's planned maintenance schedule. The davit and fall system would undergo a 5-yearly test where the load test would be to a 110% of the loaded boat capacity.

Question 17.   When would you expect a steel wire rope to be condemned?

Answer: In the event that 10% of the wires are broken in any 8 diameter lengths of the wire, it should be condemned.

Question 18.   How do you know a rope has been approved and designated for use with Life Saving Appliances?

Answer: The rope will carry a specified 'colour yarn' rove through the lay of the rope. The yarn was originally referred to as a 'Rogues Yarn', and was designated to a specific port of origin to prevent one Royal Navy ship from stealing the ropes of another Royal Navy ship, from a different port.

The term 'Rogues Yarn' still survives but for identification purpose.

Question 19.   How would you supervise the breaking out of a new coil of mooring rope?

Answer: I would instruct the Boatswain to use a suspended turntable, and flake the new rope the full length of the deck (approximately 120 fathoms in a new coil). It would then be coiled and stowed in the rope locker ready for future use.

Question 20.   Describe the operation and use of a 'pilot hoist'?

Answer: Pilot hoists are common to high sided vessels and the operation of the hoist must be carried out by a responsible Officer. Once rigged overside, the hoist must be tested prior to use. The two-way intercom from the platform to the deck would also be tested.

The pilot will have an emergency stop control on the platform in the event of incident.

Note: It should be noted that many pilots have a preference for using a pilot ladder as opposed to the hoist and it is a requirement that an option of a pilot ladder is kept readily available.

Question 21.   How would you supervise the painting of the ship's bow by use of stages?

Answer: With any operation overside, I would carry out a 'risk assessment' and make reference to the Code of Safe Working Practice

(CSWP) for relevant precautions when rigging stages. These would include the following.

Load test and inspect the stages for possible defect prior to use, ensure adequate lengths of new 'gantlines' are cut to secure stages by 'stage hitch and lowering hitch'. Order personnel to wear harness and secured lifelines. Have a stand-by man in attendance to the stage operation, and rig appropriate side ladders to accommodate stage positions.

A lifebuoy and heaving lines would be readily available for this operation.

Many ships have a steep flare under the bow region, and this operation would necessitate the rigging of a bowsing in line around the bow. Paint rollers would require man-helpers attached in order to paint extended areas.

Question 22.   When taking a docking tug, how would you secure the tugs wire towline?

Answer: Instructions from the pilot or the ship's Master may dictate the method of securing the tugs wire. However, in the absence of positive instruction it would be anticipated that the towline would be obtained initially by heaving line, followed by a rope tail messenger. The wire would then be heaved on board and turned about the bitts in figure of '8' fashion, leaving the eye clear. The turns on the bollards would then be secured by a light lashing.

Question 23.   When acting as the Mooring Officer, at the ship's aft station, what would be your main concerns and priorities?

Answer: My prime concern in any mooring operation would be the safety of personnel engaged on the mooring deck. To this end I would pay particular attention to ensure effective communications to and from the mooring station. The ropes and associated resources would be inspected to make sure that heaving lines were in place, winches fully operational, and that all personnel had been briefed on the mooring procedures.

Ropes and wires would be cleared and 'flaked' ready for running in a manner as to avoid kinking. Stoppers would be rigged and seen to be in a good condition and the whole area would be adequately illuminated during the hours of darkness.

The aft mooring deck station aboard a passenger/vehicle ferry.

Question 24.   How would you apply a chain stopper to a mooring wire when transferring the mooring from the winch drum to the 'bitts'?

Answer: The chain stopper is employed on a mooring wire by means of a 'cow hitch' and then turned up against the lay of the wire (if the chain is turned with the lay the links could cause the wire to distort).

Question 25.   When employing 'bulldog wire rope grips', how would you secure them?

Answer: When securing wire rope grips the positioning of each grip must be considered essential to the security of the hold.
   When securing grips the bolted brace part of the grip must be placed on the standing part, as illustrated below.

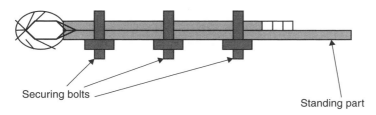

Bulldog wire rope grips.

Question 26. What would you use 'seizing wire' for?

Answer: Seizing wire is employed for various uses including: marking of anchor cables at the shackle length ends, also for mousing the bolts/pins of shackles to prevent them from coming loose. The wire can also be secured to prevent bottle screws (US Turnbuckles) from accidentally unwinding.

Question 27. When splicing an eye into a mooring rope, what tools and implements would you need to use?

Answer: Mooring ropes are heavy and of a large diameter. In order to affect an eye splice a large 'setting fid' would be needed with a heavy mallet to open up the strands of the rope in order to complete the splice.

Question 28. How would you join two wire hawsers together (without eye splicing) to take exceptional weight as in a towline?

Answer: Turn the ends of the hawsers into a 'diamond carrick bend'. Take the weight on the hawsers and then secure the tails with lashings. The use of the carrick bend is preferred to the 'double sheet bend' because it will not jam when under tension and will release easily.

Note: The weight needs to be taken before the lashings secure the tails or the lashings will be pulled adrift.

Question 29. When would you employ a Spanish eye? (Sometimes referred to as a reduced eye or a Flemish eye.)

Answer: This eye is found in a runner wire bolted onto the barrel of a cargo winch by means of a 'U' bolt.

Question 30. What hitch would you use when securing a boatswains chair to a gantline?

Answer: A double sheet bend only.

2 Questions for the Rank of Chief Mate

INTRODUCTION

Candidates who present themselves for the oral examination for Chief Mate should be aware that this rank is considered as a position of senior authority aboard the vessel. As such a higher level of responsibility over and above that of Officer of the Watch is being assessed by the Marine Examiner.

The Examiner will also be aware that the Chief Mates position aboard a vessel is considered as that of being the 'Working Boss'. As such three main areas of work are identified as being essential to such a position, namely: the **stability** of the ship, the **cargo operations** of the vessel and the **maintenance** procedures, for each and every voyage.

It is because of these topical work areas that Examiners tend to lean the questioning of candidates, towards associated activities within the Chief Officers working routine. Questions are not limited to these precise areas, but clearly the assessment must take account, that the candidate can carry out respective duties as the Ship's 1st Mate. Additionally, as with any other Certificate of Competency, a thorough knowledge of the Rule of the Road and Buoyage Systems, would also be expected.

Examiners of any senior qualification would also expect the candidate to demonstrate a level of management skill related to the nature of the work. In the case of employment within the Mercantile Marine a degree of 'Power of Command' and confidence, would also be expected qualities, that must be deemed desirable in any individual, expecting to hold a senior position.

Note: It should also be borne in mind that under the Standards of Training, Certification and Watchkeeping (STCW) guidelines persons holding an unlimited

1st Mates, Certificate of Competency may take command of a vessel under 3000 gross registered tonnage (grt). As such questions of a Master's standing, during the oral examinations, must be considered as fair and an acceptable form of assessment for this particular grade.

CERTIFICATES AND SHIP'S DOCUMENTATION

Question 1.   When joining a General Cargo ship as Chief Officer, what documents would you expect to take over from the relieved Mate?

Answer: When taking over as Chief Officer I would anticipate being supplied with the following: All ship's plans, inclusive of the Docking Plan, Plug Plan, General Arrangement, Shell Expansion, Fire Arrangement Plan, CO_2 Plan, Load Density Plans and the Rigging Plan.

All the stability criteria, inclusive of the ship's general particulars, deadweight (dwt) scale, cross curves of stability (KN and KG), statical stability information, tank capacities, ballast, fresh water and fuel arrangements. Damage stability information, together with any computer loading/discharging programmes.

All relevant working certificates such as Safety Equipment Certificate, Safety Radio Certificate, Load Line Certificate, Liferaft Certificates, Safety Ship Construction Certificate, De-Rat Exemption or De-Rat Certificate.

Note: The dates of validity would normally be noted to ensure that survey dates are not allowed to expire.

All cargo documentation including the cargo plan, cargo manifest, the Register of Cargo Handling and Lifting Appliances, The Cargo Securing Manual together with, Mates Receipts, and any Bills of Lading would also be handed over. Information on special cargoes, heavy lifts, or hazardous cargo parcels may have specific carriage or stowage instructions to consider.

Miscellaneous documents like the Log Books, tank sounding records, Crew List, Planned maintenance Schedule, etc. would normally be noted during any such handover period.

Question 2.   What is the period of validity of the De-Rat or the De-Rat Exemption Certificate?

Answer: 6 months.

Question 3. Having received the cargo manifest, prior to loading a General Cargo vessel, what items in particular would you look for, as Chief Officer?

Answer: In order of priority I would note:

- Any dangerous or hazardous goods.
- Any heavy lift items.
- Any personnel effects, valuable or special cargoes, e.g. Mails.

Question 4. When your vessel is scheduled to enter Dry Dock, what documentation would you prepare, prior to entry?

Answer: The occasion for Dry Docking the vessel would require the following plans and documents to be readily available:

(a) The Dry Dock Plan.
(b) The Shell Expansion Plan.
(c) The General Arrangement Plan.
(d) The Chief Officer's repair list.
(e) The Plug Plan.
(f) The ship's fire fighting arrangement.
(g) Tank arrangement.
(h) Relevant stability information.
(i) A list of the ship's general particulars.
(j) Rigging plan.
(k) Relevant Certificates for required surveys.
(l) Cargo Plan (if docking with cargo on board).

Question 5. If your ship is a 'tanker' vessel, what additional and specific certificate would be required prior to entering Dry Dock?

Answer: Tankers require a 'gas free' certificate prior to entry into Dry Dock.

Question 6. What information would you expect to find on the ship's 'Dry Dock Plan'?

Answer: Dry Dock Plans contain the following information: In addition to the ship's general particulars, and the ship owner's details, measurements for the overall length, breadth and depth would be included, with the air draught.

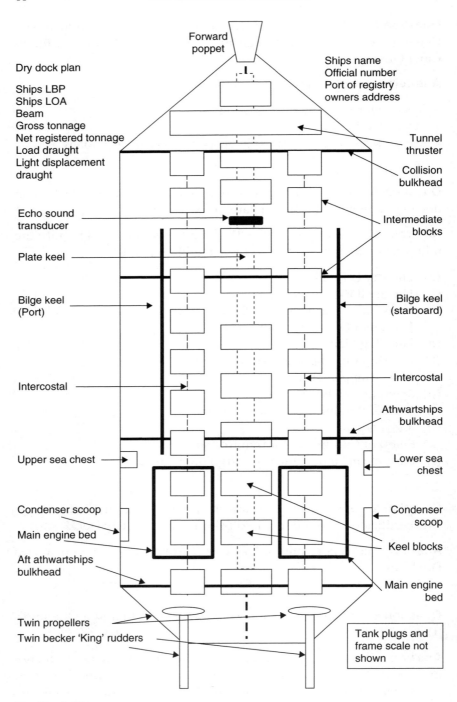

Forward poppet

Dry dock plan

Ships LBP
Ships LOA
Beam
Gross tonnage
Net registered tonnage
Load draught
Light displacement
draught

Ships name
Official number
Port of registry
owners address

Tunnel
thruster

Collision
bulkhead

Echo sound
transducer

Intermediate
blocks

Plate keel

Bilge keel
(Port)

Bilge keel
(starboard)

Intercostal

Intercostal

Athwartships
bulkhead

Upper sea chest

Lower sea
chest

Condenser scoop

Condenser
scoop

Main engine bed

Keel blocks

Aft athwartships
bulkhead

Main engine
bed

Twin propellers

Twin becker 'King' rudders

Tank plugs and
frame scale not
shown

Dry Dock Plan.

The main outline would also show the position of all Keel Blocks and docking shores, with indication of any appendages protruding from the hull.

Question 7. What information is contained in the Cargo Securing Manual?

Answer: The Cargo Securing Manual provides details on the number of lashings and securing points available on the vessel. The manual is respective to an individual vessel and will specify the distribution of lashings required per cargo space and specific weight load tests/safe working load (SWL) applicable to lashing points, pad eyes, ring bolts, etc.

Question 8. What is the Register of Cargo Handling and Lifting Appliances, and what is kept in it?

Answer: The Register is a filing system for retaining the records and certificates of all the ship's lifting apparatus, including certificates for shackles, blocks, wires, derricks, cranes, chains, hooks, etc.

Question 9. Who maintains the Register of Cargo Handling and Lifting Appliances, and who would inspect it?

Answer: The Register is kept and maintained by the Chief Officer and is liable for inspection by the cargo surveyor when carrying out a Cargo Equipment Survey. It is also liable for inspection by the External Auditor when monitoring the ship's conformity to International Safety Management (ISM) Code.

Question 10. Your vessel is about to go through a Safety Equipment Survey what documents would you prepare for use by the surveyor?

Answer: The Certificate (5-year validation with annual inspection under the Harmonised Survey System) and the 'Record of Inspection'. Liferaft and Hydrostatic Release Unit Certificates. ISM last audit report and planned maintenance schedule (if required).

Question 11.   What types of entries are made in the 'Garbage Record Book'?

Answer: Any garbage disposed of should be recorded in the Record Book. The ship's position should be recorded along with the quantity of garbage disposed and the date and time of disposal.

The method of disposal and the nature of the garbage are also required. In the event that garbage is deposited at a Port Reception and/or incinerated, a receipt for the garbage must be obtained.

Question 12.   What two documents represent compliance with the ISM Code?

Answer: The ship should have its own Safety Management Certificate (SMC) and will carry a 'copy' of the 'Document of Compliance (DoC).'

Note: The original Document of Compliance is held by the company, a separate DoC, for every class/type of vessel the company operates.

Question 13.   What on the vessel must be compatible with the Safe Manning Certificate?

Answer: The Ship's Life Saving Appliances must satisfy the number of personnel carried aboard the vessel.

Question 14.   What is the period of validity of the Liferaft Certificates and can they be extended?

Answer: The Liferaft Certificates have a period of validity of 12 months and YES, they can be extended by a period of 5 months.

Question 15.   What information and details would you expect to find on the Anchor Certificate?

Answer: The Anchor Certificate will contain the following information:

(a) The Certificate serial number.
(b) Name of the Certifying Authority.
(c) Name of the testing establishment.
(d) The mark or logo of the testing establishment, if any.

(e) Name of the Supervisor of Tests and their signature.
(f) Weight of the anchor.
(g) Type of anchor.
(h) Length of the shank in millimetres.
(i) Length of arms in millimetres.
(j) Diameter of the 'trend' in millimetres.
(k) Proof load applied, in tonnes.
(l) Weight of 'stock', if applicable.

Question 16.   What official publications must be carried by your ship?

Answer: In accord with Notice No. 18, of the Annual Summary of Notices to Mariners the ship must carry the following publications:

(a)   The Mariners Handbook.
(b)   The International Code of Signals.
(c)   The Weekly Notices to Mariners.
(d)   The Marine Guidance Notices (MGNs), The Merchant Shipping Notices (MSNs) and The Marine Information Notices (MINs).
(e)   List of Radio Signals.
(f)   List of Lights.
(g)   Sailing Directions.
(h)   Nautical Almanac.
(i)   Nautical Tables.
(j)   Tide Tables.
(k)   Tidal Stream Atlas.
(l)   Operating and maintenance manuals for navigational aids.
(m) A full set of working navigational charts.

Note: The question has asked for the official publication requirements and candidates for examination, should listen to the question carefully. Most ships carry many other useful publications such as the International Aeronautical and Marine Search and Rescue (IAMSAR) Manual, Ocean Passages of the World, and Admiralty Distance Tables. But the question did not ask what a well-found ship might carry.

Question 17.   Having completed a period in 'Dry Dock' what document would you expect to have to sign, prior to departing the dock?

Answer: The dock foreman would present the 'Authority to Flood' certificate, for signature by the ship's Chief Officer.

Note: This should not be signed until the Chief Officer is satisfied that all the essential work has been completed, that all bottom plugs have been replaced and that all personnel are clear of the dock floor.

Question 18. Your vessel has just completed taking bunkers. What documentation would you complete?

Answer: An entry to the effect of completing bunker operations must be made in the ship's Deck Log Book and in the vessels 'Oil Record Book'. The Oil Record Book entry, must have a double signature with the Master signing each page, and each separate entry being made by the operational officer, i.e. the Chief Officer or the Chief Engineer.

Question 19. During an external audit, the ISM inspector finds damage to a ventilator and orders repairs to be made within the next 3 months. What document would you expect to receive from the inspector?

Answer: The Auditor would issue a Notice of 'Non-Conformity'. This would usually carry a time limiting period. Provided the damage is rectified in the time period this notice would be cancelled by a future inspector.

Question 20. How are the ballast arrangements on the vessel monitored?

Answer: The movement of ballast is recorded in the ballast management record. Entries reflect the ship's position at the time of pumping or transferring ballast quantities. The date and time of operation as well as the identity of respective tanks involved.

Question 21. What is the period of validity of the 'Load Line Certificate'?

Answer: 5 years.

Question 22. What is the significance of the Chief Officers 'repair list'?

Answer: The repair list is an going list of essential repairs that will be carried out at an appropriate time in the future, usually the Dry Dock period.

The list is meant to protect the owners' interests and ensure that any survey work required on the vessel is not overlooked prior to the next survey.

Question 23. A Port State Control Inspector is due to visit the vessel, what would you expect to prepare on the navigational bridge prior to this inspection?

Answer: I would anticipate that the inspector would check the Chart Folio's and the 'Chart Correction Log'. He would expect to see the 'passage plan' and records of navigation warnings together with the statutory publications. Bridge equipment and the maintenance manuals with respective 'check lists' for the testing procedure of bridge equipment.

Question 24. Following an accident to a seaman aboard your vessel, what would you do?

Answer: In the case of any accident to personnel I would order the Safety Officer to investigate the circumstances and make a report of the incident to include, witness statements and photographs if appropriate. The Safety Officer would be instructed to complete an accident report form, and an entry would be made in the Deck Log Book of the essential details.

Note: In every case which involves injury to personnel the medical provision would be the first priority.

Question 25. What is a 'Mates Receipt'?

Answer: A document signed by the ship's mate or Chief Officer to acknowledge receipt of cargo on board the vessel. It forms the basis for the final Bill of Laden.

Question 26. Under the ISM convention what certificate is initially given to a new ship and what is its period of validity?

Answer: A new ship would be issued with an 'Interim Safety Management Certificate' valid for a period of 12 months.

Question 27. What organisations issue a vessel with a Certificate of Class?

Answer: The Classification Societies, e.g. Lloyds Register, American Bureau of Shipping, Bureau Veritas, etc.

Question 28. What type of vessels must have a 'Permit to Operate' and a 'Craft Operating Manual?'

Answer: High Speed Craft.

Question 29. Fast, high speed ferries must comply with which code?

Answer: The High Speed Craft (HSC) Code 1996, revised 2002.

Question 30. What type of craft are covered by the HSC Code?

Answer: High speed ferries of Category 'A' Craft (carrying not more than 450 passengers) Category 'B' craft passenger high speed other than Category 'A' types which have the capability to navigate safely in the event of damage to essential machinery. A cargo high speed craft class other than a passenger craft.

High Speed Ferry vessel seen lying port side to the Ro-Ro terminal in Barcelona, Spain.

Examples: Air cushion, hovercraft, hydrofoils and wig craft. Cater-marans, and some Trimarans may fall into these categories.

EMERGENCIES AND DAMAGE CONTROL

Question 1. Following an incident where the ship has run aground, what actions would you expect to take as the Chief Officer of the vessel?

Answer: Following a grounding incident the Chief Officer would expect to report his intention to the Master to carry out a 'damage assessment'. This assessment would expect to address the following items:

(a) The water tight integrity of the hull.
(b) The condition of the engine room either 'wet or dry'.
(c) A casualty report.
(d) Any evidence of pollution.

Subsequent actions would also include taking a full set of tank soundings, as well as overside soundings, paying particular attention to the bow and stern areas.

It is assumed that on the outcome of the Chief Officer's damage report, the Master would open up communications with relevant inter-ested parties.

The Chief Officer would advise the Master throughout this period to display the signals to indicate a 'vessel aground', and also recommend that the ship's anchors are walked back to prevent the possibility of accidental re-floating in a possibly damaged state.

Ballast adjustment may be necessary at some stage. It would also be prudent to deploy anchors to prevent accidentally, re-floating at an inappropriate time.

Question 2. What activities would the Chief Officer carry out, when the vessel is proceeding towards a distress, to recover survivors from the water?

Answer: The Chief Officer would order all hands to stand-by and assist in the following preparations:

(a) Turn out the ship's 'rescue boat' and place the boats crew on immediate stand-by to launch.
(b) Turn out the 'accommodation ladder' to effect recovery of casualties.

(c) Order the ship's medical room/hospital to prepare to receive casualties and be ready to treat for shock and hypothermia.
(d) Rig a 'guest warp' to assist boat operations.
(e) Advise the Master/Bridge Team of deck operations.
(f) Order galley staff to prepare hot food.

Question 3.   Following a fire in the ship's engine room the decision is made by the ship's Master to inject the total flood CO_2 bottle bank. Explain how the CO_2 injection system works?

Answer: The total flood system is set for immediate operation into the high risk area of the engine room. Once the decision is made to inject CO_2, the Chief Officer would be expected to shut down the boilers, fans and fuel lines and evacuate the machinery space. Following a 'roll call' of all personnel the pilot bottles would be activated by pulling the handle in the remote operating cabinet and operate the injection valve to allow ingress into the machinery space (once the cabinet is opened the alarms would be automatically activated).

This action would let CO_2 from the pilot bottles into pressurise the cylinder and push the piston downwards. The piston movement will fire the 'bottle bank' and cause CO_2 to enter the engine room.

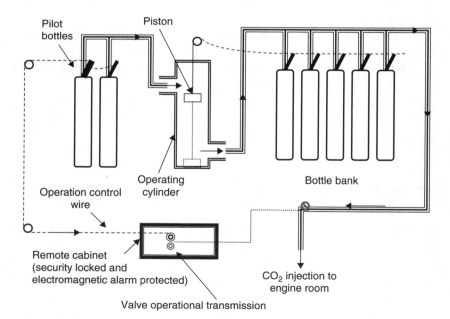

Basic CO_2, total flood, bottle bank system.

Question 4.   In the event of having to inject the total flood CO_2 into a cargo space, how would you know the amount of CO_2 to inject?

Answer: The amount of gas to inject will be defined by the CO_2 Plan, copies of which are found inside the CO_2 Bottle Room, in the Chief Officers Office and in the ship's fire fighting arrangement.

Question 5.   In the event of a fire in the engine room what would be an expected line of action for the Chief Officer?

Answer: In most cases the Chief Officer is considered the On Scene Co-ordinator (OSC) and he would probably take charge of the fire party once the alarm has been sounded.

It is in the interests of all, to tackle the fire **immediately**, on the basis that large fires were initially small fires, and such immediate action could well save the day, early. In any event the function of the Chief Officer is to establish a fire party at the fire face and try to knock out the fire by conventional means.

The Chief Officer is concerned with logistics to include communication to the men at the fire face and the navigation bridge. He is also meant to keep the fire fighting activity directed towards the fire face, and this can only be achieved if fire fighters have: (a) a fire fighting medium and (b) breathing air.

To this end the organisation of establishing a back up fire party, continuing boundary cooling, ordering the vent party to close off ventilation and holding the first aid party in readiness, all go towards the Chief Officers overall management of the situation.

Should the situation deteriorate it would also be up to the Chief Officer to recommend to the Master the use of total flood systems. In such an event, the Chief Officer would order fire teams to extract themselves from the engine room, prior to total flood activation.

Question 6.   What are the advantages and disadvantages of CO_2 total flood system?

Answer:

Advantages: Good knock down capability, a readily available supply of CO_2 around the world, comparatively cheap, cleaner than foam.

Disadvantages: Once fired at sea, no replenishment until arrival in port, non-breathable atmosphere, if used the ship is without motive power for an indefinite period.

Question 7. When advised of impending heavy weather, imminent, what actions would you take as the Chief Officer of the vessel?

Answer: With a heavy weather warning issued, the Chief Officer would address the following four areas: stability, cargo security, navigational safety and the overall security of the deck.

Stability Issues to Address
(a) Improve the vessels GM, if possible.
(b) Remove any free surface moments if possible.
(c) Ballast the vessel down.
(d) Check the freeboard deck seals on hatches and other openings.
(e) Close watertight doors.
(f) Pump out swimming pool if carried.

Cargo Security
(a) Check and tighten all deck cargo lashings.
(b) Tighten up lashing on General Cargo below decks if appropriate.
(c) Trim cargo ventilation and shut down vents if not required.

Navigation Safety
(a) Consult an advise Master regarding the aspects of re-routing.
(b) Verify vessels position.
(c) Update weather reports.
(d) Plot storm position.
(e) Update vessels position and inform shore-side authorities.
(f) Engage manual steering.
(g) Revise Estimated Time of Arrival (ETA).
(h) Secure Bridge against heavy rolling.
(i) Reduce speed in ample time to prevent 'pounding'.

Deck Security
(a) Rig lifelines.
(b) Check securing on, gangways, lifeboats, derricks/cranes, anchors, etc.
(c) Reduce manpower working on deck and start heavy weather work routine.
(d) Warn 'Heads of Departments' of impending heavy weather.
(e) Clear decks of surplus gear.
(f) Close weather deck doors.
(g) Slacken down whistle lanyards.
(h) Check all Life Saving Appliances (LSA) equipment readily available.

(i) Organise meal reliefs, if appropriate.
(j) Organise watch structure to suit three-man watch system.
(k) Note all preparations in the Log Book.

Question 8. While on a coastal passage, a navigation warning is received about a 'new danger' on your intended track. How would you expect a new danger to be identified?

Answer: New dangers are marked by the use of double 'cardinal marks' or double 'lateral marks'. One of these double marks would carry a 'RACON' morse 'D' reflective signature on the radar screen.

Question 9. What limitations are enforced on helicopter operations in offshore coastal regions?

Answer: Helicopter operations are restricted on 'range of operation' by the amount of fuel (aviation spirit) that their tanks can hold. This is further limited by the 'payload' that they carry. Also, progress against head winds could affect the endurance of operation.
   Poor visibility would ground helicopters because of the need for a visible horizon. Also storm force winds may inhibit take off, for rotary winged aircraft.
   Night flying can take place in general conditions provided the pilot is trained with Instrument Flying Rating (IFR).

Question 10. Your vessel is about to engage with a Helicopter to carry out a 'Medivac'. What deck reception preparations would you make?

Answer: The deck preparations to engage with a helicopter would include the following actions:

(a) Clean the deck area thoroughly of all loose gear.
(b) Lower any obstructive aerials from aloft.
(c) Mark the deck area of operation 'H' or 'Yellow Spot'.
(d) Display Restricted in Ability to Manoeuvre, navigation signals.
(e) Display a wind sock, call sign flags, or white smoke, as a wind directional indicator.
(f) Lower ship side rails, if appropriate.
(g) Have a fire party on stand-by, but clear of the operational area.
(h) Turn the rescue boat out board.

(i)   Designate a 'Heli-deck Landing Officer (HLO)'.
(j)   Designate a 'Hook-Handler'.
(k)   Warn department heads of ongoing activity.
(l)   Keep non-essential personnel clear of the operational area.
(m) Prepare the casualty, with documents for evacuation.

Note: The ship's navigation requirements would be handled by the Bridge
Team, under the supervision of the Master. The Search and Rescue Helicopter
Hi-Line Technique is described in MGN 161 (see Appendix C).

Question 11.   While holding the anchor watch aboard your vessel,
you see another vessel approaching at a fast speed and closing range.
What action would you anticipate taking, in the absence of the Master,
if the approaching vessel was at a 2-mile range?

Answer: I would monitor the vessel closely and sound five or more
short and rapid blasts on my ship's whistle. If the vessel did not take
immediate action to alter her course away from my position I would
order 'dead slow ahead' on the ship's engines and steam over my own
ship's anchor cable.

Note: This action would take my vessel out of the line of approach and avoid
the potential 'collision scenario'.

When at anchor the ship's engines are left on 'stop' and as such
should be readily available for an immediate order.
Alternative actions are available in this situation:

(a) Pay out on the anchor cable and let the vessel drop back
     astern.
(b) Heave in on the anchor cable and pull the vessel ahead.
(c) Go hard over with the rudder and give the vessel a sheer.

The above alternatives will take up valuable time to execute and the
closing range of the target vessel may not permit the use of these
options.

Question 12.   What emergency towing arrangement do you have
aboard a large tanker vessel, over 20,000 ton?

Answer: Large tankers must now be fitted with emergency towing
brackets in the fore and aft positions. These will generally take the
form of a 'SMIT bracket' or other weight bearing anchor point. The
ship is also expected to supply a chafe chain length, secured from this

anchor point to permit being towed. In the event that an abandon-ment of the tanker has to take place, it is anticipated that the chafe chain would be deployed prior to total abandonment to enable a tug to become attached.

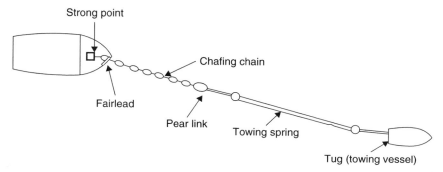

Emergency towing arrangement for tanker vessels.

Question 13. When recovering your anchor cable you discover the anchor has caught up a submarine cable. What action would you take?

Answer: Once it is realised that the anchor is fouled by a submerged cable it would be imperative to inform the Bridge immedi-ately, and in no circumstances give indication that the anchor is 'sighted and clear'.

In agreement with the Master it would be prudent to let the anchor go again, with the hope that the fouled cable will dislodge itself with this action. However, it must be realised that the anchor may not clear itself and in such circumstances one of two actions must be considered:

(a) Walk the anchor back to the bottom. Break the cable at the next joining shackle on deck. Buoy the anchor cable and deliberately sacrifice the anchor and a limited amount of cable. **Note:** It is anticipated that the cable company will recover the anchor, free of charge. The ship would be considered unseaworthy without two working bow anchors and this situation would require the spare anchor to be secured for the vessel to retain her classification.

(b) If the foul can be rectified simply, without incurring damage it may be possible to bight a soft mooring rope about the foul cable. Walk the anchor chain back to clear the obstruction, then heave the anchor home. Release the bight of rope and jettison the cable.

Question 14. While tied up alongside, working cargo, smoke is sighted coming out of the No. 2 hatch of a General Cargo vessel. The Cargo Watch Officer has raised the fire alarm. What would you do as the ship's Chief Officer?

Answer: It would be normal practice to muster the fire party and proceed to the scene of the fire. However, as the fire incident is in port, members of crew could well be ashore and this could leave the fire party deficient.

The Chief Officer would be expected to take immediate control of the situation using the manpower and the resources available and his orders and actions could expect to include any or all of the following:

Once the Alarm Has Been Sounded
(a) Stop all cargo operations aboard the vessel.
(b) Call in the local fire brigade, via the port and harbour control on very high frequency (VHF) radio, requesting immediate assistance.
(c) Remove all non-essential personnel from the ship, e.g. stevedores (check with ship's foreman that the workers are all clear).
(d) Batten down the cargo hatch which is seemingly on fire.
(e) Order the engineers to put water on deck and pressurise the fire main.
(f) Commence boundary cooling on as many sides of the cargo hatch as possible.
(g) Post a Chief Officers messenger at the head of the gangway to meet the local fire brigade on arrival.
(h) Make ready a fire envelope to include the cargo plan and the ship's fire arrangement.
(i) Have the 'International Shore Connection' readily available.
(j) Instruct Chief Engineer to make ready CO_2 for cargo hold flooding.
(k) Carry out a head count of all ship's personnel on board.
(l) Make notes of any injuries as they occur.
(m) Move up breathing apparatus to the scene, together with fire fighters.
(n) Tend fire wires fore and aft.

(o) Lift gangway clear of quayside.
(p) Place engine room on stand by.

Once the brigade has arrived it would be common practice to agree the desired method of attacking the fire with the view to bring it under control. Appropriate entries would be made into the ship's Log Book as required.

Note: No emergency scenario can expect to take account of each and every detail because each situation will be governed by a different set of circumstances. The above answer is meant only as a general guide.

Question 15. After striking a floating object, your vessel sustains damage on the waterline and a loss in watertight integrity is observed. The Master lists the vessel over and orders you to establish a collision patch over the damaged area. How would you do this?

Answer: Assuming that the vessel is not equipped with designated damage control materials, the Chief Officer would be expected to improvise to establish the patch. This could be carried out by various means and the following is a suggested method:

(a) Bolt steel bottom plates together (obtained from the engine room) and staple a rope pudding around the perimeter of the joined plates.
(b) Drill the centre of the plates to accommodate a shackle and drill the upper edge to fit suspension shackles.
(c) Cover the outer surface and inner edge with canvas.
(d) Lower the patch over the gunwale on suspension wires to cover the damaged area of the hull.
(e) Brace the patch in, by means of a 'Spanish Windlass' from the opposing side of the hold, if the cargo load permits.

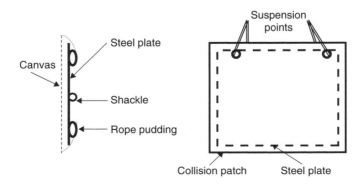

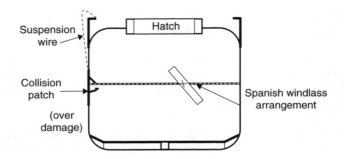

Question 16.   What would be the expected duties of the Chief Officer, in the event of his ship being involved in a collision at sea?

Answer: It would be anticipated that the Master would take the 'conn' of the vessel, if he is able. As such the Chief Officer would probably be ordered to obtain an immediate damage assessment to assess the following:

(a)   Watertight integrity of the hull.
(b)   The state of the engine room, either wet or dry.
(c)   A casualty list to include nature of injuries.
(d)   Pollution incurred, and from which tanks.

   Subsequent actions would include a detailed set of internal soundings of all the ship's tanks. Damage control parties would be formed to restore any damaged shipboard systems.
   As soon as practical, the stability of the vessel would need to be assessed taking into account the 'damaged stability' criteria.

Note: Clearly the types of ships involved in the collision will affect the nature of the required actions. Also the state of weather at the time, together with the severity of the contact between the two ships will influence considerably individual actions.

Question 17.   As a Chief Officer, describe how you would pass a towline astern, to a stricken vessel, which has suffered engine failure, when in heavy weather?

Answer: Heavy weather conditions would no doubt restrict the ship drawing too close to the stricken vessel. In such an incident it would be prudent to fire a rocket line over the target. This would subsequently allow a messenger to be attached to the rocket line. Once the messenger is passed then a 'Towing Hawser' could be secured to the messenger and subsequently passed to the distressed vessel for securing to a towing strong point.

Question 18. What do you consider the term 'risk assessment' means?

Answer: Risk assessment is a detailed and careful assessment of potential harmful factors that are contained within the nature of an operation. It is expected to classify the work and identify high, low and tolerable risk elements to personnel within the working environment. It is meant to provide an action plan which would permit ongoing operations to within limits of a tolerable risk. Check lists are employed to assess the Initial Risk and subsequent detailed parameters effecting the overall final assessment, prior to commencement of the work.

Question 19. If the need arose to abandon your vessel, what additional equipment would you order to be placed into the lifeboats, if time permitted?

Answer: Additional equipment would probably be in the form of communication items and life support gear, namely:

(a) Search and Rescue Transponder (SART).
(b) Emergency Position Indicating Radio Beacon (EPIRB).
(c) Two-way VHF walkie-talkie radio.
(d) Extra food.
(e) Blankets.
(f) Water and medical supplies.

Question 20. Having anchored your cargo vessel overnight, the windlass controls are found to have suffered massive corrosion and the ship is without spares to instigate repairs. How would you attempt to recover your anchor?

Answer: Being a cargo vessel I would investigate the possibility of improvising the cargo winches to provide the power to recover the anchor.
  This could be carried out by one or more of the following:

(a) Establishing a friction drive between the No. 1 hatch cargo winch and the windlass drum by means of a mooring rope turned up on both warping drums.

(b) Employing the topping lift of No. 1 derrick to engage in short hauls on the bight of cable at the hawse pipe. Free wheeling the gypsy to feed the cable into the locker.
(c) Employing a direct pull from a cargo winch or stores winch, to provide a direct pull on the cable via a heavy duty block and tackle arrangement. This would necessitate the rigging of an overhauling tackle to reduce the time element of the exercise.

Note: In all the above options, it would be anticipated that the ship's engines are used 'ahead' to ease the weight load on the cable when effecting recovery.

Question 21.   What orders and procedures would you expect to be contained within an emergency check list, to effect an abandonment of the ship?

Answer: An emergency checklist to abandon the vessel would probably contain the following items:

(a) Obtain the ship's position and transmit a distress alert message.
(b) Instruct crew/passengers of the order to abandon and to don warm clothing and put on life jackets.
(c) Directing them to the emergency boat stations.
(d) Turn out survival craft and prepare for immediate launch.
(e) Launch the rescue boat with crew in immersion suits.
(f) Order additional life support items to be placed into boats if time permits.
(g) Check that all lifeboat painters are stretched forward and launch survival craft when fully loaded.
(h) Brief coxswains of survival craft to remain in close proximity to the mother ship.

Question 22.   UK passenger vessels and passenger vessels, passing through UK waters are required to have a Search and Rescue (SAR) emergency response plan available for operational use (Reference: MSN 1761 M). What are the objectives of this plan?

Answer: The objectives of the SAR plan for passenger vessels are:

(a) To provide early and effective contact between the passenger vessel and the SAR services. Such contact will also take into account communications with the ship's owners and associated emergency response organisations. It will include regular communication updates to all interested parties as to the state and progressive condition of the emergency.

(b) To provide essential information, relevant to the SAR services, inclusive of voyage details and passenger numbers.

(c) To provide the vessel with relevant details of the local SAR service system, inclusive of emergency services that are available to assist with decision-making and emergency planning.

(d) To provide support and useful information in the event that the passenger vessel has to take up the role of OSC in an SAR operation.

Question 23. What are the two functions of a 'rescue boat' during the action of abandoning a ship?

Answer: The rescue boat has two functions during an abandonment:

(a) Recover persons from the water, preferably in a horizontal manner.

(b) Marshall survival craft upwind and clear of toxics or the dangers associated with capsize of the parent vessel.

Question 24. Following a minor collision a ship is proceeding towards a port of refuge when it is realised that the fore end of the vessel is flooding and that the collision bulkhead is in danger of collapse. What action would you take if you had no means or materials to shore up the collision bulkhead?

Highlight any hazards that may be associated with your solution?

Answer: Few modern merchant ships carry sufficient damage control equipment to be capable of shoring up a bulkhead. Even if employing improvised equipment like derricks or crane jibs, neither is the manpower to handle such items usually readily available.

If flooding is a feature on one side of the bulkhead it may be prudent to deliberately partially flood the next compartment aft. This would have the effect of putting an opposing pressure on the bulkhead and possibly prevent the bulkhead collapsing.

Such action will, however, increase any free surface moments affecting the ship's positive stability. Therefore, such action should simultaneously be accompanied by any improvement to the 'GM', e.g. pressing up double bottom ballast tanks.

Question 25. While on your evening watch the vessel enters known ice limits of the North Atlantic. It is during the peak of the ice season for icebergs and you have been advised by reports from the International Ice Patrol, that dangerous ice is ahead on your vessels track. What actions would you expect to take?

Answer: Such conditions would dictate that I would advise the Master of the relevant details. Although the final decision would be the Masters, I would advise him/her, in order to comply with the Safety of Life at Sea (SOLAS) requirements the ship would be expected to only proceed at a moderate speed at night, when ice is reported ahead of the vessels intended track.

A prudent Master, being aware that ice formations generally make very poor radar targets, would probably stop the vessel during the hours of darkness when inside such hazardous limits, waiting until day-light before proceeding.

A statement to this effect would also be entered into the ship's Log Book.

Note: This may seem to a candidate that this is a Master's example question but it is pointed out that Chief Officers (with unlimited Chief Mates Certificates) may take command of vessels less than 3000 grt under the current STCW Regulations.

Question 26. Following an engine room incident in open waters, while you are acting as Chief Officer aboard a dry cargo vessel, the Master requires the services of a tug. You are ordered to make prepara-tions for the vessel to be towed. What preparations and actions would you carry out and what type of towline would you employ?

Answer: It would probably not be practical to rig a towing bridle and as such a composite towline would be employed. Such a towline being constructed with the ship's own anchor cable and the combined use of the tugs towing spring. The arrangement could be established in two ways:

(a) by hanging the anchor off at the break of the foc'stle head and baring the end of the cable to secure to the towing spring, or

(b) by leaving the anchor on and securing the towing spring to the Anchor Crown 'D' shackle once walked out clear of the hawse pipe.

The first method requires extensive labour to 'hang the anchor off' and would require a level of rigging expertise and good weather conditions. While the second method is not as labour intensive and the anchor, left on the chain, would act to damp down movement of the cable and reduce any yawing, during the towing operation.

Prior to activities taking place for either method a risk assessment would be carried out. The windlass would be greased and checked beforehand and any rigging gear made ready in ample time. Rigging equipment for hanging an anchor off, would have to be of adequate safe working load and such stresses would need to be assessed.

Question 27.   When carrying out a damage assessment after the vessel runs aground you observe one of the oil tanks has fractured and is leaking. What actions would you consider appropriate to reduce the effects of the pollution?

Answer: Assuming a double bottom oil tank, it would be considered prudent to seal the upper deck scuppers to prevent oil being forced on deck by water pressure and going over the ship's side. It is assumed that the Master would contact the Designated Person Ashore (DPA) and as the Chief Officer you would recommend that Barrier/boom gear and dispersal chemicals are despatched to the vessel immediately via the ship's agents. It must be anticipated that all items of the Ship's Oil Pollution Emergency Plan (SOPEP) are carried out.

If possible, internal transfer of oil from fractured tanks into sound tanks would be carried out, as soon as practical. Similarly, external transfer from damaged tanks into a storage oil barge or shore side holding, would be arranged when available. Dispersal chemicals could be applied immediately to any oil pockets on the ship's decks. Local permission to use chemicals overside would also be sort.

Relevant entries would need to be made in the Deck Log Book, the Official Log Book, and the Oil Record Book.

Question 28.   The chief engineer informs you that a valve in the cofferdam requires routine maintenance. As the ship's Chief Officer what would you do?

Answer: Such a task inside a cofferdam must be considered as an enclosed space activity and would necessitate the space to be prepared and checked. Further, a permit to work for enclosed space entry must be issued and a risk assessment carried out, before any work could be sanctioned.

Once the space is adequately vented, illuminated and atmosphere tested, personnel could be briefed to carry out the task following all precautions as listed within the content of the permit to work. A stand-by man would be designated outside the space while the engineers are actively engaged.

Checks would also be made that this task does not overlap with other ongoing work in the same vicinity, which may lead to a conflicting hazard.

Question 29.   While on passage across the North Atlantic your vessel strikes a floating log and the number one cargo hold is bilged. What action would you take as Chief Officer?

Answer: It would be necessary to consult the 'damage stability data' and obtain the list and the ship's revised GM. Once these facts are known prudent ballast movement could be carried out to remove the list and still retain a positive GM. If the compartment contains cargo at the time of the incident, account must be taken of the permeability of the cargo.

It may be prudent to rig a collision patch over the damaged area, assuming that the damage sustained, is at, or near the water line, from the floating object.

If the damaged area can be sealed then pumping of the bilged compartment could be carried out. In any event the Master would be expected to report the incident and inform owners to make arrangements for the vessel to be repaired. A 'port of refuge' with repair facilities may be the most immediate requirement as well as being the safest option.

Question 30.   While on a voyage across the Pacific Ocean, the Master of the ship suffers a heart attack and dies. What is the expected action of the Chief Officer?

Answer: The Chief Officer would immediately assume command of the vessel and inform senior officers and the crew of the death and the change of command. An entry into the Official Log Book would be made to this effect, stating the reason why the Chief Officer has assumed command. An entry would also be made in the Log Book under the heading of Births and Deaths on board the ship, to reflect the death of the Master.

The Master's body must be isolated in a cool storage place and the ship's owners must be Informed of the incident and the current status of the vessel. Company instructions would be expected to advise on subsequent action to the Officer in Charge of the vessel. Any witness statements and photographic evidence should be retained for future enquiries.

SHIP HANDLING AND ANCHOR PRACTICE

Question 1.   How would you prepare and pass a slip wire to a mooring buoy?

Answer: Assuming that the bow is secured by soft eye mooring ropes, the slip wire would be run to the buoy on the bight.

The eye of the slip wire would have been reduced by seizing and a messenger rope would be lowered to the mooring boat with the wire. It would be normal practice for the boat men to take some slack on the wire and on the messenger to ensure smooth operations.

Once at the buoy, a boat man, in a lifejacket, would 'jump the buoy' and pass the reduced eye through the ring of the buoy, then secure the messenger to the slip wire. This is then heaved back to the parent vessel and both parts of the slip wire can be turned up on bitts.

Note: The messenger should not be passed through the ring of the buoy as this would probably cause the reduced eye to 'jam' at the buoy ring, when being hauled back by the messenger.

Slip wires are set, as last out, last in moorings, to give the vessel the ability to let itself go from mooring buoys, without the assistance of wharf men.

Question 2.   When intending to tie the vessel up on a tidal berth, what would you consider as an appropriate mooring pattern?

Answer: Assuming that the weather forecast is not adverse and the range of tide is not excessive, normal practice would be to secure the vessel with:

- four (4) headlines
- four (4) Stern lines

- a breast line each end, and
- a spring wire plus nylon pennant at each end.

Question 3.   What do you understand by the term 'Snub Round'?

Answer: The term refers to the turning of the vessel smartly, by means of letting an anchor go, at short stay. Use of helm movement towards the same side as the anchor has been used would effectively turn the vessel through 180°.

It is necessary where sea room is limited and an elliptical or short round is not an option. However, caution must be used to ensure that no underwater obstructions are shown where the anchor is to be used.

Question 4.   If your vessel found it had to take a tow in mid-ocean how would you rig up a 'composite towline'?

Answer: The 'composite towline' is established by use of the ship's anchor cable, being secured to a towing spring from the towing vessel. In order to connect the two, it may be necessary to hang the anchor off and bare the end of cable. The anchor can be 'hung off' in the hawse pipe by its own securing devices, if the vessel is fitted with a 'centre lead' in the bows. Alternatively, with no centre lead the anchor could be 'hung off' at the shoulder, from the break of the foc'stle head.

The Master may decide not to hang the anchor off at all but leave it *in situ*. This would then provide a steep catenary to the towline and could provide a dampening effect and reduce yawing movement of the towed vessel.

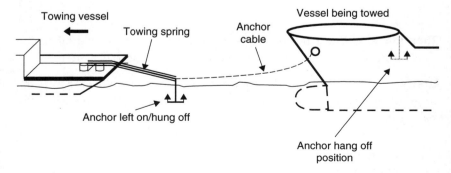

Composite towline.

Question 5.   What are the advantages and disadvantages of carrying out a Mediterranean Moor?

Answer: The advantages of the Mediterranean Moor are:

- That more vessels can berth with restricted quay space.
- Cargo ships can work both port and starboard sides into barges.
- Tanker vessels can load/discharge through stern manifolds.
- Roll on–Roll off (Ro-Ro) vessels can operate stern ramps.

The disadvantages are:

- The vessel is exposed from the shore.
- Cargo ships are denied the use of shore side cranes.
- Loading and discharge must take place into barges.
- A boat is required to go ashore.

Ferries moored stern to the quayside in Mediterranean Moor style in the Greek Island of Rhodes.

Question 6.   What is the advantage and disadvantage of using two anchors to moor the vessel?

Answer: Use of two anchors to moor the vessel is carried out to increase the holding power and prevent the vessel from dragging from her anchored position. Where a designated moor, like a running moor is executed its single purpose is to reduce the swinging room.

In any situation where two anchors are employed the disadvantage is that the risk of a 'foul hawse' is ever present.

The 'Seaward', Class 1, passenger cruise ship, seen moored at anchor with both port and starboard anchors deployed.

Question 7. A vessel moored with two anchors experiences a wind change during the night. In the morning it is realised that the cables have crossed into a foul hawse. What are the terms to describe if the cables have:

(a) Crossed once?
(b) Crossed twice?
(c) Crossed three times?

Answer:
Crossed once is termed ... 'A Cross'.
Crossed twice is termed ... 'An Elbow'.
Crossed three times is termed ... 'A Cross and Elbow'.

Note: If the vessel turned again this would be known as a 'round turn'.

Question 8.   Your vessel is under orders to moor to buoys by means of mooring ropes aft, and the anchor cable forward. How would you do this?

Answer: Initially, the vessel would secure by the use of mooring ropes both fore and aft. Once the vessel is secured to the buoys in this manner, the anchor would be hung off either at the shoulder, or in the hawse pipe, if the vessel has a centre lead 'bullring'.

Once the anchor is cleared from the cable, the bare end of the cable is flaked on deck with enough slack cable to run to the buoy. A mooring shackle would be secured to the bare end of cable, ready to secure to the ring of the buoy.

A guide wire would be passed through the cable with three or four links kept clear. Once the cable is lowered clear of the lead the guide wire from the buoy can be tensioned. The cable can be walked back to slide down towards the ring of the buoy.

A buoy jumper, with lifejacket, would then be able to secure the mooring shackle joining the bare end to the buoy ring.

The ship's bow is first secured by mooring ropes. The guide wire is then passed and the cable is walked back to slide down the guide wire to the buoy.

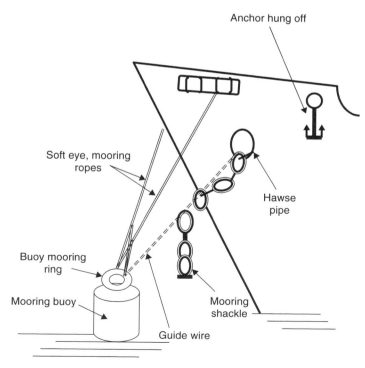

Mooring to Buoys – by means of Anchor Cable (use of 'guide wire').

Question 9. How would you moor your vessel in a tidal river, with reduced swinging room?

Answer: The vessel could be moored by either a 'running moor' or a 'standing moor', operation. If the choice is available, the running moor would be carried out because it generally provides positive control to the ship handler.

Question 10. How would you carry out a 'running moor'?

Answer: The vessel would initially stem the tidal flow and have both anchors walked back and held on the brakes of the windlass. Having previously made up an anchor plan, the ship would be manoeuvred to a position approximately five (5) shackles length, behind the designated mooring position. With engines on slow ahead, the weather anchor should be let go and the cable allowed to run, to lay out about nine (9) shackles, from this advance position stop the engines and engage the weather anchor cable in gear. Let go the second, lee anchor and provide astern propulsion. This anchor will become the riding cable as the vessel drops back astern, heaving short on the cable of the weather anchor.

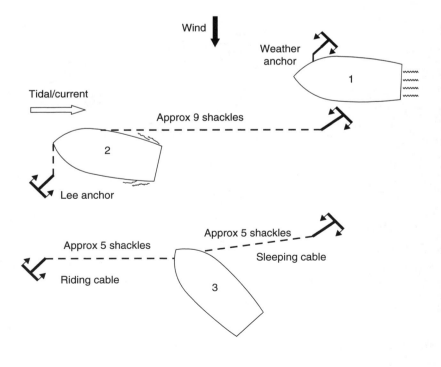

Question 11. While on anchor watch, laying to a single anchor, it is observed that the vessel is sheering about and in danger of breaking the anchor out. What would you probably recommend to the Master?

Answer: In order to control any sheering motion on the vessel, it could be recommended to lower a second anchor under foot.

Question 12. Your vessel is in transit down a long river and the helmsman reports that the steering is sluggish and slow to respond to his wheel movements. What would you surmise from this and what could you do?

Answer: Depending on the circumstances, the underkeel clearance can be expected to be somewhat reduced and as such the vessel may be experiencing excessive 'squat'. If this is the case, it might be prudent to reduce the vessel's speed as squat has been shown to be directly related to speed^2.

Question 13. If you are required to anchor your vessel in deep water, how would you proceed?

Answer: In every case of anchoring, I would expect to carry out a complete anchor plan. In the case of deep water anchoring it would be expected to walk back the anchor, in gear, all the way to the sea bottom and under no circumstances 'let go' the anchor.

Question 14. Your vessel is under repair in a port in the Far East when a tropical revolving storm is forecast as being imminent. Under normal circumstances you would let go your lines and run for the open sea. What are your options in this case?

Answer: With a disabled vessel my options would be restricted to one of two:

Remain tied up alongside. Set extra moorings out both fore and aft. Carry out and lay anchors with the assistance of tug(s) Batten the ship down for heavy weather, clear of shore side cranes and any other quayside obstructions. Plot and continue to monitor the progress of the storm.

If the port has a sheltered storm anchorage tugs may be available to manoeuvre the ship into the anchorage. Lay both anchors with maximum scope. Continue to plot and monitor the progress of the storm.

Note: In both cases continue to expedite engine repairs and return the ship to a full manoeuvring status.

Question 15.   How would you berth your vessel starboard side to, with a strong onshore wind, currently on your own starboard side and the tidal current ahead?

Answer: With the ship stemming the tidal flow you should advance parallel to the berth at a distance off, of approximately one ship's length. When the vessel's bow is in a position at a mid-point of the berth I would let the port, inshore anchor go at short stay and turn the vessel hard to port using maximum helm.

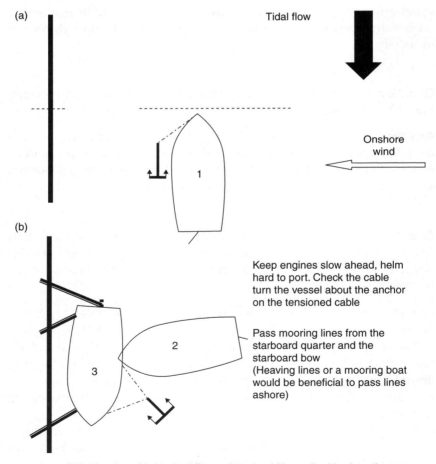

(a)

Tidal flow

Onshore wind

1

(b)

Keep engines slow ahead, helm hard to port. Check the cable turn the vessel about the anchor on the tensioned cable

Pass mooring lines from the starboard quarter and the starboard bow
(Heaving lines or a mooring boat would be beneficial to pass lines ashore)

2

3

Once the vessel is berthed the anchor should be walked back until the cable is 'up and down' to prevent obstruction of the channel

Question 16. What are the controls and their significance, which are fitted to the auto-pilot?

Answer: The auto-pilot, has several steering modes and each can be set to suit the needs of the ship handler as required.

- *Auto/manual:* Allows the user to select between the manual steering or automatic steering modes.
- *Tiller control:* An override which allows direct control of the helm and overrides the Auto control (off course alarm will activate unless cancelled before use).
- *Follow-up/non-follow-up:* Automatic return in follow-up mode. Whereas counter helm action is required in the non-follow-up mode.
- *Off course alarm:* Auto-pilots are fitted with an off course alarm system which can usually be set to operate at either 5° or 10° off the ship's desired heading.

Rudder control: This setting determines the angular measure to be given to the rudder.

Counter rudder: This control determines the amount of counter rudder to apply to be given once the vessel has started swinging, in order to check the swing to attain the correct course heading.

Permenant helm: A control used only if a constant external influence like from a beam sea is experienced. It provides helm to counteract the offset.

Weather: A counter control to compensate for the effect of weather or sea conditions which may cause adverse movement like 'yawing'.

Question 17. Where would you not engage automatic steering?

Answer: Auto-pilot must not be used in restricted waters or in conditions of poor visibility. Neither must it be employed when entering or leaving ports and harbours or other hazardous navigational area (Reference: Merchant Shipping (Automatic Pilot and Testing of Steering Gear) Regulations 1981. Additional Reference: Chapter 5, SOLAS).

Note: As the auto-pilot is interfaced with the gyro compass then manual steering should be adopted in the event of a malfunction to the gyro compass.

Question 18. How would you turn a vessel 'short round' in a restricted channel, when the ship is fitted with a right-hand fixed propeller and no bow thrust unit?

Answer: Alter the ship's head to move to the port side of the channel, as this would gain the greatest advantage when operating astern from transverse thrust, during the turn.

(a) Dead slow ahead on engines and order the helm hard to starboard.
(b) Stop engines, wheel midships.
(c) Full astern, wheel amidships, until the vessel gathers sternway, then stop engines. The effect of transverse thrust would generate a tendency for the bow to move to starboard and the stern to move to port.
(d) Wheel hard to starboard, engines full ahead to achieve the reverse heading.

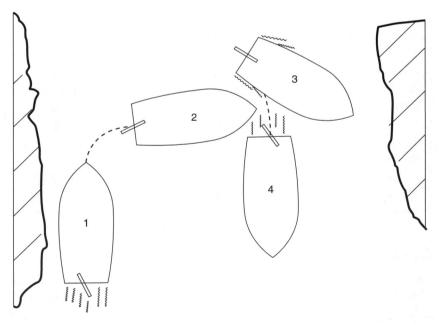

The objective of the short round is to effect a tight turn within the ships own length or as near as possible to within its own length.

Question 19. How would you carry out a 'standing moor' operation?

Answer: To carry out a standing moor, an anchor plan would be devised, and the vessel would be manoeuvred to stem the tide and pass the intended position of mooring by an approximate length of five (5) shackles of cable.

This position is approached with both anchors walked back clear of the hawse pipes. At position 1, take all way off the vessel, let the leeward anchor go and allow the vessel to drop back astern with the flow of the tidal stream, paying out the cable, to about nine (9) shackles on what will become the riding cable.

At position 2, check the ship's astern motion and place the leeward anchor in gear, prior to heaving away to shorten cable. Let go the weather anchor and use engine (if available) to move the vessel ahead while at the same time recovering cable on the riding cable and paying out on the weather anchor cable (sleeping cable).

At position 3, stop the vessel over the ground and apply the brakes to both anchor cables leaving each cable with about five shackles paid out.

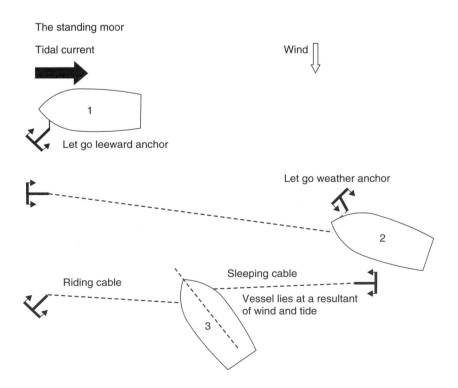

The standing moor

Tidal current

Wind

1

Let go leeward anchor

Let go weather anchor

2

Sleeping cable

Riding cable

Vessel lies at a resultant of wind and tide

3

Question 20. When making tugs fast what safety precautions and aspects would you take into consideration?

Answer: Engaging with tugs must always be considered as a high risk area of work and as such the following points would go some way to making the task as safe as possible:

(a) Clarify beforehand the method of engagement as to whether the tugs line is to be used or the ship's line and which 'lead' is intended.

(b) All persons involved in the operation should be adequately kitted out in protective clothing and briefed as to the nature of the activities involved.

(c) Adequate communications, tested beforehand, should be available between towing stations to the bridge and the towing vessel if appropriate.

(d) If the tugs line is to be used, this should be inspected to be free of defects and be seen to be of adequate strength.

(e) Throughout the operation all personnel should be advised to keep clear of bights in wires/ropes.

(f) The eye of the towline should not be placed on the 'bitts' but the wire should be set in a figure '8', turns, around the bollards. The top turns should be lightly lashed to prevent accidentally jumping off.

(g) Non-essential personnel should be kept well clear of towlines and the towing area.

Question 21. When arriving in port after a deep sea passage what instructions would you carry out regarding the mooring decks at the fore and after ends of the vessel?

Answer: As the ship's Chief Officer, I would order the deck areas to be washed down and thoroughly cleaned prior to approaching the port. It would be necessary to order the mooring lines to be coiled down from their stowage area in the rope lockers, at the respective deck stations.

All stoppers, heaving lines and fenders would be positioned and seen to be in good condition. Communications fore and aft and bridge would be tested.

The windlass would be inspected and turned over, oiled and greased as appropriate. All lights, shapes and signals would be made ready for use if required and the Master would be kept informed of the preparations made.

Question 22. What do you understand by the term 'kedging'?

Answer: The operation of 'kedging' is a stern movement of the vessel by means of an anchor layed astern of the vessel. Some ships are equipped with a stern anchor with capstan or small windlass to handle a short length of chain combined with an anchor warp.

Other vessels are known to carry a designated lighter anchor than that of the bower anchors, known as a 'kedge anchor'. These would usually lend to being carried out by the ship's boats.

Kedging is the act of dragging the vessel astern towards the kedge anchor and would usually be considered to re-float a vessel after taking the ground. The practice has been largely superseded with the advent of the more versatile tug which can be far more effective when re-floating a vessel aground.

Question 23. Your vessel receives orders to berth alongside another vessel to lighten ship. What actions and precautions would you take?

Answer: When expecting to berth alongside another vessel, the following actions are suggested:

(a) Ensure that the vessel is correctly identified and communications have been established.
(b) Advise the other vessel of the date/time of berthing to ensure reception for mooring lines and gangway.
(c) Make sure that the ship's side is well protected by fenders down its entire length.
(d) Walk back the offshore anchor to be ready to hold the vessel off and check the rate of approach.
(e) Moorings would be passed to the vessel alongside as the two vessels are drawn together. The moorings being set to include springs to prevent ranging.
(f) Once all fast it would be the duty of the offshore (outside) vessel to supply the gangway access, or alternatively this would be supplied by the vessel with the highest freeboard.
    Note: When two vessels are lying alongside it is anticipated that mutual co-operation would prevail in the provision of a safe access.
(g) Carry out a security assessment and determine a suitable security level.

Question 24.   What is synchronised rolling and what is synchronised pitching? What action would you take if either condition presented itself while you were on watch?

Answer: Synchronised rolling is when the roll period of the vessel equals the period of encounter of the waves. This is considered a highly dangerous condition and should be destroyed immediately by altering the vessels course.

Synchronised pitching is when the period of the vessel pitching, equals the period of encounter of the waves from either ahead or astern.

It must be considered extremely dangerous especially if in an area of abnormal waves. It can be overcome by reducing the ship's speed and changing the period of encounter.

Question 25.   Your vessel is under orders to moor to a buoy by means of its anchor cable. How would you hang your anchor off to bare the end of cable, if the ship is fitted with a centre lead, bullring in the eyes of the foc'stle head?

Answer: If the vessel was not fitted with a bullring, it would be necessary to hang the anchor off at the shoulder. A laborious task even with the facility of a shore side crane.

The benefit of the bullring would allow the anchor to be hung off in the hawse pipe. This task is comparatively easy, because it utilises the anchors own securing devices, like the bow stopper, devils claw and additional cable lashing points.

The cable can be broken at the first joining shackle forward of the windlass position and the bare end walked back to pass through the bullring.

Question 26.   A tanker with a right-hand fixed propeller is berthed, port side to a 'T'-shaped jetty with the tidal direction from ahead and the wind on its starboard side. If there is deep water at each end of the jetty, describe how the vessel would come off the berth into the river if no tug assistance is available?

Answer: The weight of water which forms the 'wedge of water' between the ship and the jetty will have greater power than the effect of the onshore wind. Once angled away from the jetty use of rudder and engines can be employed to move the ship in towards the open river waters.

Note: Engines should be brought to a stop while clearing the stern moorings to reduce the risk of fouling a rope in the propeller.

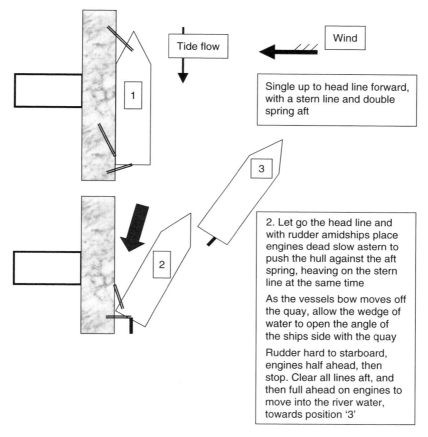

Tide flow

Wind

Single up to head line forward, with a stern line and double spring aft

1

3

2. Let go the head line and with rudder amidships place engines dead slow astern to push the hull against the aft spring, heaving on the stern line at the same time

As the vessels bow moves off the quay, allow the wedge of water to open the angle of the ships side with the quay

Rudder hard to starboard, engines half ahead, then stop. Clear all lines aft, and then full ahead on engines to move into the river water, towards position '3'

2

Taking a vessel off the berth, against the wind.

Question 27.   What are the main concerns when making a transit of a river or canal, where ships are moored against the banks of the waterway?

Answer: The main concerns in a narrow waterway are from the forces of interaction, inclusive of squat. If the ship is on passage at too high a speed the moored ships on the bank sides may even start to 'range' on their moorings. In the event that these mooring are slack to start with, the moored ships may even part their lines because of this ranging motion.

The wash from the movement of your own vessel will expect to travel along the canal or river banks, not only will this cause bank erosion but it may cause accidents to persons on the bank areas, e.g. Fishermen.

Other concerns would be with reliability of steering gear and main engine propulsion.

Question 28.   When taking a ship into Dry Dock, why do the dock authorities usually request the ship to be trimmed by the stern?

Answer: It is normal practice to have a stern trim for entering Dry Dock for several reasons:

(a)   The ship tends to handle and steer better with a stern trim.
(b)   The declivity of the dock bottom is compatible with the trim angle.
(c)   The 'Sole Piece' is an aft strength member and will be the first part of the vessels structure to make contact with the blocks. Achieved with a stern trim.

Question 29.   When conducting turning circle trials with a single right-hand fixed propeller, would you expect the vessel to turn faster and tighter to port or to starboard? (Assuming calm weather, same conditions for both port and starboard turns.)

Answer: Right-hand fixed propeller ships generally turn faster and tighter to port, than to starboard.

Question 30.   When mooring to buoys, how would you secure the moorings to the ring of the buoy?

Answer: There are several methods to secure the ropes to the buoy rings employed around the Maritime nations. Any one of the following could expect to be used:

(a)   Soft eye mooring rope or wire with a 'bow'-shaped mooring shackle.
(b)   Four metre manila lashing attached to a rope eye. The eye is passed through the ring and the two parts of the eye are secured together under the standing part. The lashing is usually completed by a slip knot for quick release.

(c) Rope eye and toggle secured under the standing part. A popular method also employs the bight of a rope (or wire) passing through the buoy ring. (In the case of a wire this could be used as a slip wire.)

CARGO WORK AND LIFTING GEAR

Question 1. What do you understand by the term 'proof load' as applied to derricks?

Answer: The proof load is that tonnage which is applied during the testing of the derricks capacity. Derricks are routinely tested at 5-year intervals by a cargo surveyor. The test imposed on the lifting gear will be the proof load and for derricks of:

Less than 20 ton SWL	Proof load = 25% in excess of the SWL
Between 20 and 50 ton SWL	Proof load = 5 ton in excess of SWL
Over 50 ton SWL	Proof load = 10% in excess of SWL

Question 2. Where would you find details of the ship's cargo handling and lifting appliances?

Answer: Register of Cargo Handling and Lifting Appliances, the Rigging Plan and marked on the appliance itself.

Question 3. When carrying out the annual inspections of derricks what would a Chief Officer expect to pay particular attention to?

Answer: An annual inspection of derricks would include a thorough visual inspection of the boom particularly the underside where contact is made with the 'crutch', as corrosion is known to occur in this region. The inspection would also note the condition of the 'spider band' and the attached 'lugs'. However, the main weight bearing components are contained in the 'blocks' and the 'gooseneck arrangement'. All the blocks would be overhauled, namely the heel block, head block and span blocks. The bushes and the axle bolts would be withdrawn from each and closely inspected for rust, corrosion, pitting or hairline cracks. The gooseneck would be drawn as being the main element of the derrick. This would be cleaned of all old grease and given a detailed inspection for any sign of corrosion or deformity. If the units are found satisfactory they would be re-greased and assembled and returned to situation.

A record of the inspection would be made in the Register of Lifting Appliances, and in the planned maintenance schedule.

Question 4.   How would you make up a loading plan for a bulk carrier?

Answer: The modern ship is equipped with a 'loadicator' or customised computer programme. The order, distribution and quantities of cargo, stores, fresh water and ballast would all be included in order to determine the overall loaded condition.

Question 5.   What information is provided by the 'loadicator'?

Answer: Following the input of cargo quantities and weights, the output from the programme would supply stress values comparable against acceptable parameters. These would include the bending moments, shear force and effects on the 'GM'.

Question 6.   When scheduled to load a heavy lift, what type of checks and precautions would you make?

Answer: As the Chief Officer I would ascertain the total weight and overall size of the load and ensure that it is within the SWL capacity of the ship's heavy lift derrick/crane (if the load is being made from a floating crane or shore side facilities over and above the ship's loading capability then it would be necessary to also check the facilities and capability at the port of discharge).

Once the size and weight of the load are known the Load Density Plan would be checked to ensure that the space for designated stowage is capable of accepting the load with regard to both size and deck weight capacity.

The stability checks would include the calculation of the maximum angle of 'heel' if using ship's gear. The GM would also be ascertained for all stages of the lift, from hoisting to landing.

The GM may need to be improved by adding water ballast to double bottom tanks, in order to compensate for any expected loss of apparent GM.

Slinging the load or any special lifting apparatus which it is intended to use, would warrant inspection and may become a consideration for leaving with the load for the purpose of discharge (often heavy loads are incorporated with a raft or cradle for transportation purposes).

Question 7. If the load concentration of a heavy lift, exceeded the tonnes per square metre, as stipulated by the 'Load Density Plan', what would you do?

Answer: The deck area for the intended stowage space can be laid with timber bearers in order to spread the load over a greater square area. It the intended stowage is in a tween deck additional under deck supports in the form of temporary additional pillars may need to be constructed. Failing this an alternative stowage position should be sought.

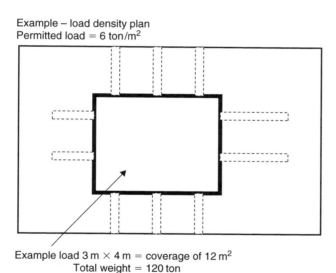

Example – load density plan
Permitted load = 6 ton/m^2

Example load 3 m × 4 m = coverage of 12 m^2
Total weight = 120 ton
Tonnes/m^2 = 10 ton (deck is overloaded)

By placing the load on bearers the deck area occupied by the load is increased to 5 m × 7 m = coverage of 35 m^2

Tonnes/m^2 = $\frac{120}{35}$ = 3.43 ton (less than the designated plan load and therefore acceptable)

Question 8. Describe the operation of loading a 60 ton bulldozer, with a conventional heavy lift, 'Jumbo derrick'?

Answer: The derrick rig would be checked thoroughly and all blocks and purchases would be seen to be overhauling and any additional

Heavy lift 'Jumbo' conventional derrick. A conventional 60 ton SWL, Jumbo
derrick stowed in the upright between the Samson Post structure. Smaller
10 ton derricks are sited on either side for working lighter cargo parcels.

rigging such as Preventor Back Stays would be secured as per the
'Rigging Plan'.

The stability check would have been completed and the maximum
angle of heel would have been calculated. Any free surface moments
would have been eliminated where possible.

The gangway would be lifted clear of the quayside and moorings
would be tended during the period of lift. Winch drivers (four) would

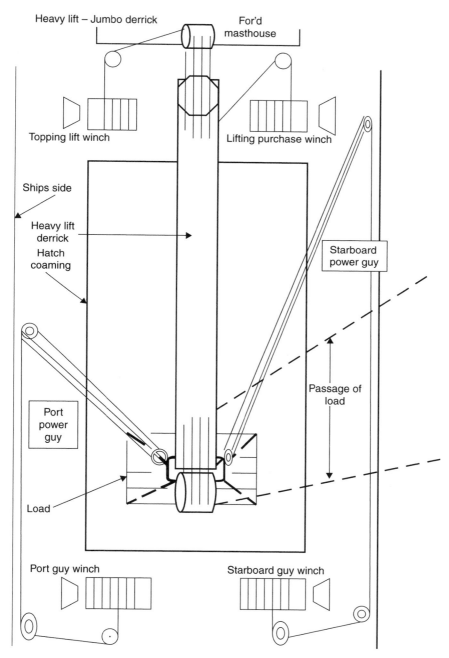

Heavy lift – Jumbo derrick.

be experienced men operating the winches in double gear and taking their instructions from the 'Hatch Foreman'.

Adequate size slings would be secured to the load at the correct lifting points. A spreader or lift bridle may be used if appropriate. Steadying lines would be secured to the lift and manned, in order to control any oscillations on the load during the hoist and landing of the heavy lift. It may prove necessary to deliberately turn the load in transit and these lines should be of adequate strength as to be able to provide positive control.

The deck stowage position would have been prepared and adequate timber bearers would be in position to provide a non-skid surface and spread the load to be within acceptable limits of the Load Density Plan.

When all was ready the derrick would be turned out to plumb the load, and the maximum angle of heel at the extreme outreach would be checked against the ship's inclinometer. Provided the conditions are acceptable, the load would be lifted, smartly, to avoid any lateral drag movement, of the load.

Note: Most Chief Officers would note the heavy lift on the cargo manifest and made time to visit the cargo warehouse to check the documentation, markings, listed weight and overall size of the load prior to commencing lift operations.

Question 9. If you were on a bulk carrier, loaded with 'iron ore' what stresses would you anticipate, which may occur during the passage?

Answer: Iron ore or other similar heavy cargoes must be loaded in proportion and in a manner conducive to the fore and aft length of the vessel. The loading plan should take account of the effects that may be incurred due to: racking stresses, bending moments, shear forces and torsional stresses.

Question 10. Why do tanker vessels engage in Tank Cleaning and what methods do they employ?

Answer: Tank cleaning is carried out to:

(a) Prevent inter-grade contamination.
(b) Permit subsequent gas freeing for entry.

(c) Provide additional ballast space.
(d) Remove solid residues and sludge.

Three methods of tank cleaning are common:

(1) Flushing with water or cargo.
(2) Seawater washing employing tank cleaning machines.
(3) Crude Oil Washing (COW).

Question 11. After washing tanks what do you do with the dirty residues?

Answer: The slops are discharged into a barge or to shore side reception facilities.

Question 12. What procedures would you adopt to load a full cargo of coal aboard a bulk carrier?

Answer: Having obtained the cargo details (grades, quantities, voyage details, etc.) from the Charterer, it would be usual practice to prepare a loading plan to take account of the ports of discharge. The holds would be cleaned and inspected before commencing any cargo operation.
   The following points would then also be assessed:

(a) The stability criteria for all conditions of loading and discharging.
(b) The distribution of grades in specific holds.
(c) Shear force and bending moments are within permissible limits.
(d) Minimum trim and air draught maintained within acceptable parameters.
(e) Ballasting and deballasting sequence to suit loading schedule.
(f) Safety procedures for coal checked and adhered to, i.e. explosion risk, spontaneous combustion and gas accumulation.
(g) Final trimming of cargo to ensure that the vessel completes in the upright condition.

Question 13. Draw a load line mark, state which side of the ship and which direction is forward?

Answer: Freeboard mark at the uppermost continuous deck. 300 mm.

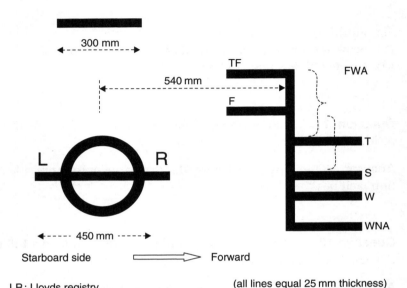

Key: LR: Lloyds registry   (all lines equal 25 mm thickness)
        TF: tropical fresh
         F: fresh
         T: tropical
         S: summer
         W: winter
      WNA: winter North Atlantic (applicable to vessels less than 100 m in length
                            trading across the North Atlantic)
      FWA: fresh water allowance

Note: Measured distance between tropical (T) and summer (S) = 1/48th summer draught
Measured distance between summer (S) and winter (W) = 1/48th summer draught
The difference between summer and fresh marks   = FWA
The difference between tropical and tropical fresh marks = FWA

Question 14. Which vessels must carry a Certificate of Fitness?

Answer: All tanker vessels, gas carriers and chemical carrying vessels must have a 'Certificate of Fitness'. It is issued by the Maritime and Coastguard Agency (MCA) and subject to annual survey, normally carried out by a Classification Society. Period of validity is 5 years with no extension permitted.

Example Certificate

Certificate No._____

INTERNATIONAL LOAD LINE CERTIFICATE

ISSUED UNDER THE PROVISIONS OF THE

INTERNATIONAL CONVENTION ON LOAD LINES, 1966
AS MODIFIED BY THE PROTOCOL OF 1988 RELATING THERETO

UNDER THE AUTHORITY OF THE GOVERNMENT OF

_____

(name of the State)

_____

(Surveyor, American Bureau of Shipping)

Particulars of Ship

Name of Ship	Distinctive Number or Letters	Port of Registry	Length (L) as defined in Article 2(8) (in meters)	IMO Number[1]

Freeboard assigned as: * { A new ship / An existing ship

Type of Ship: * { Type 'A' / Type 'B' / Type 'B' with reduced freeboard / Type 'B' with increased freeboard

*Delete whatever is inapplicable

Freeboard from Deck Line		*Load Line*
Tropical	mm (T)	mm above (S)
Summer	mm (S)	*Upper edge of line through center of ring*
Winter	mm (W)	mm below (S)
Winter North Atlantic	mm (WNA)	mm below (S)
Timber tropical	mm (LT)	mm above (LS)
Timber summer	mm (LS)	mm above (S)
Timber winter	mm (LW)	mm below (LS)
Timber winter North Atlantic	mm (LWNA)	mm below (LS)
Allowance for freshwater for all	mm	
Freeboards other than timber		
For timber freeboards	mm	

The upper edge of the deck line from which these freeboards are measured is: OPPOSITE TOP OF STEEL UPPER deck at side.

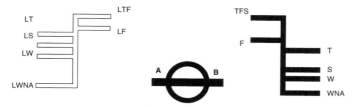

_____

[1]In accordance with the IMO Ship Identification Number Scheme, adopted by resolution A.600 (15).

Question 15. When loading fully to the ship's marks in dock water, by how much can you submerge the load line?

Answer: The ship may continue to load cargo up to the equivalent of the Dock Water Allowance.

Question 16. What is the Dock Water Allowance and how do you obtain its value?

Answer: The Dock Water Allowance (DWA) is the measured value that the summer load line disc can be submerged. Once the vessel passes from the density of the dock water into seawater the ship would rise an equivalent amount equal to the DWA. The amount the disc can be submerged is found by formula:

$$\text{DWA} = \frac{1025 - \text{density of dock water (Hydrometer Number)}}{25} \times \text{FWA}$$

Note: Examiners may give example figures and expect candidates to work the DWA.

$$\text{DWA} = \frac{1025 - 1010}{25} \times 150 \text{ mm}$$
$$= \frac{15}{25} \times 150$$
$$= 90 \text{ mm}$$

> Assume:
> Hydrometer = 1010
> FWA = 150 mm

To determine the cargo to load, this value in centimetres, can be multiplied by the tonnes per centimetre (TPC).

Question 17. What are the main dangers associated with bulk cargoes?

Answer: Bulk cargoes depending on the type, have associated hazards from the onset of loading. They include structural damage during loading and discharging periods as well as during distribution and/or trimming, to prevent shifting in a seaway.

Incorrect distribution of bulk cargoes could incur dangerous 'bending moments' and excessive 'shear forces' which could directly effect the ship's structure.

The reduction and loss of positive stability during the voyage either by cargo shift or liquefaction is a possibility with many types of cargoes, shifting being a result of bad weather and improper trimming or securing. While liquefaction of certain cargoes could be stimulated as a result of vibration and ship's motion, e.g. cargoes: fine grained materials, inclusive of fine coal if shipped in a damp condition.

Other dangers can arise from 'chemical reactions' which may give rise to either toxic or explosive gases. Other cargoes like coal, could also give rise to spontaneous combustion.

Question 18. What precautions would be taken when loading and carrying a full cargo of 'wood pulp'?

Answer: A cargo of 'wood pulp' would be loaded in accordance with the advice given in 'MSN 107' which recommends that the cargo compartments are clean and dry. Wood pulp expands considerably when wet and therefore all: air pipes and ventilation shafts should be effectively blanked off to prevent any accidental admission of water.

Question 19. What products are classed as 'Grain Cargoes' and how would you load grain in a General Cargo vessel?

Answer: Grain is defined as wheat, maize, oats, rye, barley, rice, pulses, seeds and processed forms of the above, which may behave in a similar manner.

Prior to loading grain the ship's hatches should be prepared. This would incorporate a thorough cleaning with all sweepings and residuals removed and seen to be in a dry condition throughout. The bilges should be tested and sweetened to be free of taint. These would be sealed with burlap or other similar material. The spar ceiling would be removed from the hold and stowed clear of cargo spaces. The holds would be surveyed by a cargo surveyor prior to the commencement of loading.

Grain would be loaded in accord with International Maritime Organisation (IMO) Grain Rules. These rules require a demonstration by calculation that at all times, during the state of the voyage, that the vessel will have sufficient intact stability. Sufficient to provide adequate residual dynamical stability after taking account of the adverse heeling effects caused by an assumed shift of grain, into void spaces, lying directly above the grain surfaces.

Note: Value of residual dynamical stability found from the area under the Ships Righting Lever (GZ) curve.

Stability

The grain rules specify a minimum level of acceptable stability when carrying grain products with an initial metacentric height (GM) of 0.3 m, angle of heel due to assumed shift of 12° and residual dynamical stability.

Ship's stability can be improved by removing free surface moments present with slack tanks, either press up or pump out. Additionally, fill double bottom tanks to lower 'G' to effectively increase GM.

Cargo Measures

Where the compartment is full, rig a temporary longitudinal subdivision (shifting board) or using bagged grain to form a saucer on top of the grain surface.

Where the compartment is partially full, trimming the grain flat and laying a dunnage platform over the surface, then overstowing with bagged grain or other suitable cargo.

Question 20.   Where could you obtain information on specialist types of cargoes if you lack any experience of the commodity?

Answer: Depending on the nature of the goods a variety of publications exist for reference and I would first check these out inclusive of MGNs, MSNs, The International Maritime Dangerous Goods (IMDG) Code, various IMO specified publications, Thomas's Stowage and other reputable cargo publications.

Additional sources would be via the ship's agents, direct to the shipper, the manufacturer of the goods, the Port Superintendent and the Departments of Health and Safety, and/or Environment.

Question 21.   While working cargo by derricks, a cargo runner breaks. How would you replace this runner in minimum time, without causing the vessel to suffer excessive down-time?

Answer: The boatswain would be ordered to break out a new runner wire from the stores. A heaving line would be bent-on to the broken wire then the turns on the winch would be run off. Once the broken wire is clear of the winch it can be pulled back clear of the derrick rig leaving the heaving line in place.

The new runner could then be flaked on deck and the reduced eye bent onto the heaving line. By pulling the heaving line back through the blocks, the eye of the new runner can be clamped to the barrel of the winch and run on.

Note: This method can be carried out quickly without lowering the derrick from its working position.

Question 22.   When engaged on a Ro-Ro, vehicle ferry what checks are made to ensure that the vessel retains water tight integrity, once the vessel has completed loading, prior to sailing?

Answer: Once all cargo units are on board it would be normal practice to close up the stern ramp/door, and the bow visor together with the forward cargo door. The majority of these features are closed up by hydraulics, by the duty officer. Once sealed and locked they are monitored by a 'tell tale' light display on the navigation bridge. All openings into the hull, inclusive of 'shell doors', are fitted with sensors to indicate to the bridge whether they are open or closed (closed = green light, red light = open). All such openings are also monitored by closed-circuit television (CCTV). Also shown on the bridge.

These checks are meant to show that the vehicle decks of the lower hull are all closed and sealed and that the ship has watertight integrity. These features would also be communicated to the ship's Master by word of mouth, as and when they occur.

Question 23.   When carrying the annual inspection on the ship's derricks describe how you would inspect the 'gooseneck'?

Answer: The annual inspection of lifting gear would include a thorough examination of all the blocks, shackles, wires, etc., associated with the derrick rig. The main component of the inspection would be the weight bearing, gooseneck arrangement. This would need to be drawn to expose all the moving parts for detailed inspection. The gooseneck could be drawn by use of chain blocks suspended from the underside of the 'mast table' but this method is dated and cumbersome. It is probably more practical to leave the derrick in the 'crutch', and employ the topping lift to hoist the gooseneck at the heel of the derrick.

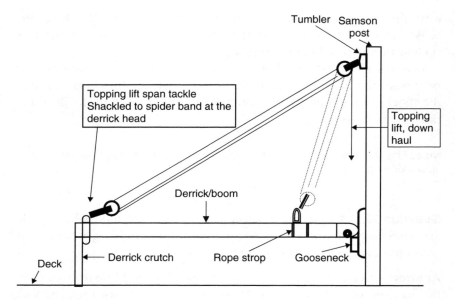

Maintenance of the gooseneck.

In order to expose the gooseneck for regular inspection and maintenance, the derrick must first be lowered into the stowed position, to rest in the crutch. Any crutch securing should be released. A rope strop should be positioned around the heel of the derrick boom and shackled onto the transferred topping lift.

Note: The topping lift is detached from the derrick head spider band and moved to the heel/stropped position.

The down haul of the topping lift is then led to a winch to hoist the derrick heel upwards and draw the elements of the gooseneck/heel block clear for inspection.

Question 24.   When engaged in overhauling and inspecting cargo blocks what instructions would you give to the boatswain, and what would you look for during your inspection?

Answer: In order to carry out a detailed inspection it would be necessary to strip the cargo blocks down completely and expose the sheave, the bush and the axle bolt. To do this the distance piece at the arse of the block should be removed and the axle bolt withdrawn. This will allow the cheek plates to move from the binding and permit the extraction of the sheave.

Once the sheave is clear, the bush (bearing) can be removed.

The inspection would follow the removal of all old grease from the grease recesses, inside the centre of the sheave and in the centre of the bush. Any rust, pitting or visible corrosion on or around the steelwork, would indicate potential problems with the block. If the corrosion elements are extensive, then the block should be condemned.

The bush would be tested with fluid to detect the presence of hairline cracks in the bearing. If none are found and the bearing is free of corrosive signs, then it should be re-greased and re-assembled prior to deploying the block in its previous position.

A note should be made in the record of the planned maintenance to the effect that the block and derrick rigging had had an annual inspection. The number and SWL should be left visible on the block, stamped on the binding and the block with its shackle should be checked and compared with the Rigging Plan.

Once re-assembled the overall condition of the block should be seen to be sound and the moving parts inclusive of the crown swivel and the sheave, should be seen to be free to rotate. The securing shackles would be moused and the rig could be returned to service.

Note: Where a block or shackle is found to be defective it should be replaced. Chief Officers are advised that the certificates for items replaced must be extracted from the 'Register of Ships Lifting Appliances and Cargo Handling Gear' and the new equipment certificate logged in its place.

Question 25. What is the principle and operational practice of a design built heavy lift ship?

Answer: These vessels are used for 'project cargo' of an exceptional nature and work on a principle similar to that of a 'floating dock'. The ship is essentially a tank system built beneath a reinforced platform deck.

Once the vessels tanks are full the vessels upper cargo deck is submerged. This allows the heavy lift, usually on a raft arrangement, to be floated over the ship. Once in position the ship's tanks are emptied and the ship rises picking up the rafted heavy lift.

The heavy lift vessel 'Sea Servant 3' engaged in the transport of the crane barge, 'Al-Baraka 1'.

Question 26.   Cargo parcels of goods listed in the IMDG Code are loaded on board your vessel at the beginning of a voyage. After several days at sea these packages are seen to be leaking. What action can you legally take?

Answer: If 'dangerous goods' are not packaged and properly marked or if shipped without the knowledge or consent of the carrier then the goods can be landed, jettisoned, destroyed or rendered innocuous by the carrier at any time before discharge.

If the goods have become a danger to the ship or other cargo they may be dealt with in a similar manner without any liability to the carrier (Reference: Carriage of Goods at Sea Act).

Question 27.   While engaged as Cargo Officer aboard a Ro-Ro vessel, a cargo tank unit, identified as carrying a hazardous chemical is observed to be leaking. What action would you take?

Answer: Emergencies of such a nature must be dealt with in accord with the IMO publications *Emergency Procedures for Ships Carrying*

Dangerous Goods (only for vessels carrying dangerous goods), and the *Medical First Aid Guide* contained in the supplement to the IMDG Code.

Assuming that the tank unit had been given a correct stowage position it would be accessible to the actions of an emergency party. The nature of the commodity would be checked to ascertain the correct chemical name, UN Number and relevant associated dangers. The ship's course may well need to be altered to allow vapour emissions to be blown overside. The product may need damping down with hose action or may not be compatible with water at all, so any action by hoses should be held off until confirmation of handling methods is acknowledged.

Communications with shore-side shippers, and/or manufactures may be desirable.

Question 28. What do you understand by the term 'angle of repose'?

Answer: The angle of repose refers to bulk cargoes and is that natural angle between the cone slope and the horizontal plane when a bulk cargo is emptied onto this plane.

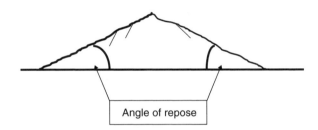

Angle of repose

An angle of repose of 35° is taken as being the dividing line for bulk cargoes of lesser or greater shifting hazard.

Question 29. The IMO has recently made recommendations for bulk carriers over 20,000 dwt and above to fit specialised equipment to facilitate the safe carriage of dry cargoes in bulk. What is this recommended equipment?

Answer: Effected 'bulk carriers' are now recommended to be fitted with:

(a) Hull Stress Monitoring Systems.
(b) Water Ingress Monitoring Systems.

Question 30.   What do you understand by the term 'Segregated Ballast Tank'?

Answer: This means a water ballast tank which is completely separated from the cargo oil and fuel oil systems. It is permanently allocated to the carriage of water ballast or cargoes other than oil or noxious substances.

3 Questions for the Rank as Master Mariner

INTRODUCTION

Once a Merchant Navy Officer has acquired sufficient sea service, he or she may present themselves as a candidate for the examination for the rank of Master Mariner. Such a position carries with it the ultimate responsibility of taking command of a ship at sea. As such, the qualification must take account of all the aspects of management of the vessel as well as the day-to-day manoeuvring, voyage economics, navigation aspects, discipline, health and safety to name but a few of the functional requirements.

The examination can be expected to be unlike previous encounters with the Marine Examiner. Yes, there will be searching questions asked, meant to reflect the overall knowledge held by the candidate. However, the examiner is making an overall assessment of the candidate's ability to command the ship, the crew and all likely operations that may affect the well-being of the vessel.

To this end discussion and debate into any form of emergency must be anticipated by candidates. It should also be realised that each and every emergency will differ, and therefore no 'pat' answer can be expected to fit every situation. The examiner is also trying to assess if the candidate can think practically, if he or she can think while under pressure and if he or she can address marine problems in a safe and logical manner.

The ethos of 'command' has been discussed and written about for decades, with many views contributing towards what makes the ultimate commander. What is that vital spark that sets one man apart from another, that spark that mirrors one candidate as a leader, above anybody else. I doubt whether anyone could define all the qualities of a ship's 'Captain', even those tried and tested Master's of ships. However,

I do think and many would agree, that the man that holds command, must first and foremost be a seaman. Whatever talents the Master has, above that of being a seaman, will know doubt enhance the quality of his command.

This examination, will most certainly be a different experience for each and every candidate and those men and women that attain this much sort after and respected qualification will soon realise that passing is only a beginning. The first command will commence a learning curve, which no other form of employment could possibly reflect.

EMERGENCY PROCEDURES

Question 1.   Following receipt of a distress message your vessel is requisitioned to assist. You acknowledge the call and proceed towards the distress area. What navigational procedures would you employ to ensure your own ship's safety while at the same time effectively moving to relieve the distress situation?

Answer: With any distress situation I would anticipate that communications will play a major role. As such I would initially acknowledge the distress call and also establish contact with the 'On Scene Co-ordinator' if appropriate.

As the Master I would place the vessel on an alert status and establish an operational 'Bridge Team' to include the engine room being placed on 'stand-by'.

I would instruct the Navigation Officer to carry out a comprehensive chart assessment, to include my own ship's position and the rendezvous position of the distressed party. Close examination of any navigation hazards affecting the area together with any low underkeel clearance areas would be prominently marked, as 'No Go' areas.

A radar watch would be established to include long-range scanning and lookouts would be posted in prominent positions on the vessel. A weather forecast would be obtained and the navigator would be instructed to obtain the expected time of sunset while on route towards the area.

The Bridge Team would operate under manual steering at best possible sea speed until closing the area. Manoeuvring speed would then be adopted (the speed of approach being faster than the speed of search and engagement).

Where an area search is expected to take place, as when the 'datum' is unconfirmed or a wider pattern is anticipated, the Master would instruct the Navigator to plot the search area together with an appropriate 'search pattern'. Track space for any search pattern being determined by the relevant circumstances.

Throughout the approach the Officer of the Watch (OOW) would be monitoring the progress and position of the vessel and an effective lookout for other traffic or potential hazards would be maintained. The echo sounder being monitored if required.

Communication updates would be ongoing and full entries made in the ship's log books.

Question 2. What factors would determine the chosen 'track space' when engaging in an Search and Rescue (SAR) search pattern?

Answer: Track space for a search operation would be based on:

(a) The target definition (size, afloat Yes/No).
(b) Day or night search time.
(c) State of visibility, rain, fog, mist or snow.
(d) The likely quality of radar target presented, if any.
(e) The height of eye and prominence of lookouts.
(f) The number of surface search units employed.
(g) The searching vessels speed of operation.
(h) Recommendations from Rescue Co-ordination Centre (RCC) and/or On Scene Co-ordinator (OSC).
(i) Recommendations from the *International Aeronautical and Marine Search and Rescue* (IAMSAR) Manual.
(j) Area and intended search time before nightfall.
(k) Availability of search lights for night operations.
(l) Master's experience.

Question 3. Having recovered two survivors from a marine disaster scene, what essential questions would you need to ask them as part of your debriefing?

Answer: Following the recovery of survivors the Master of the recovering vessel would obtain the following information:

(a) Name and rank of the survivor.
(b) Name of ship/vehicle/flight definition.
(c) Next of kin, and the address of the next of kin.
(d) Information as to cause of disaster.
(e) Total number of persons known to be aboard.
(f) Information regarding any other survivors or survival craft.
(g) Life Saving Appliance details, carried aboard the stricken vessel.

Question 4. What emergency equipment would you think could reduce the period of conducting a search pattern?

Answer: The use of an Emergency Position Indicating Radio Beacon (EPIRB) or Search and Rescue Transponder (SART) could positively identify the targets position and reduce search time. Other equipment such as flares, use of distress signals, etc., could also be effective if within visible range, but such items need a degree of self help and potential survivors would need to be conscious.

Question 5. What are the frequencies of an EPIRB?

Answer: 121.5 and 406 MHz.

Question 6. What duties would you expect to conduct when acting as an On Scene Co-ordinator in an SAR operation?

Answer: The essential function of the OSC is to provide a communication platform between the search units, the Rescue Co-ordination Centre and other interested parties.
   Essential activities would include:

(a) Maximising the information on the target and plotting the 'datum' from all the known evidence.
(b) Establishing the position and status of all search units.
(c) Advising each search unit of the co-ordinates of respective search areas.
(d) Maintaining a detailed running log of events to include communications, weather reports, search results, updates and outcomes.
(e) Plot search units operations and their endurance capability.
(f) Request resources from relevant authorities, i.e. helicopter assistance or survival equipment.
(g) Debrief survivors and amend search plans on updated information.
(h) Allocate and guard communication channels.
(i) Disperse weather reports and/or navigation warnings to search units.
(j) Direct and co-ordinate activities to return survivors to a safe haven.

Question 7. What type of facilities and conditions would suit a vessel to act as OSC?

Answer: The ideal vessel for the role of On Scene Co-ordinator would be equipped and capable of carrying out the required duties and would require the following:

(a) Adequate communication facilities on board.
(b) Sufficient manpower available.
(c) No commercial/cargo commitments.
(d) Plotting capability.
(e) No endurance restrictions.
(f) Speed overall (though this, like proximity of position, is not necessarily detrimental).
(g) Experienced Master.

Note: The ideal vessel that is considered most suitable for the role of OSC is of course the warship. It is in possession of all or most of the above requirements.

It is also pointed out that the role of co-ordinator is not that of a search and recovery unit. As such it does not need the rescue or medical facilities that search units need to have available, unless it is acting in a dual role of OSC and search unit.

Question 8.   How would you carry out a co-ordinated surface search?

Answer: A co-ordinated search involves surface craft and aircraft working in conjunction with each other. Fixed wing aircraft cannot normally land on the surface but they can often effect location quicker because of the increased air speed. However, with communication to a surface craft, recovery can be effected that much sooner.

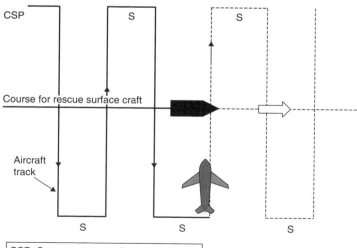

Co-ordinated surface search.

Question 9.   Your vessel is a high sided car carrier and while engaged in an SAR operation you locate a liferaft with four survivors. The weather conditions are gale force 8, increasing 9. How would you effect recovery of the survivors?

Answer: The weather conditions would prohibit the launching of the rescue boat on the grounds that it would be unsafe for my own boats crew. Under the circumstances I would order the Chief Officer to make the lifeboat ready for lowering to the water, but order the hooks for the falls to be moused. I would manoeuvre the vessel in order to create a 'lee' for the liferaft and on the same side, lower the boat to the waterline. With heaving line assistance order the boats crew to draw the liferaft alongside the lifeboat.

Transfer the raft occupants into the boat and by using the life-boat as an elevator, recover the boat and survivors to the embarkation deck.

Note: Prior to re-hoisting the boat, the raft would need to be destroyed by a knife to all the buoyancy chambers.

Question 10.   How would you determine that a 'port of refuge' was satisfactory for your vessel?

Answer: The practical aspects of choice of a 'port of refuge' would be determined by the size of the port, the available depth of water inside the port and the respective underkeel clearance for the vessel to be able to enter and berth.

Additional, preferable features of such a port would include, shelter afforded to the effected vessel and whether the port had repair facilities capable of rectifying any defects to the ship.

Question 11.   Following an engine room explosion, your engines are inoperable. The ship's position is 8 miles off a 'lee shore' and you are drifting down. What action would you take?

Answer: In these circumstances where there is no possibility of instigating repairs I would immediately make a MAYDAY with only 8 miles distance of the shore line. I would also request the assistance of a 'tug'.

It would be my intention to reduce the rate of drift towards the shore, while awaiting the tugs arrival, by taking the following actions:

(a) Ballast the fore end of the vessel to increase the windage aft. This would hopefully present the bows to the wind and reduce drift.
(b) Walk back both anchors to provide drag effect and slow the drift.

(c) If the depth reduced to shallows I would consider use of anchors for emergency holding off.

(d) Order the Chief Officer to prepare a suitable towing arrangement (probably a composite tow line).

(e) Communications to include informing owners, obtaining weather forecast and Coastguard Authority.

Question 12. Having made a distress call, what must you do once the distress situation is relieved?

Answer: Once the distress situation is resolved the distress communication must be cancelled.

Question 13. Following the loss of a 'man overboard', you take the 'conn' and complete a Williamson Turn manoeuvre but are unable to locate the man in the water. What would you now do?

Answer: Legally I am obliged to carry out a search of the immediate area. To this end I would conduct a 'sector search', as recommended by the IAMSAR Manual. During this period I would keep the RCC appraised of my activities and the results of any findings.

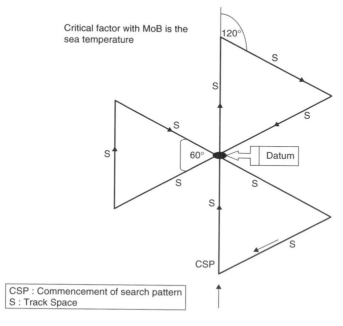

Sector search. Suggested track space 'S' = 10 minutes.

Question 14.   In the event that you would have to beach your vessel, in order to prevent a total constructive loss, what ideal conditions would you prefer?

Answer: Beaching the vessel is an extreme action and would not be carried out if an alternative action to save the vessel was available. It is an action which is employed to save the hull, with the view to instigating repairs and to re-float at a later time with improved conditions.

The ideal conditions for a beaching operation should include all or as many of the following conditions:

(a) A daylight operation.
(b) A gentle slope to the beach at the point of taking the ground.
(c) A rock-free ground area.
(d) Sheltered from prevailing weather.
(e) Current-free and/or non-tidal situation.
(f) Surf free.
(g) Communications into and out of the beach area.

Question 15.   Assuming that your vessel is in a damaged condition and you have just beached the ship. What would be your immediate actions?

Answer: My subsequent actions on taking the ground will largely be dependant on what I was able to do on running in to the shore line. Assuming that the prevailing conditions did not lend to any positive actions, I would:

(a) Order the Chief Officer to walk back both anchors to prevent accidentally re-floating off the ground into a deep water predicament.
(b) Order the Chief Officer to obtain a damage assessment, to include a full sounding of all the ship's tanks.
(c) Order the Navigator to obtain the tidal data for the next few days, paying particular attention to the heights and times of high and low waters.
(d) Open up communications with owners/agents with the view to instigating repairs. Cause an entry to be made in the Official and Deck Log Books.
(e) Order the crew to establish an oil boom (barrier equipment required) around the perimeter of the vessel.
(f) In the event barrier equipment is not available, make an improvised boom with mooring ropes.

(g) Ascertain the depth of water around the propeller.

(h) Add additional ballast to the ship to reduce the possibility of uncontrolled movement of the vessel.

(i) If and when appropriate, have tugs ordered to stand-by, especially so for when any attempt to re-float is to be made.

(j) Inform the Marine Accident Investigation Branch (MAIB) as soon as practical by use of an Incident Report Form.

(k) Display the appropriate 'aground signals' while on the beach.

(l) Inspect the lower hull and the associated ground area at low water time by boat if necessary, in order to complete the damage inspection.

Question 16.   While on passage on a Northerly course, West of the Portuguese coastline, your vessel encounters a fishing vessel on fire. Four (4) men are seen on the foc'stle head frantically waving their arms. Flames and smoke are seen coming from the aft part of the ship and the flags November/Charlie (NC) are seen flying from a midships halyard. The weather conditions are NW'ly force '8'. What action do you take?

Answer: The vessel indications are showing three international types of distress signals and as such, I would attempt to effect recovery of the men on board the fishing boat.

If the weather had permitted (force 6 or less) my first action would be to launch my rescue boat. In force, gale '8' conditions, I would consider that such action would endanger my own crew and I would consider an alternative method of recovery.

Such alternatives could involve the use of the rocket line throwing apparatus in conjunction with a messenger and hawser connected to:

(a) the liferaft of the fishing vessel (if it could be employed), or

(b) the liferaft of my own ship.

Either liferaft being secured with a towing hawser and used as a means of transport between the distress vessel and the rescue vessel (operation taking place on the lee side of the rescue ship).

If the use of the liferaft was impractical I would consider manoeuvring from a downwind position to draw my own vessel alongside the fishing boat, at a point which was at the opposite end from the flames. It would be my intention to make contact forward of my own collision bulkhead. With my increased freeboard and use of scrambling nets over the bow I would encourage the men to climb the nets and gain the security of the deck.

Note: When drawing the two vessels alongside I would not be too concerned about causing damage to the fishing vessel, assuming that the boat was probably lost to the flames already. Should my own vessel sustain damage, this would be forward of the collision bulkhead and would be considered as acceptable if the four men are recovered successfully.

Question 17.   When on a coastal passage through the English Channel the OOW reports sighting a red and white striped, round buoy on the surface. It is identified as a submarine indicator buoy. What would you do?

Answer: As Master of the vessel I would immediately take the 'conn' of the vessel and establish a Bridge Team in position. I would manoeuvre the vessel to circle the buoy, keeping my engines running. During this period I would order the OOW to establish the position of the buoy and ascertain whether it was tethered or adrift.

I would carry out a chart assessment to include the position of the buoy and note the depth in this area. Once all the information is available I would communicate to the Admiralty via the Coastguard all relevant details effecting the sighting of the buoy.

I would further operate my echo sounder, post extra lookouts and if the depth was less than 50 m, turn out the rescue boat with an emergency crew on stand-by. At reduced depth the possibility of personnel employing escape apparatus to reach the surface must be anticipated.

Additional communication may be made towards the submarine by hammer blows to the turn of the bilge. Assuming that the submarine was unable to surface the noise and vibration from the hammer action and from the propeller activity would send a positive indication to the submarine that a vessel was at the surface.

It must be anticipated that return communication from the authorities possibly with a relief warship in attendance, would relieve my merchant vessel of the situation.

Question 18.   When carrying out an emergency steering gear test drill, what would you expect to observe and do?

Answer: Emergency steering gear drills are conducted in accord with the regulations at intervals of at least three (3) months. The drill should demonstrate control of ship's steering from the steering flat compartment instead of from the navigation bridge. The communications between the two stations, steering flat/bridge, should also be tested and seen to be adequate. Any alternative power supply should also be operated and found satisfactory. Once the drill has been conducted, a statement shall be recorded in both the Official and Deck, Log Books.

Question 19. Following response to a distress situation which has been resolved, you are requested to carry out a towing operation. What factors would you consider, before accepting the towage contract?

Answer: It would be necessary to check the Charter Party and the Bills of Laden, to ensure that I am permitted to carry out a towing operation. I would further check the following:

(a) The quantity and available fuel on board my vessel to carry out the tow.
(b) Is my own cargo liable to suffer by the extended operation.
(c) Are your engines and deck machinery capable of achieving the tow.
(d) Could you still meet the Loading Port, Charter Party Clause, on time.
(e) Is the value of the towed vessel and cargo worth the effort.
(f) Owners and insurance would need to be informed as a towing operation could expect to increase premiums.
(g) Do both Masters have an agreement.

Question 20. When alongside working cargo in a port in the Far East, you are informed that a tropical revolving storm (TRS) is imminent. What options are available to you?

Answer: Any vessel, in port, in the direct path of a TRS will be limited in its options and each option would depend on variable circumstances affecting the immediate area. All options should include the following:

(a) Stopping cargo operations, closing up all hatches and re-secure cargo lashings.
(b) Remove any free surface within the vessel to improve the stability.
(c) Place the engines and crew on full alert stand-by.
(d) Continue to plot the progress of the storm.

First option – would, without doubt, be to let the moorings go and run for the open sea. The decision should be made early rather than late to avoid being caught in narrows or in the proximity of navigation hazards.

Second option – move the vessel into a 'storm anchorage' if available. Use both anchors with increased scope. Ensure the engines remain operational throughout the anchor period. Double anchor watch personnel.

Third option – remain alongside. This would not be a first or even second choice and would only happen if, say, engines were disabled and no other alternative was available. Maximise the number of moorings out, and obtain tug assistance to lay out anchors. Move the shore side cranes away from the overhang of the ship. Take on maximum ballast, with the view to make the vessel as heavy as possible and lift and stow the accommodation ladder.

Keep crew on stand-by and endeavour to make sure engines are operational.

Question 21.   While on passage in winter in high Northern latitudes your vessel starts to develop 'ice accretion' on the upper construction. What action would you take?

Answer: Ice accretion is dangerous because of the additional weight which builds up high on the superstructure. Such additional weight could well impair the vessels positive stability. Initially I would alter course South towards warmer latitudes, if possible and reduce the ship's speed to avoid wind chill factor increasing the ice build up. I would order the Chief Officer to employ the crew to clear ice formations overboard with the use of axes, shovels and steam hoses. I would also obtain an up-to-date weather forecast and investigate the options of re-routing the vessel. If sub-freezing air temperatures are being experienced, I would make a statutory report to this effect under a SECURITY priority communication.

Note: Clearing ice accretion is an extremely hazardous task and must be carried out with caution, having completed a 'risk assessment'.

Question 22.   When navigating in 'deep water' you experience a shallow sounding which is not indicated on the chart. What would you do?

Answer: I would order the navigator to note the position of the reduced sounding and report the same by means of the Hydrographical Note (H102), found in the Weekly Notices to Mariners and in the '*Mariners Handbook*'.

This report would be despatched to the Hydrographical Department respective of the chart being used.

Question 23.   Having been moored by two anchors, for some time, it is realised that the ship has swung and fouled her cables in a 'foul hawse'. What options are available to clear this situation?

Answer: If my vessel was highly manoeuvrable with twin propellers, bow thrust, etc., my first choice would be to try and steam around in opposition to the turns of the foul. A second option would be to employ the services of a tug, if available, to push the vessel around, against the foul turns in order to clear them.

A further option would be to hire a barge, preferably motorised, and break the anchor cable. Lower the bare end of chain into the barge and tow or drive it around the 'riding cable' in opposition to the foul turns.

If all previous options are not possible, break the 'sleeping cable' and dip the bare end around the riding cable, by use of easing wires. Re-connect the 'sleeping cable' before the turn of the next tide.

Question 24.   What does the 'emergency generator' or emergency power supply of the vessel provide for?

Answer: The emergency power supply must be a Self-Contained Unit and is independent of an external supply. It is usually a diesel motor with own starting system situated in a position away from the main engine room of the ship.

It provides an emergency power supply to: navigation lights and essential navigation equipment, the emergency lighting circuits, bilge and fire pumps, communications and the embarkation lights for the launching of survival craft.

Question 25.   Your vessel has been designated to be taken under tow to a repair yard for main engine repairs. The ship will retain a skeleton crew for the passage. What preparatory actions would you take, prior to engaging in being towed?

Answer: Prior to engaging the tow it would be necessary to make up a safe passage plan for the proposed operation. I would also order a full stability check to ensure that the vessel had an adequate metacentric height (GM) throughout the voyage, assuming that the vessel would be light and in ballast, making sure that any free surface effects were kept to a minimum. It would also be prudent to carry out all, or as many of the following actions:

(a)   Seal the uppermost continuous deck, with the exception of the deck scuppers.
(b)   Provide the vessel with a stern trim.
(c)   Check effective communications between the towing vessel and the towed vessel.
(d)   Ensure that adequate Life Saving Appliances are carried for the towed vessel.
(e)   A second anchor is kept ready for emergency use (assuming that the other anchor may be employed as part of the towing arrangement).
(f)   Correct navigation signals are available for day and night periods.
(g)   Lock rudder amidships, if the vessel is not steering.
(h)   Disengage propeller shafts to free rotate, to reduce drag effects.
(i)   Close all watertight doors aboard the towed vessel (MGN 35 outlines information on what to do in the case of accidents when using power-operated watertight doors – see Appendix D).
(j)   Reduce the oil content in the vessel to a minimum.
(k)   Have a secondary emergency towline arrangement available.
(l)   Contact the respective Marine Authorities, to issue navigation warnings, regarding the passage route, through international waters.
(m) Advise underwriters, who may provide an advisory 'Tow Master', to assist and accompany the towing operation.
(n)   Obtain a local and long-range weather forecast prior to the voyage.
(o)   Inspect the towing arrangement (with a Towing Master, if present) to ensure strength and securing.

Question 26.   Following a collision and damage to your own vessel you are taken to a port of refuge. What must you have on board prior to sailing from the port?

Answer: An Interim Certificate of Class. Depending on the extent of repairs it may also be necessary to 'swing the ship' to recalibrate the magnetic compass. In such circumstances a new deviation card would also be required.

Question 27.   What safety precautions are in place to prevent accidental release of the CO_2 injection system into the engine room?

Answer: The remote cabinet outside the CO_2 room is fitted with a 'break glass take key to unlock'.
Operation. Once inside the cabinet a stop valve control must be released prior to operation of the pilot bottles that activate the CO_2 bottle bank.

Question 28.   How would you increase pressure and continue the water supply to hoses fighting an engine room fire?

Answer: Shut the isolation valve to the deck line. (Usually found on the forward end bulkhead in the engine room.)

Question 29.   How would you ensure your crew are trained to handle situation disasters?

Answer: Throughout the period of the voyage it would be prudent to exercise the crew in disaster training scenarios. This could be carried out during the period of boat and fire drills.

These should be active drills with personnel being interchanged to provide multiplicity on essential tasks. Disaster/safety videos could be shown to crew. Alleyways and public rooms could carry educational and advisory posters.

Reality casualty rescues, rescue boat activity inside harbour limits, together with encouraging shore side training courses would all be expected to improve the state of readiness and efficiency of the crew.

Question 30.   You hear a distress signal and proceed at best possible speed to the last known position of the distressed vessel. When you arrive on scene nothing is found. What action would you take?

Answer: On approach I would have my Bridge Team in place and my vessel on an 'alert status' with engines on 'stand-by'. I would have posted extra lookouts and would commence an expanding square search pattern as per IAMSAR (Reference for expanding square search pattern: IAMSAR, *Guidance to Masters on Search and Rescue Operations* is also contained in the Annual Summary of Notices to Mariners, Notice No. 4).

I would inform the Marine Rescue Co-ordination Centre (MRCC) of the situation and update this report as and when evidence of the incident presents itself. Monitor my own position closely and update the weather reports, not standing my own vessel into danger.

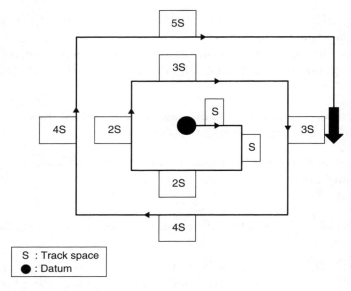

S : Track space
● : Datum

Expanding square search pattern.

THE MAGNETIC COMPASS

Question 1. How would you remove an air bubble from the liquid magnetic compass?

Answer: Invert the compass bowl in the gimbal arrangement to bring the expansion chamber uppermost. Undo the screw cap of the chamber and top up the fluid in the bowl with distilled water. This action will fill the bowl, forcing out the air bubble.

Question 2. What is the compass card made of, in a liquid magnetic compass?

Answer: Mica or melamine.

Question 3. What liquids constitute the fluid inside the liquid magnetic compass?

Answer: The liquid is made up of two parts distilled water to one part alcohol (alternatively, a modern liquid compass would use Bayol a light clear oil which lubricates the pivot and reduces bearing friction).

Question 4. What is the name of the cover that protects the bowl and the azimuth circle found on top of the compass bowl?

Answer: The cover, usually made of brass or fibre glass, is called the 'helmet'. It is fitted with two hinged windows for viewing and providing access to the bowl and azimuth ring.

Question 5. When correcting a magnetic compass for the average, conventional ship, what order of placing the correctors would you take?

Answer: The usual procedure would be to position:

(a) The 'Flinders bar' of approximately 12 in. (30.48 cm) length, into the forward, brass holder. This length would be supported by wood blocks to bring the 'pole' of the bar, level with the compass needle arrangement.
(b) The soft iron spheres, (Kelvin's balls) would be positioned midway on the side brackets and only lightly secured by the underside bolts. The size of the spheres can vary, but their centres should be level with the magnets of the card and not closer than 1¼ times the length of the longest needle.
(c) Heeling error magnets, each of a length of 9 in. (22.86 cm) are placed into the 'bucket' (they compensate for field 'R' and vertical soft iron). They also induce magnetism into the 'Flinders bar' and 'spheres' to help correct heeling error.
(d) Horizontal magnets each of 8 in. (19.32 cm) length compensate for the fore and aft and athwartships components of semi-permanent magnetism.

Question 6. When positioning the 'Flinders bar', what is the position of the top of the bar, in relation to the magnetic needle arrangement?

Answer: The top of the bar should be positioned approximately 1/12th above the needle arrangement. This position effectively brings the pole of the Flinders bar level with the card magnets.

Question 7. What do you understand by the term 'dead beat'?

Answer: The expression indicates that the compass card is steady and not being allowed to oscillate because of the fluid around the card. A 'dead beat' compass is good to use as a steering compass because it is not too sensitive (unlike a dry card compass, which is difficult to steer by).

Question 8.   Electrical current is passed into the binnacle in order to provide power to the lamp, under the frosted, glass base of the compass bowl. Why does the electrical current not magnetically affect the magnetism of the compass?

Answer: Power cables are always doubled, carrying direct current (DC). When positioned, they are set in opposing directions so that one electric field opposes the other, so cancelling each other out and having zero effect.

Question 9.   What liquid is employed in a modern liquid magnetic compass?

Answer: Bayol, which is a light clear oil. Not only will this fluid provide lubrication to the pivot but also the oily fluid makes the compass more 'dead beat' and reduces the risk of corrosion.

Question 10.   Where would you find the 'float chamber' on the liquid magnetic compass?

Answer: The float chamber is found in the centre of the compass card, under the centre 'dome'. It supports the weight of the card on the pivot and reduces friction at the pivot point. Its function is to raise the centre of gravity of the card above itself so that the card always returns to the horizontal if inclined by an external force.

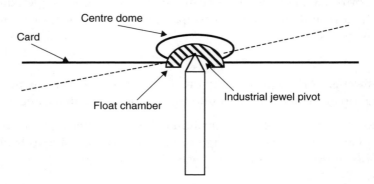

Question 11.   You are instructed to take over as Master of a ship which has been 'laid up' for 3 years. What checks would you make on the compass?

Answer: I would inspect the compass and binnacle housing for overall condition and have the ship 'swung' and corrected by a compass adjuster. It would be necessary to have the ship in an upright position for the swing with all derricks, cranes, lifeboats, etc., in their correct seagoing position.

The azimuth mirror would be checked for accuracy and correct alignment of the 'lubber line' would be ascertained. Any friction on the bearing could be noted by using a magnet at the side of the bowl, to cause a deflection, to see if it returns to its original position without sticking. The soft iron correctors should be tested for retained magnetism and any residual magnetism detected could be removed by annealing.

All moveable equipment near the compass position would be removed and the swing must not take place with other vessels within a three-cable proximity.

Question 12.   When else would you consider it necessary to 'swing' the ship to correct the compass?

Answer: The ship would normally be swung after any of the following circumstances:

(a) Following a collision or a grounding incident where major repairs are required to be made to the ship, which could affect the vessels permanent and induced magnetism.
(b) In the event of a major fire on board the ship.
(c) If engaged on a long charter trading in high latitudes, i.e. 'Hudson Bay'.
(d) After leaving the builders yard as a new ship.
(e) If loading a high capacity metallic cargo, e.g. railway lines on deck.
(f) In the event that compass errors became excessively large for no apparent reason or the compass becomes unreliable.
(g) If electrical or magnetic equipment is added or removed to/from the proximity of the magnetic compass.
(h) In the event that a period of 2 years has elapsed and the ship is without a record of deviations, or when the compass shows a physical defect when first installed.

Question 13.   Where would you place in the compass 'bucket'?

Answer: The bucket is found in the centre of the binnacle and hangs on a chain vertically beneath the centre of the compass bowl in a tube. It is used to hold the 'heeling error magnets'.

Question 14.   The fabric casing of the binnacle is usually manufactured in either wood or fibre glass resin. What is this casing called?

Answer: The whole structural fabric of the binnacle housing is referred to as the 'furniture'.

Question 15.   A liquid magnetic compass contains a mix of alcohol and distilled water. What is the purpose of this mixture?

Answer: The inclusion of alcohol in the mix is to prevent the liquid freezing when navigating in high cold latitudes, while the purpose of the distilled water is to prevent the alcohol evaporating in the warm middle latitudes.

Question 16.   The binnacle is bolted to the ship's deck through a slewing arrangement. What coefficient correction is adjusted, by slewing the directional aspect of the binnacle in its slewing feet?

Answer: By slewing the compass in its footings the correction for an 'Apparent A' can be eliminated.

Question 17.   When carrying out maintenance on or near the magnetic compass, what paints would you avoid using and why?

Answer: Black paints should not be used on or near the compass because they have a high metallic (lead) base, which could influence magnetic effect.

Question 18.   What is the normal position of the 'soft iron spheres' (Kelvin's balls)?

Answer: The spheres are normally placed in the centre of the track either side and equidistant from the compass bowl.

Question 19.   Why it is necessary to correct the magnetic compass?

Answer: The vessel has a need for an effective steering compass and correction would provide a reliable instrument for this purpose, by being provided with good, directional force.

Question 20. Having joined a ship for the first time, where would you obtain information about the compass?

Answer: Information pertinent to the compass may be obtained from:

(a) the Deviation Card;
(b) the Azimuth/Deviation Record Book on the bridge;
(c) the Deck Log Book;
(d) the Maintenance Manual, and from the compass itself.

Question 21. What is the ship's multiplier?

Answer: The difference between the directional force at the ship's position (with spheres in place) and the directional force ashore is called the 'ships multiplier', represented by the symbol λ_2. It is used to adjust weight on the vertical force instrument (VFI) needle when correcting for heeling error.

Question 22. How would you find the value of the magnetic bearing of a chosen target?

Answer: Take the bearing of the fixed object when the ship is on 8 different headings (N, NE, E, SE, S, SW, W, NW). Add the values together and divide by '8'.

Question 23. What certificates cover the magnetic compass?

Answer: The magnetic compass is covered by the Safety Equipment Certificate and is one of the navigational instruments listed in the record of inspection. Additionally, it should be noted that the Safety Ship Construction Certificate will not be issued unless the vessel is equipped with a 'type tested compass'.

Question 24. What conditions would you require for swinging the compass?

Answer: Prior to swinging the compass the ship should be noted to be in an upright condition, with all derricks/cranes, lifeboats, etc., stowed in a seagoing position. The sited position of the compass would be observed and no electrical instruments or influences are inside the specified position of the binnacle (any electrical equipment to close could give rise to an effecting magnetic field). The foundation, retaining deck bolts, should be sighted to be firm so as to prevent any unsolicited movement.

Weather conditions should be good and the intended area of swing should be free of magnetic anomalies and clear of traffic focal points. The alignment of the 'lubber line' and the azimuth mirror should be checked for correctness, prior to commencing any swing.

The overall condition of the compass bowl would be inspected and any air bubble eliminated. The gimbal arrangement should be seen to be free and to have clean bearings. The condition of the pivot would be checked by use of a magnet at the side to induce a movement and observed return to the heading.

The soft iron correctors should be inspected to ensure they are clear of retained magnetism, then placed correctly within the order of correction.

Question 25.   Where should the bucket be positioned when correcting for heeling error when the ship is at the magnetic equator?

Answer: The bucket for heeling error magnets should be at the bottom of the tube, when correction is taking place at the magnetic equator.

Question 26.   When carrying out a compass swing how far away from a chosen target should the vessel be?

Answer: The distance from target should be at least 15 miles. This will reduce bearing parallax to a minimum.

Question 27.   What reference would you use to gain information of compass standards, and required checks and inspections?

Answer: Standards and checks on both magnetic and gyro compasses can be found in Safety of Life at Sea (Convention) (SOLAS), Chapter 5, and Annex 13.

Question 28.   Why would you employ the services of a compass adjuster?

Answer: To use his experience and make use of his local knowledge.

Question 29.   What is the purpose of the 'vertical force instrument' (VFI)?

Answer: To correct for heeling error with the vessel in the upright position.

Question 30.   Describe the method of a full compass adjustment by a compass adjuster?

Answer: Prior to boarding, level the VFI while ashore. On boarding the vessel, carry out pre-swing checks. Place the Flinders bar and position spheres in mid-bracket positions. Take bowl out and position VFI to correct for heeling error. At the swinging ground establish a suitable target. Commence swing and correct coefficients. Swing again and check residuals. Produce 'deviation card' and complete documentation.

> It should be noted that candidates for Master (unlimited) are not required to demonstrate a compass correction procedure. However, in order to be competent to answer associated questions by an examiner on the use and care of various types of compasses, it may be considered useful to be able to carry out a full correction procedure.

MARINE BUSINESS AND LAW

Question 1.   What are the four legal requirements placed on the ship's Master, in the event of a collision at sea with another vessel?

Answer: The Master's legal requirements in the event of collision are to:

(a) stand-by to render all assistance to the other vessel,
(b) exchange relevant information with the Master or Officer in charge of the other vessel,
(c) report the collision incident to the MAIB,
(d) cause an entry regarding the incident to be entered into the Official Log Book (OLB).

Question 2.   What are the Master's obligations on receiving a distress message?

Answer: A distress signal must be acknowledged and entered into the log book. The Master is expected to respond to the distress and offer assistance if it is considered reasonable to do so.

Question 3.   If the Master of a vessel inside the summer load line zone receives a distress signal from inside the winter zone, is it permitted to take his vessel into the winter zone, knowing his ship would be over-loaded, in order to respond to the distress situation?

Answer: Yes. A vessel may enter a winter zone for the express pur-pose of responding to a distress situation. However, once the distress situation is resolved it is anticipated that the vessel would take the shortest and safest route to return to the summer load line zone. A notation of the 'deviation' would need to be entered into the Log Book.

Question 4.   When would a Master not have to respond to a distress signal?

Answer: Response to a distress is not required, if:

(a) it is considered unreasonable or unnecessary to do so;
(b) the distress vessel has sufficient vessels requisitioned to assist and your vessel is released from the obligation of attending;
(c) action would endanger the Master's own vessel and/or crew;
(d) where the distress is cancelled and the distress party no longer requires the attending vessel(s).

Question 5.   What are the statutory obligations placed on a Master when navigating inside known 'ice regions'?

Answer: The Master when informed that dangerous ice is ahead on his intended track, must: alter his course and proceed at a moderate speed at night. Further, if he encounters dangerous ice, he is obli-gated to make a statutory report of the type and position of this ice (Reference: SOLAS).

Question 6.   What is the period of validity of the International Oil Pollution Prevention (IOPP) Certificate?

Answer: Five (5) years.

Question 7.   With reference to the UK what ships must comply with the 1996 Marine Pollution (Convention) (MARPOL) Regulations?

Answer:
(a) All UK ships.
(b) All other ships in the territorial waters of the UK.
(c) Government ships (exemption for warships and auxiliaries).

Question 8.   Are you allowed to dispose of garbage over the ship's side?

Answer: Generally no, but food waste can be disposed of without any required need to grind or comminute, provided the ship is away from land and never within 12 nautical miles.

Note: Nothing is allowed to be discharged in Antarctica or the Arctic.

Question 9.   What entries are made in the Garbage Record Book?

Answer: Records must be kept of all discharges or incineration of garbage. The Garbage Record Book is part of the Official Log Book but may be kept separately. Entries will include:

(a) Date and time of disposal or incineration of garbage.
(b) The position of the ship at the time.
(c) A description and amount of garbage involved.
(d) Any accidental discharge or loss of garbage.

The Master must sign every page of the Garbage Record Book.

Question 10.   Under what regulations is the ship's International Tonnage Certificate issued?

Answer: Under the Regulations established by the International Tonnage Convention.

Question 11.   What is the main reason for a Master to 'Note Protest'?

Answer: The main purpose of 'Noting Protest' in the UK is to support a cargo owner's claim against underwriters.

Note: There is no legal necessity to 'Note Protest' in the UK as they are not accepted as evidence in favour of the Party, making the protest, unless both parties agree.

However, on the continent and many other countries a Note of Protest is admissible as evidence before a legal hearing, and the success of a case may well depend on Protest being made.

Question 12.   What is involved in making 'Protest'?

Answer: The procedure of making 'Protest' is carried out by the ship's Master making a statement or declaration, under oath to a Notary

Public, a Magistrate or a British Consul. The statement is related to an occurrence during the voyage, which is beyond the control of the Master, which has given or may give rise to a loss or damage.

Question 13.   When would a Master 'Note Protest'?

Answer: A 'Note of Protest' is made:

(a) When the ship has encountered heavy weather which may result in cargo damage.
(b) Whenever damage has been caused or is suspected from any cause.
(c) Where cargo has been damaged through a peril of the sea (i.e. inadequate ventilation because of the stresses of bad weather).
(d) When cargo is shipped in such a state as to be likely to deteriorate during the voyage (B/Ls would also need to be endorsed in this example).
(e) When the terms of the Charter Party (C/P) has been breached by either the Charterer, or his agent. Examples: refusal to load, or loading improper cargo.
(f) When consignees fail to discharge cargo or to take delivery and pay freight.
(g) In all cases of General Average, or failure to make a cancellation date due to heavy weather.

It should be borne in mind that the act of Noting Protest should be made as soon as possible after arrival in port. Where a cargo Protest is being made, this should be carried out before 'breaking bulk'.

Where cargo is for several ports, a Note of Protest should be made in each port.

Question 14.   When signing on a crew, the Master thinks he has been presented with a fraudulent Certificate of Competency. How can he ascertain the validity of the qualification?

Answer: On inspection, the Master would take note of the full name and certificate number, together with the date of birth of the person presenting the credentials. The Master would contact the Marine Authority of issue, and confirm the personal details of the Officer presenting the papers.

Question 15.   What is General Average?

Answer: Is a sum of money that all parties to the venture have to pay to any one member who suffers a partial loss during the voyage. If a cargo owner does not pay his contribution, then the ship owner will have a 'lien' on the cargo.

Question 16.   As Master of a ship you are expected to report certain meteorological phenomena. What weather features would you report?

Answer: As Master I would report the following features:

(a) The sighting of dangerous ice.
(b) Storm force winds of force '10' or over for which no report has been issued.
(c) Sub-freezing air temperatures (that could give rise to ice accretion).

Question 17.   If a member of your crew died on the passage, what would you do?

Answer: In the event of a death of a crew member it would be the responsibility of the Master to complete the report form Return of Births and Deaths (RBD) 1 and deliver it to a Superintendent and, Consul, or Shipping Master at the earliest opportunity. The Master would further cause an entry to be made into the Official Log Book, which is consistent with the RBD 1 report.

The body should be kept isolated and under security until it can be landed. If a post mortem is carried out at any time a copy of the report and any other associated medical details should accompany the body when landed.

An inquiry into the death may be required and if so, a report of this inquiry is to be made.

Question 18.   Three members of the crew make a complaint about the food on the ship. What would be the actions of the Master?

Answer: If only one man makes a complaint the Master is not legally obliged to act. However, when three men or more complain, the Master must investigate the grounds for the complaint and if it is found proved, take such action as will rectify the problem.

He is then expected to inform the complainant of his actions and obtain their agreement to satisfaction, that the action taken has been adequate. In the event of that they are *not* satisfied with the action taken, they may take their compliant to a higher authority, namely a proper Officer, i.e. Port Superintendent.

Whatever the outcome the Master must enter the details of the complaint into the Official Log Book.

Question 19. What Certificates are issued by the Marine Authority (Maritime and Coastguard Agency (MCA))?

Answer: Safety Equipment Certificate, Safe Manning, Document of Compliance, Safety Management Certificate, Cargo Ship Safety Construction Certificate.

Question 20. What certificates are issued by the Classification Society?

Answer: International Tonnage Certificates, Load Line Certificate, Cargo Ship Safety Radio Certificate.

Note: One or more of the Safety Convention Certificates are issued on behalf of the Marine Authority (UK, the MCA; US, United States Coast Guard).

Question 21. On a tanker vessel what certificate must you carry to show that you comply with the MARPOL Convention?

Answer: The vessel is required to have the International Oil Pollution Prevention Certificate (IOPPC).

Question 22. What sanctions could a Master impose if a seafarer was found to be guilty of a breach of the 'Code of Conduct'?

Answer: Any sanction imposed by the Master would be dependent on the nature and degree of the breach of the Code. The punishment to fit the crime, so to speak and would consist of one of the following:

(a) A formal (oral) warning and a record made in the Official Log Book.
(b) A written reprimand, also recorded in the Official Log Book.
(c) Dismissal from the vessel, either immediately (if in a UK port or an overseas port) or at the next port of call.

CARGO SHIP SAFETY EQUIPMENT CERTIFICATE

THIS CERTIFICATE SHALL BE SUPPLEMENTED BY A RECORD OF EQUIPMENT (FORM E)

ISSUED UNDER THE PROVISIONS OF THE

INTERNATIONAL CONVENTION FOR THE SAFETY OF LIFE AT SEA, 1974,
AS MODIFIED BY THE PROTOCOL OF 1988 RELATING THERETO

UNDER THE AUTHORITY OF THE GOVERNMENT OF

_____
(Name of the state)

by _____
(Surveyor, American Bureau of Shipping)

Particulars of ship

Name of Ship	Distinctive Number or Letters	Port of registry	Gross tonnage a) according to function[1] b) according to tonnage[2]

Deadweight of ship (Metric Tons)[3]	Length of Ship (Regulation III/3.10)	IMO Number	Date on which keel was laid[4]

Type of Ship[5]

Bulk Carrier
Oil tanker
Chemical tanker
Gas Carrier
Cargo ship other than any of the above

THIS IS TO CERTIFY:

1   That the ship has been surveyed in accordance with the requirements of Regulation I/8, of the Convention.
2   That the survey showed that:

2.1   the ship complied with the requirements of the Convention as regards fire safety systems and appliances and fire control plans;

2.2   the life-saving appliances and the equipment of the lifeboats, liferafts and rescue boats were provided in accordance with the requirements of the Convention;

_____

[1] The above gross tonnage has been determined in accordance with the International Convention on Tonnage Measurement of Ships, 1969.
[2] The above gross tonnage has been determined by the authorities of the Administration in accordance with the national tonnage rules which were in force prior to the coming into force for existing ships of the International Convention on Tonnage Measurement of Ships, 1969.
[3] For oil tankers, chemical tankers and gas carriers only.
[4] Insert the date of expiry as specified by the Administration in accordance with Regulation 1/14(a) of the Convention. The day and the month of the date correspond to the anniversary date as defined in Regulation 1/2(n) of the Convention, unless amended in accordance with Regulation 1/14(h).
[5] Delete as appropriate.

Question 23.   How often would you expect to carry out inspections of the crew accommodations?

Answer: Inspections must be carried out at least at every seven-day (7-day) intervals, by the Master or his designated deputy. Such inspections must be recorded in the Official Log Book, with the name of the inspector and any findings that did not comply with the regulations.

Question 24.   When taking over a ship as Master, what entries would be made into the Official Log Book?

Answer: The outgoing Master would cause an entry to be made in the narrative section, to the effect that he has delivered to me (the incoming Master) all documents and keys relating to both the ship and crew. Both Masters would sign the entry.

The incoming Master would then add his name and certificate number, to the list on the front cover of the log book.

Question 25.   What entry would be made in the Official Log Book with regard to disciplinary action taken, following a breach of the Code of Conduct?

Answer: The log book entry would include full details of the alleged breach and results and findings of any subsequent enquiry. The sanction(s) if any, taken by the Master in response to the breach of the code would also be entered.

The seafarer involved in the case must be given copies of the log book entries affecting the case and these must be acknowledged by a receipt signing.

Question 26.   When taking over as Master of a vessel, how would you know that the ship is compliant with the International Safety Management (ISM) Code?

Answer: If the ship is compliant with ISM, a valid Safety Management Certificate, will be strategically displayed along with a copy of the companies Document of Compliance (DoC).

SAFETY MANAGEMENT CERTIFICATE

Issued under the provisions of the INTERNATIONAL CONVENTION
FOR THE SAFETY OF LIFE AT SEA, 1974, as amended
under the authority of the Government of

_____

by the AMERICAN BUREAU OF SHIPPING

Name of Ship: _____

Distinctive Number or Letters: _____

Port of Registry: _____

Type of Ship[1]:   _____

Gross Tonnage: _____

IMO Number: _____

Name and address of company: _____

                                       _____

                                       _____

                                       _____

                                       _____

                          (see paragraph 1.1.2 of the ISM Code)

THIS IS TO CERTIFY that the Safety Management System of the ship has been audited
and that it complies with the requirements of the International management code for the
Safe Operation of Ships and for Pollution Prevention (ISM code), adopted by the
International Maritime Organization by resolution A.741(1B), as amended, following
verification that the document of compliance for the company is applicable to this
type of ship.

This Safety Management Certificate is valid until _____ subject to
periodical verification and the validity of the Document of Compliance.

Issued at: _____

Date of Issue: _____

_____
(Signature of the duly authorized official issuing the certificate)

_____

[1]Insert the type of ship from among the following: Passenger Ship; Passenger High
Speed Craft; Cargo high speed craft; Bulk Carrier; Oil Tanker; Chemical tanker;
Gas Carrier; Mobile Offshore Drilling Unit; Other Cargo Ship

The Merchant Shipping Act　　SIGNAL LETTERS: ___

CERTIFICATE OF REGISTRY

SHIP'S PARTICULARS

Official Number: IMO Number: Port Number:	Name of Ship: GRT:　　NRT:	Description of Ship:
Registered dimensions: Length　　　metres Breadth　　　metres Depth　　　metres	Where Built: Date Keel Laid:	Previous Registration: Former Name: Hull No:

ENGINE PARTICULARS

Description of Engine: Make and Model: Number:	Maker: Year made:	Number of Shafts: BHP: Estimated Speed:

OWNER'S PARTICULARS

Name and Address:		Number of Shares:

Issued at _____

On _____

_____
Registrar of Ships

Notice: A Certificate of Registry is not a document of title. It shall be used only
for the lawful navigation of the ship and shall not be subject to detention by reason
of title, lien, charge or interest whatsoever had or claimed by any owner, mortgagee
or other person to, on or in the ship.

Question 27.   What is the period of validity of the Safety Management Certificate?

Answer: Five years.

Question 28.   What compatibility must a ship have, prior to the issue of a Safe Manning Certificate?

Answer: Prior to issuing a Safe Manning Certificate (SMC), the surveyor would ensure that adequate Life Saving Appliances were in place on the vessel for the certificated number of personnel that the ship has capacity for.

Question 29.   What is the function of the Certificate of Registry?

Answer: The Certificate of Registry is issued by a Government to establish nationality and ownership of a vessel.

Question 30.   What is a Charter Party?

Answer: The Charter Party is a formal agreement to rent, hire or lease a ship. There are various types of Charter, including: Time Charter, Bareboat Charter or Open Charter.

It is written up with condition clauses that the Master of the vessel would be expected to abide by, while executing the voyage.

SHIP HANDLING AND MOORING

Question 1.   What is and where would you find the 'ganger length'?

Answer: The ganger length is that length of anchor chain found between the Anchor Crown 'D' shackle and the first joining shackle of the cable.

Question 2.   What is a 'gob rope' used for?

Answer: A 'gob rope' is used by a tug to change the position of the towing position from midships to the aft end of the tug. The purpose of this is to prevent the tug from capsizing caused by the direction of the towline 'girting' the tug.

A tug operating with a single 'gob wire rope' in conjunction with a heavy-duty shackle over the towline.

Question 3. What are the advantages of controllable pitch propellers (CPP) over and above a conventional right hand, fixed blade propeller?

Answer: Use of CPP provides several advantages over a fixed blade, although they are more expensive to install. Advantages include:

(a) Immediate control of the vessel by the OOW.
(b) The ship can be stopped, without stopping the engine.
(c) Shaft alternators can be used with a constant speed shaft, thereby saving on the cost of auxiliary fuel for generators.
(d) Air start bottles are unlikely to cause a problem during continuous manoeuvres.
(e) Bridge wing and central control positions provide better ship handling.

Question 4. Prior to going into an anchorage to moor the ship, what preparations would you do?

Bridge wing control station for the operation of CPP's, bow thrust and emergency stops. Additional monitors and sensors display ship's movement elements.

Answer: When it is the intention to use the ship's anchors I would construct a clear and objective 'anchor plan', to take account of the following considerations:

(a) The position of letting go or walking back the anchor would be defined.
(b) The depth of water on site would be noted to estimate scope of cable.
(c) The state of tide at the time of intended anchoring, together with the rise of tide between the high water and low water marks.
(d) The type of holding ground as shown on the chart.
(e) That the intended anchorage is clear of underwater obstructions.
(f) That there is an adequate swinging room, clear of surface obstructions.
(g) With the ship's draught, the underkeel clearance throughout the operation is adequate.
(h) Whether to use one or two anchors.

(i)   The proximity of other shipping or through traffic.
(j)   The position fixing methods available.
(k)   The speed of approach and positions of reducing speed.
(l)   The types of anchors being used and there respective holding power.
(m) Any local hazards that could effect a safe anchorage, e.g. outfalls.
(n)   The wind direction and local weather conditions at the time of operation.
(o)   The shelter offered by the proposed anchorage site.
(p)   That the anchor party is briefed as to the relevant details and signals to display.

Question 5.   How would you expect your Watch Officers to ensure that the vessel does not drag her anchor(s) and move position?

Answer: It is normal practice to leave instructions and 'Night Standing Orders' for the OOW to monitor the ship's position by primary and secondary means, throughout the period of each watch.

The position of the ship being fixed by:

(a) Visual Anchor Bearings
(b) Radar Range and Bearing
(c) Global Positioning System (GPS).

Note: The anchor bearings being written onto the chart and entered into the Deck Log Book.

Question 6.   What checks and precautions would you expect an OOW to take in the event of suspecting the vessel to be dragging her anchor?

Answer: I would anticipate that the OOW had re-checked the anchor bearings, and if in any doubt would call and advise the Master accordingly.

The Master could relieve the Watch Officer to go forward to feel if the cable was experiencing excessive vibration, to further confirm that the anchor is dragging. Radar observation and position change would identify ship movement.

A hand lead, lowered to the sea bed from the bridge wing could also give indication of dragging, by leading forward towards the bow as the vessel drags.

Question 7.   In the event that the vessel is found to be dragging her anchor, what action would you take?

Answer: If dragging the anchor is confirmed, the initial action would be to pay out more anchor cable. If the ship continues to drag, a second anchor could be used at 'short stay'.

However, in the event dragging still continues, it would be prudent to recover both anchors and move to either a better, more sheltered anchorage or move to open waters and steam up and down, until the weather abates.

If in coastal regions it is some times possible to seek the lee of the land and gain shelter there.

Question 8.   What is 'squat' and how can you reduce it?

Answer: Squat is a form of interaction which occurs between the underside of the vessel and the closeness of the sea bottom to the keel. It is a shallow water effect on the ship's hull which could influence the steering of the vessel and the overall control of the vessel. The effect is generally amplified by the speed of the ship over the ground, combined with underkeel clearance and blockage factor in canals/rivers, etc.

Squat effect has been directly linked to speed^2 and to this end a positive and immediate reduction in speed will reduce or even eliminate detrimental effects of squat in shallow waters. Alternatively the vessel should seek deeper waters where the interactive effects of the sea bottom make squat effect, insignificant.

Question 9.   What is 'blockage factor' in a canal?

Answer: Blockage factor is caused by the volume of the ship's hull, occupying a greater part of the cross-sectional area of a waterway.

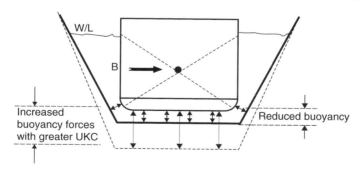

Blockage factor illustrated. B: position of the centre of buoyancy; UKC: underkeel clearance; W/L: water line.

The illustration shows that because the underkeel clearance is small the volume of water under the keel is small and would not have the same buoyancy effect on the hull as noted in deeper water.

Bearing in mind that the position of buoyancy is defined as the geometric centre of the underwater volume. If the vessel is heeled by external forces the water plane will increase, the position of 'B' would move upwards, but at the same time, also outwards towards the angle of heel. This leaves the low side, at the turn of the bilge, liable to contact with the ground.

Question 10. How would you enter your ship into a dock from a tidal river?

Answer: Depending on overall circumstances, most vessels would stem the tide and lay alongside the river wall of the dock, then warp the vessel forward into the dock entrance.

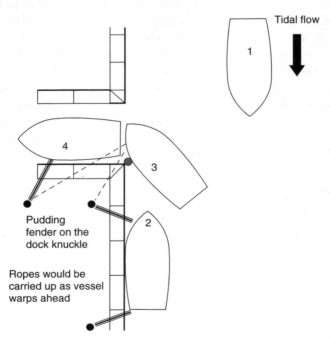

Question 11. When about to engage with a helicopter to receive the 'Marine Pilot', by vertical hoist method, what course would you adopt?

Answer: Air to surface operations of this nature would normally be dictated by the direction of the wind and the available deck space for landing and receiving the 'Pilot' on board.

It would be anticipated that the ship should alter course to position the wind 2 to 3 points off the port bow, provided the ship had adequate sea room and underkeel clearance was not going to be infringed.

Note: Helicopters have the winch over the access doorway on their starboard side and would want to engage their starboard to your port side. At the same time they would wish to head just into the wind to retain tighter control on the aircraft.

A puma helicopter engages over the port side, deck area of a tanker vessel, to lower the Marine Pilot. Deck space does not lend to a land on situation, but would in any event be exceptionally clean and free of loose objects. The danger of 'downdraft' from the aircraft rotors is well known to cause loose objects to fly with possible dangerous consequences.

Question 12. When operating astern propulsion, at what moment in time will you be able to detect that the vessel has gathered 'sternway'?

Answer: Sternway would be detected when the wash from the propellers is sighted at a position abeam the bridge.

Question 13. Your vessel is secured to a weak jetty. Two tugs are available to assist. How would you unberth?

Answer: If the condition of the berth had been realised prior to docking it would have been prudent to use a 'baltic moor' configuration.

As presented, the use of the two tugs would be employed to pull the vessel off the berth without use of ship's engines. Once clear of the berth then engines could be engaged and the tugs dismissed.

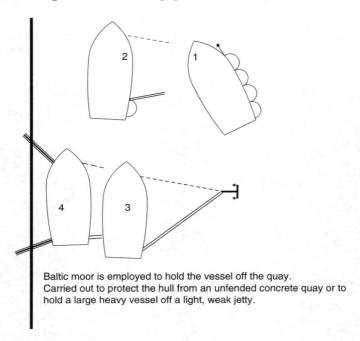

Baltic moor is employed to hold the vessel off the quay.
Carried out to protect the hull from an unfended concrete quay or to hold a large heavy vessel off a light, weak jetty.

Question 14. Following a test on the emergency steering gear, the connection pin shears during the disconnection from the steering flat to the bridge. The bridge is then informed that steering cannot be returned until a new pin can be manufactured. What options are available to you and what actions would you take in open sea conditions?

Answer: Such circumstances where the loss of effective steering control is experienced extremely limit the Master's actions. Such actions, as they may be, will depend on a variety of factors, not least the weather and the geography.

In all options the ship should display not under command (NUC) lights or shapes until steerage control can be regained. In congested waters the vessel would stop engines and not attempt to proceed without effective steering.

Option 1. Twin screw/propeller vessels can attempt to steer by engines, under NUC signals and while in open, non-congested waters.

Option 2. Stop engines and await repairs to be effected.

Option 3. Stop engines and anchor the vessel if the depth of water permits.

In all cases of such a situation arising, the ship's position should be obtained. A statement should be entered in the ship's Deck Log Book and the Official Log Book. In certain circumstances it may be necessary to make a SECURITY, navigation warning signal.

With repairs underway, it would not be anticipated that tug assistance would be required.

Question 15.   What are the anticipated dangers when making a tug fast at the forward end, when the mother vessel is under way and making way?

Answer: The main concern with the engagement of tugs would be from interaction. This is especially important when making the forward tug fast as the pressure cushion at the break of the foc'stle head will be at its maximum and counter helm action, at this time, by the tug master, could allow the tug to be drawn under the flare of the bow.

Question 16.   Following a grounding incident your tanker vessel has received bottom and side damage to the outer hull. Pollution is evident from the damaged tanks. What action would you expect to take as Master of the vessel?

Answer: Assuming that no risk to life is present the Master's priority would be to direct his attentions to reducing the pollution effects to the environment. This could be carried out in many ways and the following methods are suggested:

(a) Order the upper deck scuppers to be sealed and prevent access overside for any oil from damaged tanks being pressured upwards through air pipes or sounding pipes.

(b) Transfer oil from damaged tanks internally, into known structurally sound tanks.

(c) Request shuttle tankers or oil barges to attend, to transfer oil externally.

(d) Make use of anti-pollution chemicals and order more supplies to be flown in to the area to combat on board pollution.

(e) Order barrier/boom apparatus to be deployed if available (alternative improvisation – use mooring ropes to encompass the spillage area).

(f) Commence clean up operations soonest, to include oil recovery vessels, skimmers, and the like.

(g) Instigate repairs (or temporary repairs) to damaged areas as soon as practical, without causing any additional fire risk.

(h) Contact the Marine Pollution Control Unit (MPCU) and seek advice as to improving anti-pollution methods.

(i) Cause an entry to be made into the Oil Record Book to reflect the incident and what actions have been taken.

(j) Establish a fire patrol in the area, from the onset of the incident.

(k) Complete an incident report to the MAIB.

Communications

It must be assumed that communications following the grounding incident have included contact with owners/underwriters/charter party, etc.

Local Coastguards via the Coast Radio Station should have received an 'urgency' call. A position report being made and a weather forecast obtained. Requests for tugs, skimmers, barges and specialist vessels may be appropriate, together with oil pollution effective chemicals and barrier equipment.

Question 17. How would you moor your single right hand fixed blade propeller vessel between two mooring buoys in a tidal river. Assume that your vessel is stemming the tidal flow direction?

Answer: Once instructions to moor between buoys is received, I would order the assistance of a 'mooring boat' together with the services of a 'buoy jumper'.

Note: The buoy jumper should be wearing a lifejacket.

Manoeuvre the vessel to bring the inner mooring buoy abeam of the break of the foc'stle head and off the port bow. Pass a head line through a centre lead to the mooring boat for running and securing to the buoy.

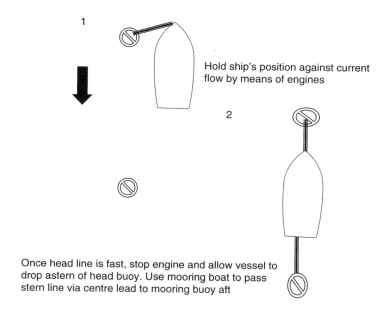

1

Hold ship's position against current flow by means of engines

2

Once head line is fast, stop engine and allow vessel to drop astern of head buoy. Use mooring boat to pass stern line via centre lead to mooring buoy aft

Question 18.   When lying at anchor your vessel is required to provide a lee for barges to work general cargo. How could you achieve this?

Answer: A 'lee' could be provided to the vessel by 'pointing ship'. This operation is achieved by running a stern mooring wire from 'bitts' aft back up through the hawse pipe and shackling it onto the anchor cable. The cable is then veered to provide the vessel with a directional heading off the weather and give a lee for the operational use of barges or boats alongside.

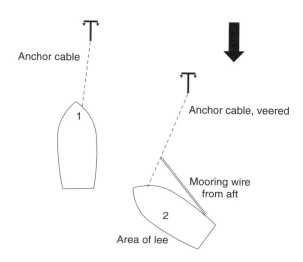

Anchor cable

1

Anchor cable, veered

Mooring wire from aft

2

Area of lee

Question 19.   How would you anchor a very large crude carrier (VLCC) tanker vessel in wind over tide conditions?

Answer: It must be assumed that a VLCC or other large vessel would be equipped with heavy-duty anchors and cables and as such the choice of anchor would be walked back.

Prior to approaching the anchorage an anchor plan would have been formulated and the vessel would conform to the salient points of the plan.

A suggested approach is given below.

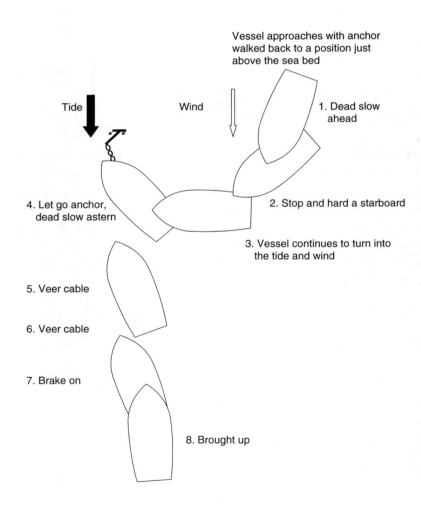

Vessel approaches with anchor walked back to a position just above the sea bed

Tide

Wind

1. Dead slow ahead

4. Let go anchor, dead slow astern

2. Stop and hard a starboard

3. Vessel continues to turn into the tide and wind

5. Veer cable

6. Veer cable

7. Brake on

8. Brought up

Question 20. When berthing and manoeuvring a large VLCC tanker you would expect to engage tugs to assist. How many tugs would you consider as a necessary requirement and how would they be deployed?

Answer: A large vessel such as a VLCC would normally engage a minimum of four (4) tugs. These would probably be deployed initially, one from each bow pulling directly ahead. A stern tug made fast aft, probably through the centre lead to act as a braking and steerage tug while

The British Petroleum (BP) Tanker, 'British Alliance' manoeuvres with four tugs in attendance.

the fourth tug would remain in attendance in a stand-by mode, to be brought in to push or assist as required.

Once in close proximity of the berth, it would be anticipated that the tugs are repositioned, to have one forward (offshore side), one aft, centre lead. While two engaged in pushing on the offshore side, positioned either side of midships.

Question 21.   When in command of a modern vessel equipped with bow thrust and twin CPP, describe how you would achieve a Mediterranean Moor.

Answer: With enhanced manoeuvring equipment like controllable pitch propellers together with 'bow thrust' the approach to the mooring can be made with either port side or starboard side to the quay at a distance off, of about two ships' lengths.

Both anchors should be walked back clear of the hawse pipes and held on the windlass brakes. Once the centre position of the intended berth is reached the way should be taken off the ship, prior to commencing a turn in the offshore direction.

The inshore engine should be placed ahead, with the offshore engine placed astern. Maximum bow thrust 100% should be given in order to turn the vessel about the midships point.

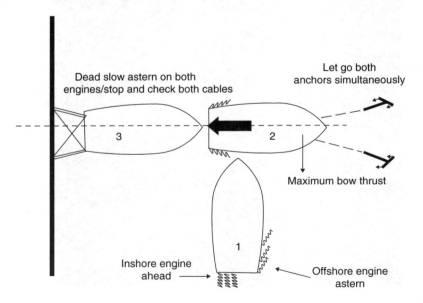

At position 3 the vessel should be within heaving line range of the quayside and moorings can be passed to secure the stern. Once all fast aft, tension cables at the fore end to render stern moorings taught.

Question 22.   How would you carry out a 'Williamson Turn' to effect a man overboard recovery action?

Answer: Assuming that the OOW has carried out the essential actions of placing the engines on stand-by. Releasing the man overboard (MoB) lifebuoy and smoke from the bridge wing. Raising the general alarm altering the helm over to the side to which the man fell.

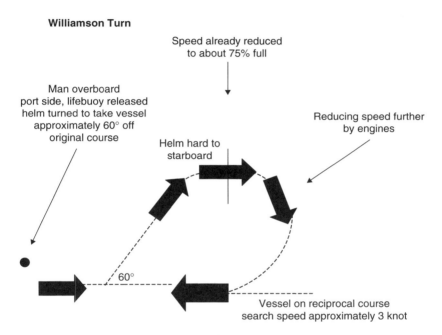

On approach to the MoB position, the Chief Officer would be ordered to turn out the rescue boat (weather permitting) and prepare for immediate launch with boats crew wearing lifejackets and immersion suits.

The ships hospital would be ordered onto an alert status and be ready to treat for shock and hypothermia.

Question 23.   What would you consider as a high holding power anchor, and why?

Answer: High holding power anchors are notably the AC14 type, and specialist anchors like Bruce, Flipper Delta Anchors and types found extensively in the offshore environment.

A conventional anchor is estimated to provide four (4) times its own weight in holding power, whereas a high holding power anchor, depending on type can expect to provide considerably higher, e.g. AC14 estimated to provide ten (10) times its own weight.

If the comparison is made between the conventional, cast, stockless anchor and the AC14, it will be seen that the AC14, is a constructed, prefabricated anchor, which provides a greater surface area to the arms and flukes. Weight for weight, a greater arm/fluke area would seem to hold an increased ground area.

Question 24.   What actions could you take to reduce drift, if your vessel lost engine power while off a 'lee shore'?

Answer: Following a report on the state of the engines from the Chief Engineer, would determine an appropriate line of action. Initially the following immediate actions would be anticipated to reduce the rate of drift.

The vessel must of course display NUC signals and obtain the current position. Switch on and monitor the echo sounder then:

(a) ballast the fore end of the vessel with the view to weather vane the vessel;
(b) walk back both anchors to effect a drogue effect;
(c) open up communications and call for a Tug to stand-by, if available;
(d) if continuing to close the shoreline, walk back an anchor with the view to 'hanging up'.

Such a scenario would dictate early communications under either distress or urgency priority signals to make the relevant authorities aware of the prevailing situation.

Question 25.   When moored with two anchors, as in a running moor or standing moor, how often will the vessel swing, and how would you ensure that she swings in the required direction?

Answer: The vessel can expect to swing every 6 hours to 6¼ hours, and it would be prudent to give the vessel a sheer (rudder action) to ensure that the vessel turns in the desired direction without fouling the cables.

Question 26.   While Master of a VLCC your engines are disabled and you need a tow to prevent being blown onto a 'lee shore'. What emergency towing arrangement do you have on board this vessel?

Answer: A VLCC would be over the statutory tonnage of 20,000 where tankers are required to be fitted with emergency towing arrangements.

These would include a strong anchor point (usually a 'SMIT' bracket), together with a length of chafing chain and a purpose designated lead, to connect a towline.

Question 27. All ships of 300 GT, engaged on international voyages and all vessels over 500 GT must eventually be fitted with Automatic Identification Systems (AIS). What will this provide to observing ships?

Answer: AIS is an information providing system which will supply observing vessels with: the ship's identity, its type, its position course and speed. AIS will further supply the navigational status of the ship and other safety related information automatically to appropriately equipped vessels, aircraft and shore side stations.

Question 28. When carrying out a turning circle with your vessel where would you expect to obtain the advance, the transfer, and the drift angle information, prior to commencing the manoeuvre?

Answer: The vessels trials would be normally documented when the vessel is new. Amongst these would be the ship's characteristics including details of the turning circles to both port and starboard.

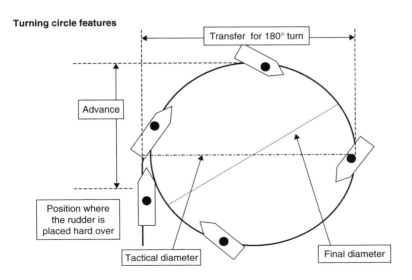

Turning circle features

Transfer for 180° turn

Advance

Position where the rudder is placed hard over

Tactical diameter

Final diameter

The path of the stern is well outside the perimeter of the turning circle. The circle being that which is described by the ships compass platform as the vessel moves through 360°.

Question 29. State how you would berth your own vessel starboard side to, between two ships already secured alongside.

Your own vessel is in a position (1) stemming the ebb tidal stream. A mooring boat is available, and the vessel is fitted with a right hand fixed bladed propeller.

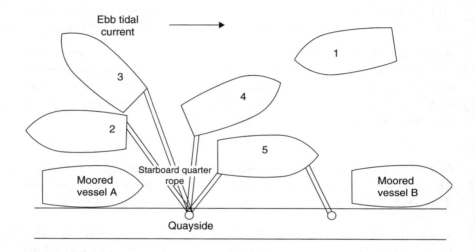

Answer:

(a) The vessel must be manoeuvred to stem the tidal current as in position (1).

(b) Manoeuvre the ship to a position (2) parallel to the moored vessel A.

(c) Run the best ships mooring rope from the starboard quarter to the quayside with the aid of the mooring boat (2) and keep this quarter rope tight, above the water surface.

(d) Slow astern on main engines – then stop. This movement should bring the vessels stern in towards the quayside by means of 'transverse thrust'. The bow should therefore move to starboard, outward, to bring the current onto the ship's port bow; position (3).

(e) The vessel should turn with current effective on the port side and no slack given on the quarter rope to complete an 'ebb swing' position (4).

(f) Run the forward head line (position (5)) and draw the vessel alongside from the fore and aft mooring positions.

Note: Where the manoeuvre is required when an 'offshore wind' is present, use of the offshore anchor would reduce the rate of approach towards the berth.

If an 'onshore wind' is present the first bow line would probably need to be carried aft to allow it to be passed ashore or alternatively use the same mooring boat which was initially employed to run a long drift on the head line.

If no mooring boat was available for berthing, the quarter line could be passed, first to the moored vessel 'A', and then onto the quayside.

Question 30.   When taking the vessel to an anchorage it is intended to use a single anchor. What is the minimum scope of cable that would be employed and what factors would possibly cause an increase in the amount of cable to use?

Answer: As a general rule of thumb the minimum amount of scope paid out when at a single anchor is considered to be 4 times the depth of water. However, it is stressed that this is a minimum figure and would be increased where any of the following factors are found to exist:

(a) Strong tidal/current conditions.
(b) Large rise and fall of the tide.
(c) Poor holding ground for the anchor.
(d) A bad weather forecast.
(e) A lengthy period of stay.
(f) A low holding power type of anchor as opposed to a high holding power anchor.
(g) A non-sheltered anchorage position.
(h) A Master's preference for increased chain deployment.

4 Miscellaneous Questions for all Ranks

INTRODUCTION

Many marine topics are common to one or more grade of certificate or qualification. Also, it should be borne in mind that the examiners can be expected to ask questions on previous qualification grades to ensure that the candidate's prior knowledge and his/her competence as a Junior Officer is evident.

The details expected when answering certain questions must also be anticipated as being a variable. As such an examiner may expect a very comprehensive answer from say a Master Mariner, whereas a more limited answer could be equally acceptable on the same question when directed to an Officer of the Watch (OOW).

Neither can every question easily fall to a single rank. Different ship types tend to generate selective operational questions, i.e. Tankers and Roll on–Roll off (Ro-Ro), vessels. The obvious area of guidance must therefore be the respective syllabuses for the relevant examination. Hence, this section on miscellaneous questions includes a variety of topics effecting various ship types and scenarios, which must be considered as being within the realm of 'fairness'.

As with any assessment, it must be fair and it must be valid. Marine examiners are aware of these parameters when carrying out examinations and usually ensure that questioning of the candidates always falls within the categories of fairness and validity. They are equally aware that no one man or women can expect to know all the answers to every topic and question. Clearly, within the conduct of any examination a level of common sense must be seen to exist on the part of both the candidate and the examiner.

MISCELLANEOUS MARINE

Question 1. What is the radar signature you would expect to receive from a Search and Rescue Transponder (SART)?

174

Answer: Twelve dots on the screen issuing from the SART up to a range of 5 nautical miles (assuming SART at 1 m above sea level). Once under the mile range from the SART the signature would turn to one of concentric circles on the screen.

Question 2.   What 'statutory' publications are you expected to carry aboard a British Ship?

Answer:
(a) A full set of working charts.
(b) Relevant sailing directions.
(c) Annual Summary of Notices to Mariners.
(d) Mariners Handbook.
(e) Admiralty List of Radio Signals (all volumes).
(f) Admiralty List of Lights and Fog Signals.
(g) Admiralty Tide Tables.
(h) Tidal Stream Atlases.
(i) The International Code of Signals.
(j) Marine Guidance Notices (MGNs), Merchant Shipping Notices (MSNs), Marine Information Notices (MINs).
(k) Maintenance manuals for navigation instruments and equipment.
(l) Nautical Tables.
(m) Nautical Almanac.
(n) Code of Safe Working Practice.

Question 3.   A vessel aground is advised by the Regulations for the Prevention of Collision at Sea, that it may sound an appropriate whistle signal. What would you consider as 'an appropriate whistle signal' in these circumstances?

Answer: The vessel aground could probably use 'U' or 'L' as an appropriate sound signal.

Question 4.   What does ECDIS stand for?

Answer: An accepted abbreviation is Electronic Chart Display and Information System.

Question 5.   Where would you expect to find an 'oxter plate' on the ship's construction?

Answer: An 'oxter plate' is the 'S'-shaped plate found in a position on the ship's hull, on either quarter. It is a shell plate, sited from above the propeller towards the gunwale.

Question 6.   How would a new danger be identified under the current buoyage system?

Answer: New dangers are marked with 'double cardinal' or 'double lateral' marks.

Question 7.   What do you consider the most important navigation instrument aboard the vessel?

Answer: The magnetic compass.

Question 8.   According to the Collision Regulations, do ships have to carry an all-round manoeuvring light?

Answer: No. The Regulations stipulate the ship 'may carry', not 'must carry'.

Note: The vessel has a statutory obligation to carry an 'Aldis Lamp' in order to comply with the necessary capability to supplement whistle signals.

Question 9.   Where would you expect to encounter a 'stealer plate' in the ship's construction?

Answer: A 'stealer plate' is a reducing plate. It is normally found at the fore and aft ends of the vessel. It may be a side strake of the hull, but it is more often a deck stringer plate, reducing say three stringers to two, at the fine lines of the bow.

Question 10.   What publication is concerned with safe operations in all shipboard departments?

Answer: The Code of Safe Working Practice.

Question 11.   What type of vessel would operate with a spectacle frame and an 'A' frame in its construction?

Answer: Twin screw/propeller vessels have the tail end propeller shafts supported by either an 'A' Frame and/or a 'spectacle frame'.

Question 12.   What stops the inert gas (IG) of a tanker's IG System (IGS), flowing back along the line towards the accommodation block?

Answer: All IGSs operate with a deck water seal which prevents back pressure moving gas backwards in the system, as with a non-return valve.

Question 13.   Describe the procedure for launching a davit launched liferaft?

Answer: The davit launched liferaft is a method of launching life-rafts popular on passenger vessels and ferries. The procedure for launching is given below:

(a) Manhandle the liferaft in its canister under the wire fall of the davit.
(b) Pull off the sealing patch of the canister and pull out the secur-ing shackle of the liferaft.
(c) Secure the fall hook to the exposed shackle.
(d) Pull out and tie off the container retaining lines to the side rails.
(e) Pull out and secure the bowsing-in lines to the deck cleats provided.
(f) Pull out the short painter and tie off at the embarkation deck.
(g) Hoist the liferaft canister clear above the deck.
(h) Turn out the davit by the handle provided, to its designed limit (usually about 70° off the ship's fore and aft line).
(i) Inflate the liferaft by giving a sharp tug on the painter (the two halves of the canister should fall away to either side of the ship being retained by the 'container retaining lines' secured at the rails).
(j) Tension the bowsing-in lines to ensure that the liferaft is flush against the ship's sides.

Note: Some liferafts have bowsing-in lines secured to a boarding flap.

(k) The person in charge of the liferaft should then carry out inter-nal checks on the condition of the buoyancy chambers for any defects and ensure that the inside is well ventilated and not containing CO_2.

(l)   A further check must be made overside to ensure that the water surface beneath the liferaft is clear of debris and it is safe to launch.

(m) Load the liferaft in a stable manner checking that all personnel have no sharp objects on their person.

(n)   When fully loaded, detach the bowsing-in lines and the painter and cast them into the access point of the raft.

(o)   Commence lowering the liferaft on the fall towards the surface.

(p)   Approximately 2–3 m from the surface, the person in charge of the liferaft should pull down on the lanyard from the release hook.

Note: This effectively unlocks the hook arrangement, but the sheer weight inside the liferaft does not allow the shackle to release from the hook at this time.

(q)   Continue to lower to the surface. As the buoyancy effects the underside of the liferaft the hook arrangement (spring loaded) retracts from the shackle, to effect the release of the liferaft.

Note: It would be considered prudent for the person in charge of the liferaft to have two well-built men on the paddles to manoeuvre the craft away from the ship's side as soon as the liferaft reaches the surface and releases.

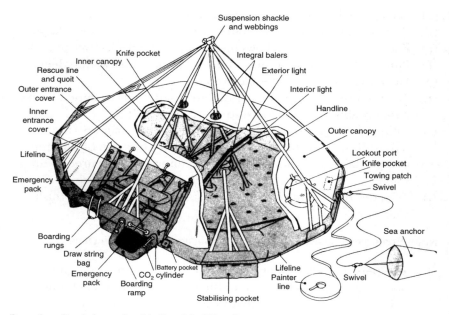

Beaufort Davit launched inflatable liferaft.

Question 14.   What lights would you expect to see at night, exhibited from an offshore installation?

Answer: Offshore installations show an all round 10 and/or 15 miles range all round, white light. In addition, they also exhibit a red light on each corner, all lights flashing 'U' in the morse code.

It should also be pointed out that the name plate of the installation is usually illuminated in a prominent manner and the rig will most certainly be operating under deck working lights, assuming a 'hot platform'.

Example of 'offshore installation' a permanent feature (non-mobile) drilling operation. Easily identified by the prominent features of drill tower, deck cranes, heavy support structure, heli-deck and accommodation block.

Question 15.   When would you expect to use a 'Hi-Line Operation'?

Answer: A Hi-Line Operation is conducted when engaging with a helicopter. It is widely used when there are a number of persons to evacuate, as opposed to a single person lift. It would also be used in bad weather or if the surface vessel was obstructed by construction features or rigging obstructions.

Question 16.   What is the effective range of Search and Rescue (SAR) Helicopters?

Answer: Different types of Helicopters have variable ranges, but they all depend on the fuel and related payload capacity. Some aircraft may extend their range with the addition of emergency fuel tanks. Generally, speaking, the European SAR Helicopters are the Sikorsky S61N, 'Sea King' variety with an operational range of 250 nautical miles. The more modern aircraft is the 'Merlin' (EH101) a five-bladed rotor, triple engine helicopter, with an operational range of up to 500 nautical miles.

Note: Range capability varies with fuel capacity, weather conditions, payload, etc. and assumes a two-way trip returning to the departure position. All aircraft have a reserve fuel capacity, and it is at the pilots discretion when he decides to cease operations and turn for home.

Only one rotary winged aircraft, the HH53C/D, 'Sea Stallions' operated by the US military have a mid air refuelling capability at the present time.

The Sikorsy 'Jayhawk' below operates with the US Coastguard. It is a Medium Range Recovery aircraft operating up to 300 nautical miles offshore, with a 45-minute on scene endurance. With a crew of four it can transport up to six survivors.

Question 17. On a Passenger (Class 1) vessel, how would you muster 2000 passengers and make them ready in the survival craft to abandon the vessel?

Answer: Passengers are usually mustered at their 'emergency stations' in the public rooms like lounges, cinemas, bars, etc. which are close to the boat embarkation deck. Here they can be kept generally controlled and monitored. Lifejackets can be checked and names taken prior to being led in 'Crocodile Formation' in batches of 25 towards survival craft.

Note: Twenty-five people are about as much as any one person could be expected to control under abandonment circumstances. Also, the survival craft are often constructed to take 25 persons or multiples of 25 persons as a complete complement.

Passengers mustered at an assembly station, in lifejackets being checked off muster lists and being kept informed of activities by the ship's P/A system.

Question 18. What information would you expect to find on the front cover of the 'Official Log Book'?

Answer: The format of the front cover of the Official Log Book contains the following:

(a) The ship's name, Port of Registry and the official number.
(b) The Gross and Registered (Net) Tonnages.

(c) The name of Master(s) and the respective number of Certificate of Competency.

(d) The name and address of the registered, managing owner; or the ship's husband or manager.

(e) The date and place at which the Log Book is opened.

(f) The date and place at which the Log Book is closed.

(g) Date and official stamp of the superintendent accepting delivery.

(h) Date received by the Register General of Shipping and Seaman.

Question 19.   What are the duties of the Safety Officer aboard the vessel?

Answer: The function of the Safety Officer is to primarily promote a safety culture aboard the ship. This may be carried out by regular drills and training exercises. Promotion poster displays, holding active safety meetings or making use of the Training (Video) Manual.

The Safety Officer would also be a member of the Safety Committee, under the Chairmanship of the Master, and could expect to draw up the agenda for the meeting. He would normally take the minutes of the meeting and give a safety report at this time. Such a report would include details of any investigation undertaken following an accident. Recommendations from accident findings would be a cause for deliberation by the Safety Committee.

Accident reports, obtaining witness statements and taking photographs to support any incident, all fall to the duties of the Safety Officer. The position of the Safety Officer is an appointment and he/she cannot resign this position.

In the event the Safety Officer observes unsafe activity on the vessel he has the authority to stop this work immediately. Only the Master can order the resumption of said work.

His duty is also to maintain a log account and file of all accidents and accident reports.

Question 20.   What precautions and safety actions will you take when about to take on 'bunkers'?

Answer: A vessel can take on bunkers from a bunker barge on the offshore side or alternatively from shore side facilities. In any event the following activities should be carried out:

(a) Seal all deck scuppers before commencing to take on bunkers.

(b) Display the red light signal or 'B' Bravo Flag by day.

(c)   Additional 'No Smoking' signs displayed at the gangway and deck outlets.

(d)   No unauthorised personnel allowed on board and gangway watch set.

(e)   Three-way communication link tested between (i) the manifold; (ii) the pumping station and (iii) the tank top ullage port.

(f)   Ships Oil Pollution Emergency Plan (SOPEP) checklist observed.

(g)   Fire precautions set in a position of readiness.

(h)   Drip trays in position under flange/pipe connections.

(i)   Anti-spillage equipment readily available.

(j)   Double access established.

(k)   Adequate manpower on deck throughout, especially during topping off.

(l)   Log Book entries made on commencement and finish.

(m)   Notation in the Oil Record Book on completion.

Question 21.   What are the factors that must be taken into consideration when determining the construction of sea watches?

Answer: The responsibility of the ship's watch structure lies with the Master and the established system will be constructed taking into account all the prevailing circumstances at the time. Ideally, the following factors will influence the overall structure:

(a)   The geographic position with the associated navigational hazards present.

(b)   The state of visibility affected by fog, rain, sleet, snow or haze.

(c)   Day or night conditions.

(d)   The traffic density and the proximity of focal points.

(e)   The number and experience of watchkeeping personnel available.

(f)   The need for a continuous radar watch or not.

(g)   The possibility of 'fatigue' affecting watch keepers.

(h)   The level of navigational duties anticipated.

(i)   The need for a Bridge Team, as with special operations, i.e. SAR operations.

Question 22.   What is 'gale force' on the Beaufort Wind Scale?

Answer: Gale force is recognised as force '8'.

Question 23.   What do you understand as being the function of the International Safety Management (ISM)?

Answer: The ISM system is a safety culture affecting both the shore side and the sailing side of the Maritime Industry. It is monitored by 'Auditors' who are both internal and external to the ship owning company. These 'Auditors' carry out periodic checks into all operations of marine activity and provide evidence of compliance with the issue of a Safety Management Certificate to individual, compliant vessels.

   A 'Document of Compliance (DoC)' is also issued for each class of vessel, that the company manages. It should be noted that the original DoC is held by the shipping company, but the company ships of class would carry a copy of the DoC.

Question 24.   Following an abandon ship situation, you are the last person into a liferaft. What would be the first action to take place?

Answer: Assuming I was to take charge of the liferaft, I would expect to order the following immediate actions:

(a) Cut the liferafts painter to release the raft.
(b) Stream the sea anchor (drogue) and manoeuvre the raft away.
(c) Batten down the access points.
(d) Maintain and manage the liferaft.

Question 25.   How would you beach a liferaft after abandonment from the parent vessel?

Answer: When in charge of the liferaft, it would be necessary to:

(a) Order all personnel to don and secure lifejackets.
(b) Inflate the double floor.
(c) Open the access doorways.
(d) Man the paddles on approach.

This task is extremely hazardous at any time but especially at night or in surf. Ideally, the beach area should be free of rocks and the approach should be made slowly tripping the sea anchor (drogue) periodically as the landing is approached.

Question 26.   What is the range of the lights fitted to lifejackets and liferafts, as seen on a dark night, with a clear atmosphere?

Answer: Lifejacket lights in these conditions should be detected at about 1 nautical mile. Liferafts being positioned at an increased height above sea level would be detected at about 2 nautical miles.

Question 27.   Under the Standards of Training, Certification and Watchkeeping (STCW) Convention, watch keepers must be given designated time off duty so that they do not become fatigued. What are the designated time off periods?

Answer: Watch keepers must be given a period of ten (10) hours off duty, of which six (6) hours must be continuous (Reference: STCW).

Question 28.   What pyrotechnic would you not use from a survival craft if your location was being sort by a rescue helicopter?

Answer: Persons should not use 'rocket parachute flares' when aircraft are in close proximity. The recommended signal for attracting the attention of aircraft would be a 'red hand flare' at night and the 'orange smoke float' during the daytime.

Question 29.   What information would you find on a deviation card?

Answer: Information on the deviation card would include:

(a) The ship's name, the name of the compass adjuster.
(b) The position of the swing.
(c) The number and position of all correctors.
(d) A table or curve of deviations and the signature of the adjuster.

Question 30.   What would be included in the Masters 'standing orders' for the OOW when the vessel is under pilotage?

Answer:
(a) The OOW remains the Masters representative despite the presence of the pilot and in the absence of the Master from the bridge.

(b) The OOW maintains an effective lookout throughout the watch and pilotage period by all available means.
(c) The OOW will continuously monitor the ship's position and ensure that the vessel is not stood into danger.
(d) The OOW will ensure that the pilot's instructions are carried out in a correct manner provided that they do not endanger the ship's progress.
(e) The OOW will continue to monitor the performance of bridge equipments and instruments, and report any defects to the Master.

GENERAL SHIPBOARD OPERATIONS (APPLICABLE TO ALL MERCANTILE MARINE OFFICER RANKS)

Question 1. What is the procedure and period of validity under the Harmonised Survey System to effect the Safety Equipment Certificate?

Answer: The Certificate is issued at intervals of 5 years. However, the vessel will undergo an annual inspection and this inspection would be endorsed and dated, on each occasion, by the surveyor, a new Certificate being issued at the 5-year interval.

The survey and validity of the certificate would be based on the 'Record of Inspection', which contains details of all the ship's safety equipment.

Note: The 'Record of Inspection' (Supplementary Form 'E') is usually contained behind the certificate, which is displayed on the bulkhead.

Question 2. What are the main questions discussed between the Master of the ship and the Marine Pilot during the initial Master/Pilot exchange?

Answer: Following introduction and an exchange of documentary credentials for administration purposes (e.g. see Appendix E), it would be normal policy for relevant details to be discussed:

(a) The Pilot Card, listing the ship's criteria, handling facilities, specialised equipment, engine details, critical revolutions and respective vessel speeds.
(b) The mutual agreement of the proposed passage plan to be seen to be either acceptable or requiring amendments from the Pilots

local knowledge. Adequate under keel clearance throughout the passage being a prominent issue.

(c) Details of current navigation warnings, special operations and any specific communication systems in operation, e.g. Vessel Traffic Services (VTS) check positions if such a system is in place.

(d) Current status of the ship's course, engine condition, anchors, Bridge Team, any equipment defects, instrumentation familiarity and details of gyro errors, etc.

(e) Voyage/docking details such as to taking tugs yes/no, if so at what rendezvous, docking pilot being taken on, anchors to be employed, what side to, moorings and gangway details, etc.

Question 3.   When making up a 'passage plan' what principles would you adhere to and what specific details would you pay particular attention to?

Answer: The 'passage plan' would be constructed under the four main principles of:

- Appraisal
- Planning
- Execution
- Monitoring

Specific attention must be paid to adequate under keel clearance throughout the period of passage from 'Berth to Berth' positions. The plan would highlight 'No-Go' areas and contain relevant contingencies for dealing with respective, possible emergencies and be security assessed.

Navigation warnings, focal points and areas of specific operations would be highlighted within the final plan. Communication points, radar conspicuous targets and position monitoring methods would be noted on the chart.

Question 4.   What constitutes a safe access to the ship?

Answer: The ship will rig either the gangway or the accommodation ladder in order to provide ship to shore access. In the case of the accommodation ladder, the inclination from the horizontal should not be greater than 55° whereas, the MoT gangway should not exceed 30°.

In either case each type of access must be provided with adequate illumination during the hours of darkness. A lifebuoy and line should be kept close for immediate readiness and in every case the rig should be protected by a 'safety gangway net'.

It is also essential to provide gangway security to any access to the ship and this is usually carried out by either a shore side watchman or crew security personnel inclusive of the Officer of the Deck.

Question 5.　How would you recover a boat in heavy weather?

Answer:　Passenger vessels are equipped with hanging off pendants and recovery strops, and these could be quickly manufactured for use with cargo vessels. Nylon strops would have the equivalent safe working load (SWL) to support the weight of the boat to allow a transfer of weight onto the hanging off pendants. This would effectively allow the boat falls to be resecured with the boat clear of the inherent dangers of the surface.

Question 6.　When carrying out maintenance work on the radar masts, what precautions would you take?

Answer:　It is expected practise when work is being carried out on the radar mast that the radar fuses are pulled and a note is left over the radar Plan Position Indicator (PPI) screen advising of the ongoing work.

Question 7.　What would you look for when carrying out a ship's bottom inspection, when the vessel is in Dry Dock?

Answer:　Specific items, such as tank plugs, echo sounder transducers, bilge keels, sea chest gratings, stabiliser units and bow/stern thrusters, would all warrant particular attention.

The degree of weed and/or barnacle coverage would generate the cleaning of the underwater hull and this would then permit sighting of any fractures, or deep indentation to shell plates. Overall the condition of coatings, inclusive of anti-fouling and the boot topping would be noted.

Once the bottom area is cleaned, the quality of sacrificial anodes could also be assessed as to the need for renewal. These would know doubt be inspected with the propeller, rudder and stern tube arrangements during the early proceedings following docking.

Bow thrust units exposed for inspection during a routine Dry Docking. The vessel is situated on blocks following bottom cleaning and hull coating.

Question 8. When in high latitudes what evidence would present itself to the OOW, that ice was in close proximity to the vessels position?

Answer: When in high latitudes in the North or Southern hemispheres, it must be anticipated that the sea temperature will drop to about the $0°$. This in itself would indicate the close presence of ice.

Other features, such as wildlife, seal, walrus, snow petrel, etc., would all indicate that ice was in close proximity.

The 'Officer of the Watch' may also see an 'ice blink' or ice fragments and this coupled with the geographic position and the seasonal period for ice being relevant would provide positive evidence of ice formations.

Question 9. What bridge routine could a Master instigate to ensure that the vessel did not meet a tropical revolving storm (TRS), unexpectedly?

Answer: If a ship is known to be entering a region where TRS is possible and it is the season for these storms the Master may specify within bridge standing orders the following requirements:

(a) The Master should be informed if any evidence of a Tropical Storm is observed by the OOW.

(b) That any change in the diurnal range should be reported to the Master, and in particular if the barograph was seen to drop more than 3 mbar, in 3 hours.
(c) All weather forecasts, Navtex reports, advising on changing weather patterns must be passed to the Master immediately.

Question 10.   When carrying out an inspection of the galley what would the Master pay particular attention to?

Answer: Ship's Masters would be aware that food poisoning could effect the whole crew and prevent the ship from operating at maximum efficiency. Bearing this in mind an inspection would expect to find a level of overall cleanliness in and around the galley and pantry areas.

Fridges, handling rooms and cool chambers must be seen to be at correct temperatures. Dry store rooms should be free of taint and odour. Utensils and appliances should be noted to be clean and in covered stowage positions.

Cooked and uncooked meats should be in separate compartments, while fire appliances should be sighted to be readily accessible.

Question 11.   How would the bridge and engine room watch organisation be established on a new ship?

Answer: Watchkeeping organisation is structured in accordance with the company standing orders. The operation would be established by the Master meeting the officers in the first instance. Each Officer being asked to read and acknowledge by signature the standing orders.

Additionally, night and daily orders would be issued by the Master as appropriate to the vessels position and respective geography.

Question 12.   Your vessel is about to be inspected by a Port State Control Officer, what would you expect the inspector to be interested in and looking to see?

Answer: A Port State Control Inspector would carry out the inspection in accord with the checklist carried on the navigation bridge.

This would include any or all of the following items:

(a) The Chart Management System and respective correction logs.
(b) Passage plan operations and records.

(c) Equipment and navigation instruments.
(d) Life saving appliances, inclusive of SARTs, Emergency Position Indicating Radio Beacons (EPIRBs), lifeboats, liferafts, release units, etc. (records of drills and boats being manoeuvred in the water).
(e) Fire plans, fire fighting equipment and training.
(f) Mooring equipment, including anchor handling gear.
(g) The overall condition of the vessel throughout its length.
(h) Log Books and ship's records.
(i) International Ship and Port Facility Security (ISPS) security assessment.

Question 13.   What do you understand by the term 'water ballast management system' and what are the dangers associated with it?

Answer: Water ballast management is designed to control the spread of micro-organisms by monitoring what is pumped out into the oceans and where it is being taken on and discharged.

These actions need to be recorded in the water ballast management log. Ships are now being fitted with ballast water treatment systems to satisfy environmental conditions, new tonnage being equipped with a water ballast management plan.

The inherent dangers with the movement of large volumes of fluid are free surface effect, incurred stresses within the ship's structural length, over pressurising of tanks and salt water corrosive affects.

Question 14.   What procedures and safety checks would you expect to take, prior to making an entry into an enclosed space?

Answer: Entry into enclosed spaces is considered an extremely dangerous activity and has been the cause of many accidents involving fatalities in the past. Chapter 17 of the *Code of Safe Working Practice for Merchants* (H.M. Stationery Office, UK) provides detailed information regarding correct procedures to adopt.

In any event it would be expected that the following actions and precautions are adopted:

(a) A 'risk assessment' of the activity must be carried out prior to entry.
(b) The recommended checklist, within the 'permit to work' should be adhered to.

(c) The atmosphere of the intended space for entry must be tested for oxygen content and the presence of toxic gases.

(d) The space must be vented in every case and the ventilation system must be seen to be adequate.

Note: This is usually carried out days before entry is due to take place.

(e) Reduce the number of persons on the activity to only those persons deemed as essential to carry out the intended task.

(f) Designate a 'stand-by man' to be stationed outside the entrance of the space in order to raise the alarm in the event of problems being incurred by the work party once inside the space.

(g) Post the 'permit to work', copy at the entrance of the space.

(h) Ensure that the space is adequately illuminated prior to entry being allowed.

(i) Resuscitation equipment should be readily available for emergency use at the entrance to the space.

(j) Test communications between the stand-by man, and the work party before and after entry is made (communication equipment and torches should be intrinsically safe in their operation).

(k) Emergency alarms and communications should be clearly understood by all persons concerned with the operation.

In the event entry is to be made with Self-Contained Breathing Apparatus (SCBA), full precautions and safety checks must be made in conjunction with the wearer. Once the task is completed the permit to work must be cancelled.

Question 15.   When loading deck cargo what references would you employ to ensure that the safety of the vessel is not impaired?

Answer: Deck cargoes are loaded and shipped in many forms and the type of cargo can reflect specific hazards. Generally, all cargo parcels must be adequately secured against shifting in bad weather and reference should be made to any or all of the following:

(a) The Merchant Shipping (Load Lines) (Deck Cargo) Regulations 1968.

(b) Relevant MGNs and MSNs, especially M1167.

(c) MSNs relating to Timber Deck Cargoes, where relevant.

(d) Shippers and companies recommendations.

(e) The International Maritime Dangerous Goods (IMDG) Code if appropriate.

(f) The Ship's own 'Cargo Securing Manual'.

(g) *The Lashing and Securing of Deck Cargoes* (Nautical Institute Publication) by Captain J.R. Knott, BA FNI.

Question 16.   What is the purpose and function of the construction of a 'cargo plan', for a general cargo vessel?

Answer: The plan which is colour coded for the respective ports of discharge, will identify respective cargo parcels for that specific port. It is meant to show the weight of cargo and/or the number of units for discharge.

The plan clearly illustrates the cargo distribution throughout the vessel and allows the allocation of labour to permit a balanced discharge procedure. The pictorial display would expect to highlight incompatible cargoes and also show sensitive cargoes in the event of a cargo hold fire occurring. Space allocation on the proposed plan, prior to commencement of loading would permit hold, tween deck and deep tank spaces, to be correctly prepared beforehand.

Question 17.   What maintenance is carried out on the total flood CO_2 system?

Answer: The total flood system and the gang release is maintained under the ship's 'planned maintenance system'. The CO_2 room or bottle bank store, is visually inspected monthly and in conjunction with fire drills. The system also under goes an annual test by checking the lines and nozzles by connecting the compressed air line. The bottles are also checked for any leakage of gas by either weighing the individual bottles or by use of an ultra sonic level indicator. Every 10 years the bottle containers would also be subject to a hydrodynamic test.

Question 18.   What recording procedures should be followed by a tanker vessel loading or transferring oil cargo?

Answer: In accordance with Marine Pollution (MARPOL) 73/78, Annex 1, Appendix III, any loading of oil cargo must be supported by recording:

(a) The place of loading.

(b) The type of oil loaded and the identity of tank(s).

(c) The total quantity of oil loaded. State total quantity added and the total content of tank(s).

When transferring oil cargo during a voyage, the movement of oil cargo must be supported by recording:

(a) The identity of the tanks that the oil is being taken from.
(b) The identity of the tank that the oil is being transferred to.
(c) The total quantity of oil transferred.
(d) The total quantity of oil in tanks.

Whether the tanks of origin have been emptied or the quantity of oil which has been retained within the tank from which it was transferred.

Question 19.   What do you understand by the term 'special area'?

Answer: In accord with Regulation 10, of MARPOL, special areas are designated sea areas where discharge of oil and garbage is prohibited or severely restricted by specific provision. Such special areas include:

(a) The Mediterranean Sea.
(b) The Baltic Sea.
(c) The Black Sea.
(d) The Red Sea inclusive of the Gulfs of Suez and Aqaba.
(e) The Gulfs Area, between the Gulf of Aden and the Arabian Sea.
(f) The Antarctic Area (Sea area South of Latitude 60°S).
(g) North West European waters inclusive of the North Sea, The Irish Sea, the Celtic Sea and the English Channel with the North East Atlantic, immediately to the West of Ireland.

Question 20.   What activities and procedures must be conducted during a routine fire drill aboard the vessel?

Answer: Fire drills must be conducted in accord with Safety of Life at Sea (SOLAS) Chapter III, Regulation 19, 3.4.2. and include the following activities:

(a) All persons must report to stations as described in the 'muster list'.
(b) Start and operate the emergency fire pump and affect the required two jets of water to show that the system is in correct working order.
(c) Checking of the Fireman's Outfit together with other personal rescue equipment.

(d) Checking and testing communication equipment.
(e) Operation and checking of all watertight doors, fire dampers and ventilation systems.
(f) Checking that the necessary arrangements for abandonment of the vessel are in place.

Any faults and defects found during a drill must be rectified and all equipment must be brought back to an operational status following the drill period.

Question 21. How would the five yearly test on a derrick be carried out?

Answer: The five yearly test on the lifting appliances are conducted by a cargo surveyor or an equivalent competent person (class surveyor) appointed by the Marine Authority. The type of test to be conducted would be a proof load test which could be achieved by operating the derrick through its working radius, as per rigging plan, with the proof load weight suspended. Alternatively, a static test could be carried out which employs the derrick being guyed off and a dynamometer anchored to a fixed point between the deck and the runner wire. As the runner is heaved the dynamometer will record the weight applied, equivalent to the 'proof load'.

Provide the lifting appliance shows no deformation or adverse indications of defect the appliance would be passed and a certificate issued.

Question 22. What procedures and company policy are in place for monitoring your ship's position?

Answer: Company 'standing orders' and the Masters night orders tend to reflect the policy of monitoring the ship's position. Any of the following principles should be taken into account when fixing the ship's position, respective to whether the ship is coastal or in open deep sea waters:

(a) Minimum of three (3) position lines (P/Ls) should be engaged for visual fixing.
(b) Buoys and floating marks should not be used for obtaining bearings.
(c) Primary and secondary position fixing methods should be employed.

(d) Where Global Positioning Systems (GPS) are employed the respective datum should be checked prior to application.
(e) Position fixes should be corroborated by echo sounder whenever appropriate.
(f) Position transfers should be checked against bearing and distance from one chart against latitude and longitude with the other.
(g) The interval for position fixing should be appropriate to the geography and reflect all navigation hazards.
(h) In the event that a position obtained is doubtful or suspect, the Master should be informed.
(i) Where a position obtained is suspect, it should not be relied upon and an alternative position should be obtained as soon as practical.
(j) Noon, together with morning and evening twilight positions should be entered in the Deck Log Book.
(k) Wherever continuous position, real time position fixing, can be obtained it should be exercised.

Question 23.   What safeguards are exercised by your vessel regarding the discharge of sewage into the seas?

Answer: In respect of Annex IV of MARPOL 73/78, all vessels over 200 grt and carrying more than ten (10) persons would need an International Sewage Pollution Prevention Certificate (valid for 5 years). Prevention equipment on board would stop drainage from:

• toilets, urinals and WCs.
• medicinal premises.
• live stock areas.

The system and equipment is subject to periodical inspections, and the plant must meet International Maritime Organisation (IMO) standards. Holding tanks, comminuter and type of treatment meeting the standards of Annex IV, MARPOL.

No discharge being permitted within 4 miles of land unless an approved plant is in operation. Between 4 and 12 miles sewage must be comminuted and disinfected.

Question 24.   What is contained in the Shipboard Oil Pollution Emergency Plan (SOPEP)?

Answer: In accord with Regulation 26, of Annex 1, MARPOL, the SOPEP will be written in the working language of the ship's Master and must contain:

(a) The procedure to be followed by the Master or other persons having charge of the ship to report an oil pollution incident as required under Article 8, and protocol 1 of the present convention.
(b) A list of the Authorities and Designated Persons ashore to be contacted in the event of a pollution incident (emergency numbers).
(c) A detailed description of the actions to be taken immediately by persons on board to reduce or control the discharge of oil following the incident.
(d) The procedures and point of contact on the ship, for co-ordinating shipboard action with national and local authorities in combating the pollution.

Note: The above is generally covered by a working checklist to ensure that in the event of an incident all required procedures are covered and no actions are overlooked.

Question 25.   When does a ship's Master not have to respond to a distress signal which has been received on board?

Answer: In the event that the ship receiving the distress signal is unable, or in the special circumstances of the case, considers it unreasonable, or unnecessary to proceed to the assistance of the person(s) in distress, then the Master must enter into the Log Book the reason for failing to proceed to the distress scene.

Question 26.   What dangers are the Masters of ship's expected to report when they are encountered on the high seas?

Answer: Under SOLAS, Chapter 5, Regulation 2, Masters are obliged to communicate information on navigation dangers. Such dangers include the following:

(a) dangerous ice;
(b) a dangerous derelict;
(c) sub-freezing air temperatures associated with gale force winds likely to cause ice accretion;

(d) gale force winds of storm force 10 or above, for which no report
     has been issued;
(e) any other direct danger to navigation;
(f) such danger messages must contain the nature and position of
     the danger, together with the time and date of observation.

Question 27.   If circumstances dictated how would you engage in a
towing operation with a tanker of 50,000 tonnes deadweight?

Answer: Assuming that my Charter Party allowed my vessel to engage
in towing and delays to the loading port are not likely, a towing spring
could be passed to the tanker and secured to its emergency towing
arrangement.

Note: All tankers of 20,000 tonnes deadweight are required to be fitted with
emergency towing arrangements both fore and aft.

   Such towing arrangements would include a Strongpoint, chafing
chain and adequate lead.

Question 28.   How is on board training carried out aboard the vessel?

Answer: In house training of crew members takes place by means of
the following methods:

(a) Accident Prevention, poster displays – managed by the Safety
     Officer.
(b) Active boat and fire drills – inclusive of equipment demonstra-
     tions by Deck Officers.
(c) Safety Manual (Video) shown at periodic intervals.
(d) Distance learning study time allocated to Cadets.
(e) Junior Officers encouraged to understudy Senior Officers when
     ever practical.
(f) Crew briefings on new equipment fitted to the vessel.
(g) Alternative job share, operating during drills.
(h) Shore side training courses encouraged whenever possible.

Question 29.   A new 3rd Officer joins the vessel. How would he/she
be made familiar with the ship and their expected duties?

Answer: It is normal company policy for the outgoing Officer to carry
out a detailed and listed handover procedure. The new Officer would

be given a tour of the vessels decks and compartments. This would include updates on the condition of cargo, currently in the vessel.

The Officer would be shown the navigation bridge and made familiar with relevant instrumentation. Charts and publications would be discussed and respective duties would be explained.

All life saving and fire appliances would be pointed out together with identification of the individual Officers muster station.

A copy of the company standing orders would be made available for the new Officer to read and subsequently sign, once they have been read.

Question 30.   What are the offences and penalties that exist for over-loading of the ship?

Answer: In the event that a ship proceeds or attempts to proceed to sea in contravention of the loadline regulations, the Master or Owner will be liable on summary conviction, to a fine not exceeding £5000 (statutory maximum) or on conviction of indictment to an unlimited fine.

The ship may also be detained until it is has been surveyed and marked or until she is no longer overloaded.

The Master or Owner of a UK ship overloaded, may on summary conviction, be fined up to the statutory maximum of £5000 having regard to the earning capacity of the overload, be fined additionally £1000 for each complete centimetre by which she is overloaded.

If the Master, Owner or other associated person is charged with over-loading the vessel where it is considered to be 'dangerously unsafe' then they will be guilty of an offence, punishable by a fine of £50,000 on summary conviction or 2 years imprisonment, plus an unlimited fine on conviction on indictment.

Question 31.   The ISPS Code came into effect from July 2004. What are the shipboard requirements under this mandatory code?

Answer: The ship is required to have ship-based security plans, a ship security Officer, reporting to a company security Officer, and specialised on board equipment.

Question 32.   Under the ISPS Code, what actions and activities would you expect to be in place on board the ship and in ports of arrival?

Answer: It would be anticipated that the control of access in and out of the port and direct access to the ship is monitored tightly. Cargo security provisions should be in place and security communications during the length of stay of the ship, in any port.

Question 33.   Can the Master act as the 'ships security Officer'?

Answer: Yes.

Question 34.   What type of security risk would you expect to be prepared for aboard the following vessels: Ro-Ro ships, passenger vessels, tankers?

Answer:
• Ro-Ro ships are subject to attack by the car bomb.
• Passenger vessels are subject to terrorist insurgents.
• Tankers are vulnerable to small boat explosive attack causing pollution.

Question 35.   How many security levels are there and what is the significance of each level?

Answer: Their are three levels of security readiness:

Security level 1. Means that level for which minimum appropriate measures shall be maintained at all times.

Security level 2. Means that level at which appropriate, additional protective security measures shall be maintained for a period of time as a result of heightened risk of a security incident.

Security level 3. Means that level for which further specific protective security measures are to be maintained for a limited period of time when a security incident is probable or imminent.

(It may not be possible to identify the specific target with this level.)

CERTIFICATE NO: _____

INTERNATIONAL SHIP SECURITY CERTIFICATE

Issued under the provisions of the
INTERNATIONAL CODE FOR THE SECURITY OF SHIPS AND OF PORT FACILITIES (ISPS CODE)

under the authority of the Government of

_____
(name of state)

by the AMERICAN BUREAU OF SHIPPING

Name of Ship: _____

Distinctive Number or Letters: _____

Port of Registry: _____

Type of Ship[1]: _____

Gross Tonnage: _____

IMO Number: _____

Name and Address of Company: _____

_____

_____

_____
(see paragraph 1.1.2 of the ISM Code)

THIS IS TO CERTIFY THAT:

the security system and any associated security equipment of the ship have been verified in
accordance with section 19.1 of part A of the ISPS Code;
the verification showed that the security system and any associated security equipment of the ship is
in all respects satisfactory and that the ship complies with the applicable requirements of chapter XI-2
of the Convention and part A of the ISPS Code;
the ship is provided with an approved Ship Security Plan.

This Certificate is valid until _____, subject to verification in accordance with section
19.1.1 of part A of the ISPS Code.

Date of the initial/renewal verification on which this certificate is based:_____
(dd/mm/yyyy)

Issued at: _____

Date of Issue: _____

_____
(Signature of the duly authorized official issuing the certificate)

_____

[1] Insert the type of ship from among the following: Passenger Ship; Passenger High Speed Craft; Cargo High Speed
Craft; Bulk Carrier; Oil Tanker; Chemical Tanker; Gas Carrier; Mobile Offshore Drilling Unit; Other Cargo Ship.

Bulk Carriers

Question 1.   How and why do you carry out water ballast management operations?

Answer: Exchange of ballast water is currently compulsory for Australia, the US and Canada, mandatory reporting being compulsory for the US.

The main concerns from the ship's point of view in changing ballast water over, is that the stability of the vessel may be impaired and to this end a ballast management plan is the basis for the operational activity. Ballast water being changed to ensure that harmful microbes and organic matter are not carried from say temperate zones to tropical zones and allowed to contaminate local waters with environmentally, undesirable bacteria or unwanted plant growth. Where the method of 'emptying out and refilling' is used the possibility of generating serious hull stresses exist, with the generation of added free surface moments during the operation, causing a reduction in the ship's 'metacentric height (GM)'.

Question 2.   You are expected to load coal on your bulk carrier. What types of coal would you be concerned about and what are the particular hazards associated with such a cargo?

Answer: There are various types of coal inclusive of anthracite, lignite, coal slurry or duff, as well as the graded coals (coke is another form which the gases and benzol have been removed).

The main hazards are that most coals (other than coke) are liable to spontaneous combustion and emit methane gas. Such gases must be vented. The smaller particle coals are liable to shift and if the moisture content is high the cargo could possible act as a liquid with any excessive ship's vibration.

The cargo requires certain precautions and these could be referenced from the Code of Safe Working Practice for Bulk Cargoes. Special equipment should be placed on board in the form of methane detector-meters, cargo thermometers, extra SCBA, face protector masks, etc.

Question 3.   The vessel contains certain stability criteria, which may be in a stability book form. Must this information and criteria be approved?

Answer: Yes. Such stability information must be approved by the Marine Authority of the ship's Flag State.

Question 4.   What documentation would be required for your bulk carrier if you are scheduled to load bulk grain?

Answer: As a dedicated bulk carrier the ship would require a Document of Authorisation to load the grain cargo.

Note: Vessels other than dedicated 'bulk carriers' would require approval by the National Authority, in order to load a grain cargo.

Question 5.   How would you draw up a loading plan for a bulk carrier?

Answer: The loading plan is based on company recommendation and the ship design. The method employed is devised so as not to incur concentration of stresses to any particular part of the vessel and would inter-co-ordinated with prudent ballast and deballasting operations. In parallel with the loading plan, the deballast sequence would be worked to be compatible with the proposed cargo operation.

Both the sequential cargo loads and the ballast loads would be entered into the loadicator (computerised loading data) to provide the GM, bending moments and shear forces throughout the period of loading.

Example of gas and chemical carriers. The bulk carrier 'Alpha Afovos' lies port side too alongside the grain silo's in Barcelona, Spain. The ship is seen being discharged of bulk grain by means of the grain elevators.

Gas and Chemical Carriers

Question 1.   What fixed fire fighting equipment would you expect to be carried on a gas carrier?

Answer: Gas carriers employ a 'Dry Chemical Powder' system as a fixed installation, incorporating the requirements of the International Gas Code.

Question 2.   What maintenance would you expect to carry out on the Dry Chemical Powder system of gas carrier?

Answer: The Powder system would have a visual inspection on a monthly basis and every 3 months the powder tank/container would be opened to check that the powder is not congealing or caking.

The system would also be subject to annual shore service which would include a powder analysis to ensure the moisture content was to high. Actuator valves and pressure relief valves would be subject to inspection and test under the ship's planned maintenance schedule.

Question 3.   What general requirements are required for the lifeboats on gas carriers, tankers and chemical carriers?

Answer: Such vessels would be expected to carry totally enclosed lifeboats. These craft would normally be fitted with a compressed air supply sufficient for a full complement and to allow the use of the boats engine (compressed air operation good for at least 10 minutes). The boats would also be equipped with a water sprinkler system for operation on the outside of the boats form. They would expect to operate with an on-load, off-load, release system.

Question 4.   How many SCBA would you expect to carry aboard a chemical carrier?

Answer: It is normal practice for each crew member to have his own B/A set so the number, with spare sets, would be a variable. These are normally stored in a B/A room equipped with compressor and maintenance facilities.

Question 5.   When about to load bulk chemicals, what checks would you expect to make?

Answer: Ensure that correct information and data on the cargo type is available and that suitable protective clothing and equipment is ready for use. Counter measures against personnel contact would have been agreed together with the automatic shut down procedures known. All alarm systems and gauges are correctly set and in good order and portable vapour detection equipment is readily available. Full fire fighting facilities are ready for immediate use and the transfer pipelines are in good order.

Example of gas carriers. Two liquid natural gas (LNG) carriers lay alongside each other inside the Dubia Shipyard complex. The prominent domes over the cargo tanks tend to define the type of ship and give a clinical distinction.

Oil Tanker Vessels
Question 1.   When acting as Chief Officer aboard a tanker what preparations and actions would you take, when receiving orders to load?

Answer: It is normal practice to cover the loading by taking account of the cargo requirements: quantity, density, temperature and respective tank capacities. The concern would then be towards the pumping arrangements for both the cargo and for any ballast movement together with the associated deck equipment. Manifold connections, etc. Such activity would be monitored under the loading checklist where all safety precautions and specified safety equipment was seen to be in place.

The loading operation would be adequately covered by sufficient deck/engineering personnel in place especially during the period of 'topping off'.

Particular items of concern would be the preparation of a sequential loading plan. The oxygen content inside tanks would be checked (to be less than 5%) and the overfill alarms tested prior to commencing actual loading. Pumping into designated tanks being started slowly and allowed to build up once the risk of back pressures are reduced.

Question 2.   While alongside the oil terminal what safety precautions will be kept on hand, during loading or discharging operations?

Answer: A secondary means of escape[1] would be in place, in addition to the ship to shore gangway. Fire wires would be rigged at the fore and aft ends of the vessel, while respective fire extinguishers would be placed in the proximity of the manifolds.

A hose would be on stand-by, connected to the hydrant and fire main on the deck area of the manifold position. A communication link between the pumping station, manifold and the tank monitor would be established with emergency pump stopping capability and communications confirmed.

All the SOPEP equipment would be in place and the emergency contact numbers of the Designated Person Ashore (DPA) would be available. The offshore lifeboat would be turned out and lowered to the embarkation deck.

Question 3.   What type of fixed installation do tankers have for fighting fire on deck and what maintenance would be applicable to this installation?

Answer: Oil tankers would carry a foam system for deck fires.

The maintenance for such a system is covered by the planned maintenance schedule of the vessel. This would include the inspection and check of all foam pumps and valve alignments. General instructions for

---

[1]For example, a pilot ladder may be considered as a secondary means of access. If such is the case, this would be in place and secured, but would not be deployed overside, because of the security risk.

operations would be posted and a liquid level check would be made on the foam tank.

Company manuals require a six (6) monthly foam discharge test and an annual foam sample analysis would be made.

Where foam monitors are covering a heli-deck such monitors must be turned away from the landing operation area.

The largest tanker in the world the 'Jahre Viking' is manoeuvred with tugs off Dubia Dry Docks. The vessel has recently been converted to a Floating Storage Unit.

Question 4. What tankers are required to have a Crude Oil Washing (COW) system and what additional system must they also be fitted with?

Answer: All tankers over 20,000 tons deadweight must have a COW system and they must also be fitted with an inert gas system.

Question 5. Which Ships carry an Oil Record Book(ORB) and what entries are made in this book?

Answer: Every oil tanker of 150, and every ship of 400 or over, must carry an ORB. In the case of a tanker, the vessel would be expected to carry two Record Books, one for the oil cargoes, the other for recording bunkers.

Entries in the Oil Record Books are required to have a double signature, one of which will be by the ship's Master. Entries will record any movement of oil in or out of the vessel either accidental or deliberate, inclusive of internal transfers.

Passenger Vessels

Question 1.   In general, what additional requirements are required by passenger vessels over and above the life saving appliance requirements of a Class 7 vessel?

Answer: Passenger vessels must additionally have a double 'Public Address' (P/A) system, for advising all passengers and a separate system to advise crew on emergencies and shipboard operations.

They should further operate a fire patrol system on board the passenger vessel and they will carry a designated rescue boat either side with fixed radio facilities.

Question 2.   When must lifeboat drills and musters take place aboard a passenger vessel?

Answer: Where passengers are scheduled to be on board for more than 24 hours a muster of passengers must take place within 24 hours of their embarkation. An abandon ship drill must take place weekly. Passenger ships must provide instructions to passengers of how to don

Partially enclosed lifeboats seen being lowered to the water from the boat deck of the passenger vessel 'Queen Mary 2', in Southampton Water.

their lifejackets and be guided as to the action they should take on hearing the general emergency alarm signal.

Ro-Ro passenger ferries must give abandon ship instruction prior to the vessel sailing.

Question 3. Many passenger vessels carry davit launched liferafts. Are the crew expected to train with such equipment and if so how is this carried out?

Answer: Yes. The crew are expected to train in the use of davit launched liferafts at intervals of not more than 4 months. A special liferaft would be placed on board for use as a training raft and would not be included in forming part of the vessels life saving equipment.

Note: On vessels of Class II and II(A) engaged on regular voyages, the training should include the inflation of one of the ship's liferafts when in port. After such an exercise the liferaft would be sent for servicing.

Example of a davit launched liferaft station, with open deck aspects aboard a Class 1, passenger vessel. The liferafts are racked from where the view is taken. The bulwark is hinged to swing inwards either side to allow passenger access once the raft is inflated overside.

Question 4.   Why would you think a passenger vessel would probably be a good choice, as an On Scene Co-ordinator (OSC), in the event of a SAR operation developing?

Answer: Next to a warship a passenger vessel is likely to be far better equipped than most any other commercial vessel. This would be especially so if he was in a position to take on the role of 'On Scene Commander'. The passenger vessel would have the manpower to carry out the duties and could expect to have the endurance capabilities. Its main function would be communications which are usually in abundance on Class 1, vessels. The 'Bridge Team' aboard the vessel would probably have longer range plotting facilities and a selection of superior navigation aids to perform the task of OSC.

Should his position permit direct involvement the passenger ship may have a doctor and additional medical facilities on board?

The downside is that passengers may be delayed, especially if the ship is on a tight schedule. However, the potential speed within the ship could, eliminate concerns about tight docking times.

Note: Passenger vessels are expected to carry an Emergency SAR Operational Plan.

Question 5.   Do the crew of a passenger vessel, who are regularly in contact with passengers require any special training?

Answer: Yes. Under the STCW Convention crew members who deal with passengers should be trained in Crowd Control, survival craft handling and first aid. Since the ISPS Code has been implemented specific crew members have also been trained in matters of shipboard security.

Container Vessels
Question 1.   As a Master of a container vessel, what would you see as being some of the greatest problems of being in command?

Answer: From the seamanship point of view, ship handling with a large container stack on deck, in strong winds could be a distinct problem, even with bow thrust and tugs in attendance.

Another concern would be in the winter season when in high latitudes, where the danger of ice accretion is always present. Added weight on the container stack could be detrimental to the ship's positive stability.

The third aspect of a container ship is that the containers themselves are vulnerable to actions from terrorists or illegal immigrants.

The container vessel 'Lykes Commader' seen discharging containers by means of gantry cranes, while lying alongside the container terminal in Barcelona, Spain.

These are anticipated problems over and above the lashing of the containers, personnel problems and other routine tasks that form the role of the shipmaster.

Question 2.   When loading a container vessel prior to sailing, what are your main concerns as a Deck Officer?

Answer: My first concern would be for the safety of the personnel, especially container lashing gangs when containers are loaded on deck. As a responsible Officer it would be essential that deck stowed containers are well secured and to this end I would note the contents of MGN 157, regarding the safety of personnel during container securing operations and the IMO MSC/Circ. 886.

Question 3.   When at sea would you consider carrying out a helicopter transfer from the top of the container stack?

Answer: Such an operation would be highly undesirable. The container stack is usually not set in an even stow and the top containers could be in excess of 12 m high (40 ft). It should be realised in such an exposed position with the vessel stopped a minimum of a force four (4) wind would be experienced by persons on top of the stack. In exposed conditions with a slight wind force 1 to 2 on the Beaufort Scale, this would effect personnel as if it was a force of 6 to 7.

Once a helicopter was on scene the downdraft from the rotors would turn the top of the container stack into hurricane force conditions and it must be considered extremely hazardous. Such an operation could not be conducted safely without exposing the crew to a very high and intolerable accident risk.

Question 4.   Can containers be packed with Hazardous (Dangerous) Goods?

Answer: Yes. But they must be declared as dangerous goods and the container would need to be provided with a packing certificate to effect that the goods have been packaged, labelled and stowed in accord with the IMDG Code. Depending on the nature of the goods being shipped, would dictate the position of stowage.

Question 5.   Describe the constructional and operational features that you would expect to find aboard a large container vessel?

Answer: The larger container vessel will probably not be fitted with its own container cranes and rely on the use of terminal gantry cranes

The container vessel 'P & O Nedlloyd Susana' lies port side too in Lisbon, Portugal. The vessel is seen loading and discharging containers by use of the terminal gantry cranes. The ship's own container cranes are turned outboard so as not to interfere with the cargo operation.

to load and discharge. The container stack height on deck will be restricted to not obscuring the viewing operation from the navigation bridge. While access fore and aft through the length of the vessel will be achieved by an under deck passage from the all aft accommodation to the fore end store rooms and mooring deck.

Large container vessels are now designed at over 12,000 TEU size and such vessels would probably incur some draught restrictions in some ports around the world.

Special features on some ships will include pontoon hatch covers which seal the uppermost continuous deck (designs also include deck-less container vessels where the containers are just stowed in cell guides above and below the usual deck positions). Other features include wing tanks, loading computer systems, for container tracking. Some have a duct keel arrangement and most have a high engine power ratio for maintaining regular sailing schedules.

Smaller vessels would carry their own container pedestal or mobile gantry cranes.

High Speed Craft, Ro-Ro and Car Carriers

Question 1.   Many modern ferries and High Speed Craft (HSC) are fitted with twin controllable pitch propellers and operate Unmanned Machinery Spaces (UMS). What are the advantages to the watch Officer aboard a vessel which is so equipped?

Answer: The handling of the ship, by the Officer of the Watch, is easier and immediate. It is good for anti-collision manoeuvres as the speed of the vessel can be reduced quickly and effectively with the bridge controls. The vessel can also be stopped over the ground without having to stop the machinery plant. This means that the number of air starts, as when docking, are reduced and not restrictive to ship handling scenarios.

Question 2.   Car carriers and some ferries are very high-sided hulls. If an incident occurred in rough weather how would you attempt to recover a man over board?

Answer: On any vessel the weather conditions would dictate the possible use of the ship's rescue boat. Conditions of force six (6) or over would endanger the lives of own crew and would probably not permit use of the boat. With such a high-sided vessel, the risk would be amplified.

If a Master found himself in such a predicament he may want to attempt a rescue but at the same time would have the welfare of his own crew to consider.

A solution may be in the use of the rocket line throwing apparatus. In such circumstances the line could be fired over the casualty in the water and provided the person is conscious and can secure the line, the person could be drawn alongside.

A lifeboat could be lowered, but not released and used as a boarding platform for the casualty. Once aboard the lifeboat it could be hoisted as an elevator to effect recovery.

Note: Handling of the ship to create a 'lee' for such an operation would be considered essential. Though it is pointed out that high-sided vessels can expect to set down quickly and the faster the operation can be concluded the better.

Question 3.   Car carriers generally have numerous deck levels. What other special features do you associate with car carrying vessels?

Answer: Car carriers are usually of a high freeboard. The ships are also fitted with angled stern ramps and many are fitted with additional side ramps to either port or starboard. Vehicle decks are fitted with water tight doors which are alarmed and fitted with indicators to the bridge.

Car carrier – Vehicle Ramp. Angled vehicle ramp seen deployed from the Grimaldi Car Carrier, 'Republic Di Genova'. The scene is shown in Falmouth Dry Dock, where the vessel was booked in for routine maintenance.

All garage spaces have internal angled ramps to allow vehicle movement throughout the vessels cargo areas. Some vessels, if fitted with a lower hold space, may also be fitted with a vehicle elevator system.

Cargo securing chains are retained on board, for use with heavy vehicle loads if and when carried.

Question 4.   What documentation is required to be carried by a High Speed Craft (HSC)?

Answer: HSC must have the following three items in order to operate:

(1) **Safety Certificate.** This Certificate is issued after an initial survey to ensure that the vessel complies with the HSC Code (period of validity 5 years).

(2) **Permit to Operate HSC.** This will specify the name of the operator and state the route and maximum range on which the vessel is engaged. It will stipulate any weather restrictions which could curtail operations. The passenger capacity and manning levels would be reiterated in the permit (both the permit and the Safety Certificate are issued by the Marine Authority of the country where the craft is registered).

(3) **Craft Operating Manual.** This is a manual that contains the vessels details and describes any equipment on board. Damage control procedures would be listed together with descriptions of machinery and remote systems. All fire protection systems, loading procedures, communication equipment, etc. would all be included in the manual.

Note: For further reference on the operation of HSC the reader should see Chapter 18 of the HSC Code.

Question 5.   What do you understand by the term 'Ro-Ro, cargo space'?

Answer: A Ro-Ro cargo space is defined as a space which is not normally subdivided in any way and which extends to a substantial length or the entire length of the ship. It allows the loading and unloading of vehicles, road cars and trailers and/or rail tankers, containers, pallets, demountable tanks or other similar stowage units, in a horizontal direction.

Example Ro-Ro, cargo space partly loaded with vehicles in lanes.

SPECIALIST VESSELS ASSOCIATED WITH THE RULE OF THE ROAD (APPLICABLE TO ALL DECK OFFICER RANKS)

Question 1. When altering the vessels course away from a mine clearance vessel, what minimum passing distance would you consider appropriate?

Answer: A minimum passing distance, clear of a mine clearance vessel, engaged in mine clearance activity would be 1000 m.

Question 2. A vessel exhibits the International Code Flags 'YG' (Yankee, Golf). What would this mean to you?

Answer: This signal would indicate my vessel is not complying with the traffic separation scheme. Immediately check my own vessels position and ascertain that the ship's course is correct and that the vessel is not infringing Regulation '10' of The Regulations for the Prevention of Collisions at Sea (ColRegs).

Question 3.   When sighting another vessel at sea what are your first actions?

Answer: It would be normal practice to identify the target and ascertain whether 'Risk of Collision' existed between my own ship and the target vessel. In accordance with the Regulations, in the event that risk of collision did exist, the OOW would decide which ship was the 'Give Way' vessel and which ship was the 'stand-on' vessel. A Radar Plot or Automatic Radar Plotting Aids (ARPA) acquisition would be made on the target.

Question 4.   During the watch at sea, observation shows that a vessel constrained by its draught, is on a collision course with a trawler engaged in fishing. No risk of collision exists with the observers ship, but which of the other two vessels would you expect to keep out of the way and which would be the 'stand-on' vessel? Justify your answer.

Answer: The vessel constrained by its draught could expect to be designated the give way vessel and the trawler could expect to stand-on.
   The reason for this is found in Regulation 6, concerning safe speed. The vessel constrained by its draught, is defined as a Power-Driven Vessel (Regulation 3 definitions) as such it must be proceeding at a safe speed for the prevailing circumstances and it must therefore be capable of stopping in adequate time to avoid collision with the trawler.
   The trawler on the other hand could not necessarily stop, because of the nature of his operation, may cause fouling of his propellers.

Question 5.   How would you join and enter a traffic separation scheme?

Answer: Traffic separation schemes are joined and left at the extremities. However, if circumstances dictate and it is to be joined in the middle, the ship must do so, at a narrow an angle as possible to the direction of traffic flow.

Question 6.   What prevents the light from the starboard navigation side light being seen on the port side of the vessel?

Answer: Navigation sidelights are screened by a 'matt black' screen plate of 1 m length. The end of the screen is chocked to prevent light passage.

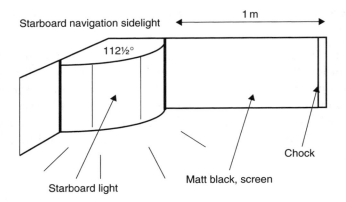

Question 7. Two trawlers are operating in close proximity. Each vessel is flying the following signals. What are they doing?

Answer: When each vessel indicates the following signals, it signifies that they are engaged in fishing and pair trawling.

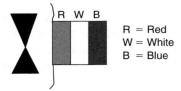

Question 8. When approaching a hidden bend in a river passage, the lookout reports hearing one (1) prolonged blast followed by two (2) short blasts, at intervals of not more than 2 minutes, from a position around the bend. What would you do as OOW?

Answer: This is a fog signal, and it must be assumed that poor visibility lies in the river around the bend. As such the OOW must prepare the bridge for entering poor visibility, as per the Regulations for the Prevention of Collision at Sea.

Question 9. When navigating at reduced speed in conditions of poor visibility you detect a fog signal apparently four points forward of the ship's beam, on the starboard side. No target is visible on the radar screen. What would you do, as OOW?

Answer: The OOW should immediately stop the vessels ahead motion, and take all way off the ship.

Once the way is off the vessel and she is not making way over the ground, the ship's fog signal should be changed from the previous one (1) prolonged blast to two (2) prolonged blasts at intervals not exceeding 2 minutes.

It would be prudent action to advise the Master, increase/double look-outs and change ranges on the radar, in order to pin-point the position of the target. Additionally, increase the frequency of the ship's fog signals.

Question 10. What indication could be detected by the OOW of reduced visibility conditions beginning to set in?

Answer: By inspection of the Masthead Steaming, navigation lights it will be noticed that back scattering of light is occurring in front of the light position.

Question 11. When approaching a 'pilot station', where your vessel does *not* want the pilot. What actions would you expect of the OOW?

Answer: When passing through the Pilot Roads, the OOW should inform the pilot station, out of courtesy, that the vessel is intending to pass through.

Additionally, the following actions should take place:

(a) Brief lookouts in the Bridge Team to watch for small pilot cutters.
(b) Reduce the ship's speed passing through the roads.
(c) Advise the Master of the situation/position.
(d) Record in the Log Book the reduction of speed, position and lookout briefs.

Question 12. How could the Officer of the Watch distinguish the difference between a vessel engaged in 'trawling' and a 'vessel engaged in fishing, other than a trawler', during the hours of daylight?

Answer: The vessel engaged in trawling is engaged in dragging a dredge net or other apparatus through the water, for which a degree of speed is required to keep the apparatus clear of the propeller. It must therefore be moving through the water at a minimum speed of about 3 knot, such movement would create a bow wave noticeable through binoculars.

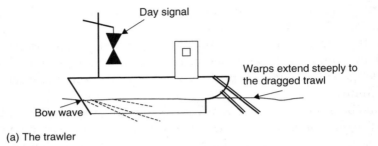

(a) The trawler

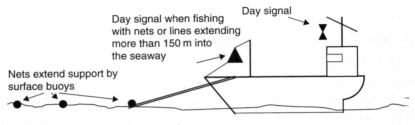

(b) Fishing vessel, other than a trawler

A vessel engaged in fishing other than a trawler, would have little or no way on her with a line of heavy nets out. This would not allow excessive way on the vessel and movement would be difficult to detect through binoculars.

Trawlers show the two black cones apex together signal, by day, the same as vessels engaged in fishing other than trawling. But never show the additional 'black cone' apex upwards in the direction of the gear.

Warps to the trawl net tend to be visible at a steep, acute angle, right aft of the trawler. No such warps are usually sighted on the fishing vessel which is not trawling.

Question 13. If your vessel had to cross a traffic separation scheme, how would you do it?

Answer: Traffic separation schemes can be crossed, but must be crossed at right angles to the general flow of traffic in the scheme.

Question 14. What do you understand to be a 'Wing-in-Ground (WIG) craft'?

Answer: The term WIG craft stands for 'Wing-in-Ground' craft. This means a multimodal craft which in its main operational mode, flies in close proximity to the surface by utilizing surface-effect action.

WIG craft design

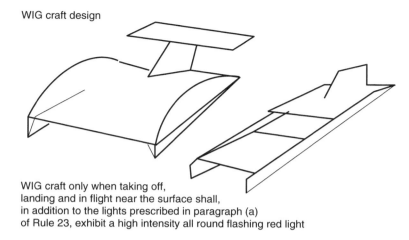

WIG craft only when taking off, landing and in flight near the surface shall, in addition to the lights prescribed in paragraph (a) of Rule 23, exhibit a high intensity all round flashing red light

Question 15. Which vessels must comply with the Regulations for the Prevention of Collision at Sea?

Answer: All vessels upon the high seas and in all waters connected therewith navigable by seagoing vessels.

Question 16. While in open waters you sight a vessel flying the International Code Flags (NOVEMBER, CHARLIE) NC. What action would you expect your vessel to take?

Answer: 'NC' is a recognised 'distress signal'. On sighting of this signal it would be expected that my vessel would render immediate assistance to the distressed vessel. Such assistance would depend on the nature of the distress and the prevailing circumstances. The Master would be immediately informed and the engines placed on stand-by mode.

Question 17. The Officer of the Watch reports a vessel aground two (2) points off the starboard bow, showing a day signal of three black balls in a vertical line where they can best be seen. Would you expect to alter course to assist this vessel?

Answer: No. The vessel is aground, not in distress, or it would display a distress signal. However, I would contact the grounded vessel to obtain any essential information from the ship which could effect the safe navigation of my own vessel, i.e. what the draught of the aground vessel was and what time she grounded. Very high frequency (VHF) contact being made following station identification.

Question 18.   Which vessels are directed by Rule 10 of the ColRegs (Appendix B), not to impede the safe passage of a power-driven vessel following a traffic lane?

Answer: Vessels of less than twenty (20) metres length, sailing vessels and vessels engaged in fishing, are so directed not to impede the safe passage of a power-driven vessel, following the lane.

Question 19.   What classes/types of vessel are considered to be 'restricted in ability to manoeuvre'?

Answer: The Regulations give provision for six (6) types of vessel to be considered as restricted in ability to manoeuvre. They are a vessel engaged in:

(a) laying, servicing or picking up a navigation mark, submarine cable, or pipeline;
(b) dredging, surveying or underwater operations;
(c) replenishment or transferring persons, provisions or cargo while under way;
(d) the launching or recovery of aircraft;
(e) mine clearance operations;
(f) a towing operation such as severely restricts the towing vessel and her tow in their ability to deviate from their course.

Question 20.   A sailing vessel is sighted showing a Black cone signal in the fore part, with the apex pointing downward. What would you assume this to mean?

Answer: The observation would indicate that the vessel was under sail and power at the same time.

Question 21.   A vessel engaged in towing is being approached by another vessel which appears to be heading towards the area of the towline. How can the towing vessel draw the attention of the approaching vessel to the danger?

Answer: The towing vessel could direct a search light towards the towline, to draw attention to the danger of the towing operation (Reference: Regulation 36, ColRegs).

Question 22.   A vessel is engaged in underwater operations with diving activity ongoing. How would she indicate her activities to approaching vessels by day?

Answer: The vessel would exhibit the restricted in ability to manoeuvre shapes, namely Ball, Diamond, Ball black shapes and the 'A' (Alpha) Flag, or a rigid replica of the 'A' Flag.

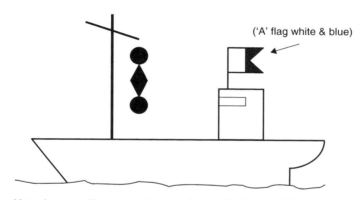

('A' flag white & blue)

Vessel engaged in underwater operations with diving activity

Question 23.   Can a vessel make a departure from the Regulations for the Prevention of Collision at Sea?

Answer: Yes. Under the direction of Regulation 2, a vessel may make a departure from the Anti-Collision Regulations to avoid immediate danger.

Question 24.   While on route towards Japan, your ship encounters a vessel engaged in fishing, other than a trawler, with its nets extended more than 150 m into the seaway. You observe this fishing craft 'port side open' at approximately four compass points off your own port bow. Its nets are seen to be across your intended track and a land mass is on your own Port side.

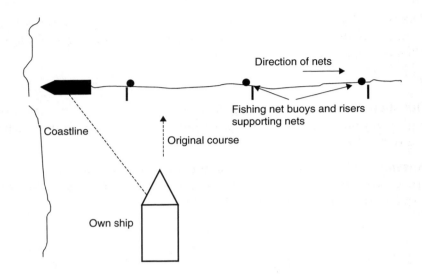

What action could your vessel take knowing that Japanese fishing boats have there nets extending up to 90 nautical miles into the sea?

Answer: The land mass on the ship's port side restricts an alteration of course to port. Such a restriction would force the ship to cross the nets of the fishing vessel. As such the Officer of the Watch, should:

(a) Inform the Master of the vessel.
(b) Direct the ship's course to pass between the fishing net buoys.
(c) Cross the nets at a right angle to spend as little time as possible over nets.
(d) Zero pitch on propellers or stop propellers when passing over nets.

It should be noted that such action as crossing fishing nets is highly undesirable and alternative action should be taken wherever possible. The above answer is suggested only where the mariner has no other alternative course of action.

Question 25.   Your power-driven vessel meets a sailing vessel end on right ahead. The wind direction is approximately four compass points off your own port bow.
Following observations of a steady compass bearing, clearly risk of collision is deemed to exist. What action would your vessel expect to take?

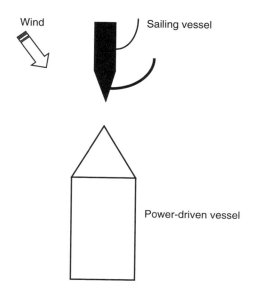

Answer: The power-driven vessel should sound two short blasts on the ship's whistle, and make an upwind alteration to port, giving a wide berth to the sailing vessel (Reference: Power-driven vessel gives way to sailing vessel Regulation 18a).

Note: The sailing vessel cannot sail directly into the wind.

Question 26. Your vessel encounters a fishing vessel by day, which exhibits the usual day signal for a vessel engaged in fishing but in addition shows the International Code Flag 'P'. What does this mean?

Answer: The Code Flag PAPA (P) when shown by a fishing vessel signifies that the vessel has become fast by her nets on an obstruction.

Question 27. What craft would exhibit a 'high intensity, all round flashing red light'?

Answer: This signal is shown by WIG craft, when taking off, landing, or in flight near the surface.

Question 28. A sailing vessel under way and making way at night, engages her engine in conjunction with her sails. How would the vessel change her navigational lights?

Answer: Once the engine is brought into operation the vessel is effectively considered as a power-driven vessel and she would show lights as for a power-driven vessel of her length.

Note: If the sailing vessel was operating under sail and showing the optional sailing lights, these must be turned off with the engine engaged.

Question 29. If two sailing vessels are on the same tack, and a risk of collision is present, which of the vessels will keep out of the way of the other?

Answer: That sailing vessel of the two, which is to windward of the other, would normally become the give way vessel.

Question 30. What is the fog signal given by a vessel being towed?

Answer: The vessel which is under tow would sound the fog signal of one prolonged blast plus three short blasts on the ship's whistle, immediately after the fog signal made by the tug.
   The towed vessel would only make the signal if manned.

Note: This signal is effectively made at intervals not greater than 2 minutes, as that is the designated interval of the signal made by the towing vessel.

MISCELLANEOUS BUOYAGE

Question 1. How would you mark a new danger in open waters, with navigable water all around?

Answer: The new danger is marked by double cardinal marks.

Question 2. What is the recommended passing distance about an isolated danger mark?

Answer: As wide a berth as possible.

Note: Any action taken would only proceed after a chart inspection.

Question 3.   When proceeding past a long obstruction, moving with the direction of buoyage, what would you expect to see between the south cardinal buoy and the east cardinal buoy?

Answer: Port hand, lateral marks.

Question 4.   For what uses is a 'special mark' deployed?

Answer: Outfalls, marking a Channel within a Channel, practice 'Firing Zones' or marina limits, etc.

Question 5.   When heading East across the North Sea, in reduced visibility, you see an 'east cardinal buoy' right ahead. What would be your action as Officer of the Watch?

Answer: Stop, take all way off the ship immediately. Advise the Master, and carry out a chart inspection to ensure that the buoy is in the correct position. Ascertain the vessels position, and check the under keel clearance by echo sounder. The situation would mean that the vessel is on top of the danger. The only known safe water is directly astern, and the vessel would probably have to navigate clear, stern-first. A check on the state of tide as to whether it is rising or falling could influence the outcome. Remaining in the present position is not an option.

Question 6.   When entering a buoyed channel you see two port hand, lateral marks, positioned close together. What does this signify?

Answer: A 'new danger' inside the channel on the port hand side.

Question 7.   When approaching a new danger, marked by double 'cardinal marks', it is noted that a radar signature is being emitted from one of the two marks. What is this radar feature?

Answer: A new danger is fitted with a RACON 'D' morse code signal, showing at a reflected signature range of 1 nautical mile.

Question 8.   What does IALA stand for?

Answer: International Association of Lighthouse Authorities.

Question 9.   What is the topmark of a spherical 'safewater mark'?

Answer: This buoy is already spherical and as such does not show any topmark.

Question 10.   What do you understand by the term 'local direction of buoyage'?

Answer: The direction of buoyage in a local area like the estuary of a river.

Question 11.   Where would you find the direction of buoyage indicated?

Answer: On the navigation chart.

Question 12.   Describe the symbol for the 'direction of buoyage' as found on the chart?

Answer: A block arrow with two small circles either side of the point, marked on the chart in 'magenta'.

Question 13.   What are the problems of using 'spar buoys' in ice regions, like the Baltic Sea, in winter?

Answer: Spar buoys very often become submerged by ice floes pushing the buoy under the surface. It is easy to sustain damage and may lose any topmark if fitted. It is also liable to become discoloured and may prove difficult to discern.

Note: Any floating mark employed in ice regions is liable to sustain damage or movement. As such it becomes extremely unreliable for navigation purposes and should only be used with extreme caution having first verified the buoy's position. Floating marks should never be solely used to monitor the ship's position in any event.

Question 14.   What type of buoys would you expect to mark the sides of a TSS?

Answer: Special marks, marking a channel within a channel.

Question 15.   A vessel is steering 270° and sights a south cardinal mark, right ahead. What action should the vessel take?

Answer: Carry out an immediate chart assessment and expect to alter course to port, passing to the South of the Buoy.

Question 16.   When leaving harbour a vessel sights a port hand preferred channel mark (preferred channel to starboard – System A). What action would you expect the vessel to take?

Answer: Alter course to port and remain in the deep water channel (treat the mark as a port hand buoy and leave it to starboard when departing the harbour).

Question 17.   Is the ship entering or leaving the Port System A?

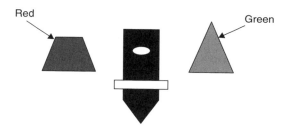

Answer: The vessel is leaving the Port and moving against the direction of buoyage.

Question 18.   In the diagram below, is the ship entering or leaving port (System B)?

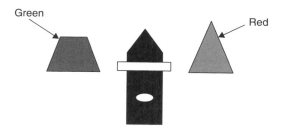

Answer: The vessel is entering the port and moving with the direction of buoyage.

Question 19. A vessel is steering 135° and sights an east cardinal mark, right ahead. What action would you expect the vessel to take?

Answer: Alter course to port and pass to the East of the mark.

Question 20. A buoy is noted to be out of position, from that given on the chart. What should the Master of the vessel do?

Answer: The Master would transmit via a Coast Radio Station a Navigation (Security) Warning. He would also report the hazard to the Hydrographic Office by means of the 'Hydrographic Note' found in the Weekly Notices to Mariners or the Mariners Handbook.

Question 21. The south cardinal buoy has a light sequence which contains six (6) short flashes followed by one (1) long flash. No other cardinal buoy has a long flash. What is the significance of the long flash on the south cardinal?

Answer: To distinguish the buoy from the other cardinal marks.

Question 22. While on watch an isolated danger is sighted right ahead. What is the buoys topmark and what action should the OOW take?

Answer: The buoy would show two (2) black spheres in a vertical line. Such a sighting would warrant a chart inspection and if not expected, the Master would be advised. An alteration of the ship's course would be made preferably to starboard depending on the geography and the circumstances found with the chart assessment (an alteration to starboard would keep the vessels starboard side clear in the event of additional traffic becoming a problem).

Question 23. Where would you expect to encounter 'System B' buoyage?

Answer: The Americas (North and South) and the Japan/Philippines areas.

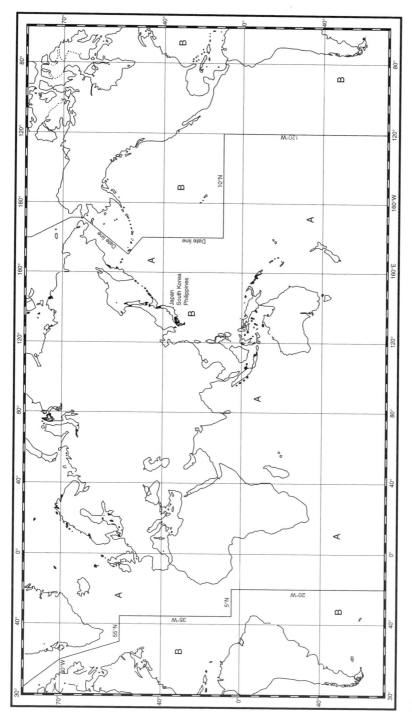

The IALA Maritime Buoyage Systems – Regions A and B. Reproduced with permission from IALA.

Question 24.   Why would a conical buoy carry a conical topmark?

Answer: To extenuate the shape and meaning of the buoy.

Question 25.   What type of buoy could be seen as a barrel shape?

Answer: A special mark buoy, yellow with a yellow St. Andrew's cross, as a topmark, is sometimes displayed as a barrel shape.

Appendix A: Conduct of Candidates

Extracts from MGN 69, regarding the Eligibility and Conduct of Candidates to be Examined for the Oral (Certificate of Competency) Examinations. The Syllabuses appear in the format followed in the book.

All references to 'Parts' in this document are to other Parts of this series of Training and Certification Guidance Notes

1 General

1.1 The Merchant Shipping (Training and Certification) Regulations 1997 (the Regulations) implement in the UK some of the requirements of the International Convention on Standards of Training, Certification and Watchkeeping (STCW) for Seafarers 1978, as amended in 1995 (STCW 95 Code, available from the Publications Department, International Maritime Organisation, 4 Albert Embankment, London SE1 7SR) and its associated code. STCW 95 and the Regulations introduce a new certificate structure applicable to Masters, Deck and Engineer Officers and ratings, which is explained fully in other Parts of this series of Guidance Notes.

1.2 The issue of a Certificate of Competency, particularly a first certificate, is generally the final stage in the following procedure:

1.2.1 demonstration of the required standard of physical fitness (by passing a medical examination/sight test);

1.2.2 completion of the initial training requirements;

1.2.3 completion of the appropriate watchkeeping and/or sea service;

1.2.4 successful completion of the approved training programmes and assessments;

1.2.5 successful completion of all ancillary training as set out in Parts 2 (deck) and 3 (engineer);

1.2.6 success in the Maritime and Coastguard Agency (MCA) oral examination (not required for ratings certification under STCW 95 Regulations II/4 and III/4).

1.3 The MCA oral examination is aimed at ensuring the candidate's ability to undertake the duties appropriate to the Officer of the Watch (OOW), Chief Mate, Master, Second Engineer or Chief Engineer. Oral examinations are part of the procedure for the attainment of all MCA certificates of competency, and all candidates must demonstrate an adequate knowledge of the English language.

1.4 The examination syllabuses are divided into topics. Each topic contains a group of tasks, duties and responsibilities considered necessary for ship operation, Safety of Life at Sea (SOLAS) or protection of the marine environment. As indicated in the preamble to each examination syllabus, the examination will be conducted from a particular perspective and this will be based upon the level of responsibility assumed, i.e. either management level (Master, Chief Engineer, Chief Mate or Second Engineer) or operational level (Officer in charge of a navigational or engineering watch).

1.5 Candidates seeking STCW 95 certificates of competency as a **Deck Officer** will follow the oral examination syllabuses A–E contained in Appendix A of this Note. At the date of this Marine Guidance Notice (MGN), syllabuses F–H are still being developed. Further details of requirements for Deck Officers are set out in Part 2.

1.6 Candidates seeking STCW 95 certificates of competency as a **Marine Engineer Officer** will follow the oral examination syllabuses contained at Appendix B of this Note. Further details of requirements for Engineer Officers are set out in Part 3.

1.7 Appendix C to this Note contains addresses of the MCA Marine Offices where oral examinations are held.

1.8 Until 31 December 1999, candidates who commenced seagoing service or approved education and training programmes prior to 1 August 1998 were examined using the oral syllabuses required for STCW 78 certificates of competency Classes 1 to 5.

2 Applications for MCA Oral Examinations

2.1 Before being admitted to the MCA oral examination candidates must be in possession of a Notice of Eligibility (NOE). Details of the application procedure for obtaining an NOE can be found in Part 9. This NOE will be required by the MCA examiner as evidence that the candidate fulfils the oral examination entry requirements and must be sent to the Marine Office undertaking the examination when making an appointment. A candidate attending college may arrange for an oral examination appointment through the college.

2.2 A candidate not attending college should apply for an appointment by sending the NOE to the Marine Office of his or her choice (listed at Appendix C) stating a range of dates when he or she is available for examination, although it cannot be guaranteed that an examination will be arranged on one of the requested dates. As wide a range of dates as possible should be given to afford the examiner the maximum opportunity to arrange an appointment convenient to the candidate.

2.3 An NOE is only valid for one oral examination attempt. A new one should be obtained for any subsequent attempt (see paragraph 3.6).

2.4 When attending for examination, the following documents should be produced for scrutiny by the examiner:
   (a) NOE;
   (b) discharge book or passport (if a discharge book is not held);
   (c) Certificate of Competency (if one is held);

(d) Deck or Engineer (as appropriate) Record Book, if an approved course of training has been followed, or Vocational Qualification (VQ) portfolio of evidence (as appropriate).

3 Conduct of Oral Examinations

3.1 The oral examination will in all cases be conducted in English by an examiner from the MCA, generally at an MCA Marine Office. However, where appropriate, MCA has the discretion to use other venues.

3.2 Examiners will use the appropriate examination syllabuses, as detailed in paragraphs 1.5 to 1.6.

3.3 The result of the oral examination will be entered on the NOE by the MCA examiner. A candidate failing the oral examination will receive verbal feedback from the examiner, indicating the function(s)/topic(s) in which the candidate was deemed to have failed.

3.4 A candidate passing the oral examination, and holding an NOE carrying a red endorsement to the effect that they have met all the requirements for the issue of a Certificate of Competency prior to attending the oral examination, should give their existing Certificate of Competency (if held) to the examiner, who will make arrangements for a Certificate of Competency to be issued within three working days.

3.5 A candidate passing the oral examination, but not holding an NOE carrying the red endorsement, will have the Notice returned to him or her. The Notice should be retained until all the requirements have been met and should be sent together with relevant documentation and existing Certificate of Competency (if held) to the Seafarer Standards Branch of the MCA at the address given at the beginning of this MGN.

3.6 If a candidate fails the oral examination and wishes to resit the examination, the NOE (showing the 'failed' entry) together with the relevant fee, should be sent to the Seafarer Standards Branch and a new NOE will be issued. Candidates will not be reexamined within 2 weeks of having failed.

3.7 A candidate failing the oral examination through serious weakness may, at the examiner's discretion, be given a time penalty which may include a requirement to complete a period of sea service before becoming eligible to resit the examination.

3.8 A candidate not appearing for an oral examination at the appointed time may be failed by default unless reasonable proof can be provided that the failure to attend was unavoidable.

3.9 Any candidate involved in irregular behaviour (such as cheating) will be failed in the oral examination and the circumstances reported to the MCA's Chief Examiner. The circumstances of reported cases will be considered individually and such consideration may result in the candidate being barred from sitting the oral examination, either for a specific period, or until further sea service has been completed by the candidate.

4 Further Advice

4.1 Further information, if required, may be obtained from the MCA at any Marine Office or at the address given at the beginning of this MGN.

STCW REGULATIONS II/I: SYLLABUS DECK C (OOW – SHIPS OF 500 GT AND ABOVE)

Candidates should demonstrate the ability to apply the knowledge outlined in this oral examination syllabus by appropriate responses, anticipations and reactions to a range of routine, non-routine and contingency scenarios as presented by the examiner, from the perspective of **OOW – Ships of 500 GT and above**.

TOPIC 1: NAVIGATION

1 Plan and Conduct a Passage Including Position Determination

(a) Passage planning with respect to the use of navigational publications including navigational charts (including Electronic Chart Display and Information System (ECDIS) and Raster Chart Display System (RCDS)), sailing directions, light lists, tide tables, radio navigational warnings and ships' routeing information.

(b) The requirements of ship routeing and mandatory reporting systems.

(c) International Association of Classification Societies (IALA) systems of maritime buoyage.

(d) Electronic navigational systems – limitations and sources of error, methods of correction.

(e) Limitations of electronic chart systems including ECDIS and RCDS navigational chart systems.

(f) Radar and Automatic Radar Plotting Aids (ARPA) – practical use of, modes of operation, limitations, sources of error and parallel indexing.

(g) To use an azimuth mirror for taking bearings including the determination of compass errors.

(h) To use a sextant, identify and correct errors.

(i) Sources of meteorological information, ability to use and interpret information obtained from ship borne meteorological instruments (the instruments supplied by the Meteorological Office will be taken as standard), knowledge of characteristics of various weather systems, reporting and recording systems.

2 Maintain a Safe Navigational Watch

(a) A thorough knowledge of the principles of navigational watchkeeping at sea, including under pilotage, and watchkeeping at anchor and in port.

(b) A thorough knowledge of the content, application and intent of the International Regulations for Preventing Collisions at Sea.

(c) Radar and ARPA – practical use of, modes of operation, limitations, sources of error, plotting and parallel indexing.

(d) Understand the use of bridge equipment including rate of turn indicators, course recorders, echo sounders and NAVTEX.

(e) Knowledge of steering control systems including automatic pilot, operational procedures and change-over from manual to automatic control and vice-versa – adjustment of controls for optimum performance.

(f) Knowledge and application of the International Chamber of Shipping (ICS) Bridge Procedures Guide.

3 Compasses
(a) Use, care and limitations of the magnetic and gyro compasses, and associated equipment including automatic pilot.

4 Manoeuvre the Ship
(a) Preparation for getting under way, duties prior to proceeding to sea, making harbour, entering a dock, berthing alongside quays, jetties, or other ships, and securing to buoys.
(b) Use and care of mooring lines and associated equipment.
(c) Helm orders, conning the ship, effects of propellers on the steering of a ship, effects of wind and current, stopping, going astern, turning short round, interaction and squat, manoeuvring in the vicinity of pilot vessels and other craft, embarking and disembarking a pilot.
(d) Action in event of failure of bridge control, telegraph or steering, emergency steering arrangements.
(e) Proper procedures for anchoring.

TOPIC 2: CARGO HANDLING AND STOWAGE

1 Loading and Unloading of Cargoes
(a) Use and care of synthetic fibre and wire ropes, ascertaining of safe working loads.
(b) Basic knowledge of the regulations and recommendations affecting cargo handling, stowage, securing and carriage including the International Maritime Dangerous Goods (IMDG) Code.
(c) Use of the hydrometer.

TOPIC 3: RESPONSE TO EMERGENCIES

1 Response to Navigational Emergencies
(a) Initial action following: man overboard, collision, grounding, flooding or major mechanical damage and receipt of a distress message; initial damage assessment and control, protection of the marine environment.
(b) Precautions for the protection and safety of passengers in emergency situations.
(c) Use of the International Aeronautical and Marine Search and Rescue (IAMSAR) Manual (Volume III), distress and emergency signals, Search and Rescue (SAR) around the UK and worldwide.

2 Response to Other Emergencies
(a) Understanding of the organisational procedures for emergency parties and drills.

(b)   Knowledge of fire prevention, use and care of fire-fighting appliances, the shut-down and isolation of plant and equipment, escape and breathing apparatus, fire and safety plans.
(c)   Knowledge of classes and chemistry of fire.
(d)   Understanding of action to be taken in the event of fire including fires involving oil.
(e)   Use and care of life saving appliances and equipment including hand held radios, Emergency Position Indicating Radio Beacons (EPIRBs), Search and Rescue Transponders (SARTs), immersion suits and thermal protective aids, and rocket line throwing apparatus.
(f)   Meaning of markings on survival craft and associated equipment.
(g)   Correct use of distress signals and awareness of penalties for misuse.
(h)   Launch and manage survival craft, recover rescue boats at sea.
(i)   Precautions for the protection and safety of passengers in emergencies.
(j)   Knowledge of the contents of SOLAS training manuals and maintenance logs.
(k)   Basic principles of survival.
(l)   Appreciation of action to be taken when emergencies arise in port.
(m) Sources of medical information available.

3 Communications
(a)   Use of distress and emergency signals, International Code of Signals and the International Maritime Organisation (IMO) Standard Marine Communication Phrases.
(b)   Emergency communications within the Global Maritime Distress and Safety System (GMDSS) Regulations.

TOPIC 4: ONBOARD SHIP OPERATIONS

1 Pollution Prevention Requirements
(a)   Precautions to be taken to prevent pollution of the marine environment as required by the Marine Pollution (MARPOL) Conventions including Restricted Areas and the disposal of pollutants.
(b)   Basic understanding of the Ships Oil Pollution Emergency Plan (SOPEP) Manual, Garbage Management Plan and anti-pollution equipment.

2 Seaworthiness of the Ship
(a)   Understand fundamentals of watertight integrity and the closing of all openings including hatch covers, access hatches and watertight doors.
(b)   Preparations for heavy weather.

3 Legislative Requirements
(a)   Contents and use of Merchant Shipping Notices, Marine Guidance Notes, Marine Information Notes and Annual Summary of Admiralty Notices to Mariners.
(b)   Knowledge and application of current Merchant Shipping Health and Safety legislation and the Code of Safe Working Practices for Merchant Seamen.

(c) Basic knowledge of relevant IMO conventions concerning SOLAS and protection of the marine environment.
(d) Purpose and application of the International Safety Management (ISM) Code.
(e) Purpose of Flag State and Port State Control.

STCW REGULATION II/2: SYLLABUS DECK B (CHIEF MATE – UNLIMITED AND MASTER – UNLIMITED – SHIPS LESS THAN 3000 GT)

Candidates should demonstrate the ability to apply the knowledge outlined in this oral examination syllabus and oral examination syllabus **Deck C**, by the appropriate responses, anticipations and reactions to a range of routine, non-routine and contingency scenarios as presented by the examiner, from the perspective of **Chief Mate** and **Master**.

TOPIC 1: NAVIGATION

1 Plan and Conduct Safe Navigation
(a) Passage planning with respect to the use of navigational publications including navigational charts (including ECDIS and RCDS), sailing directions, light lists, tide tables, radio navigational warnings and ships' routeing information.
(b) The requirements of ship routeing and mandatory reporting systems.
(c) IALA systems of maritime buoyage.
(d) Electronic navigational systems – limitations and sources of error, methods of correction.
(e) Radar and ARPA – practical use of, modes of operation, limitations, sources of error and parallel indexing.
(f) Sources of meteorological information, ability to use and interpret information obtained from ship borne meteorological instruments (the instruments supplied by the Meteorological Office will be taken as standard), knowledge of characteristics of various weather systems, reporting and recording systems.

2 Establishing Safe Navigational Watchkeeping Arrangements and Procedures
(a) A thorough knowledge of the principles of navigational watchkeeping at sea, including under pilotage, and watchkeeping at anchor and in port.
(b) A thorough knowledge of the content, application and intent of the International Regulations for Preventing Collisions at Sea.
(c) Conduct in and near traffic separation schemes and vessel traffic service (VTS) areas.
(d) Understand the use of bridge equipment including rate of turn indicators, course recorders, echo sounders and NAVTEX.

(e) Knowledge of steering control systems including automatic pilot, operational procedures and change-over from manual to automatic control and vice-versa, adjustment of controls for optimum performance.
(f) Knowledge and application of the ICS Bridge Procedures Guide.
(g) A knowledge of principles of establishing a safe engineering watch at sea, anchor and in port.

3 Compasses
(a) Use, care and limitations of the magnetic and gyro compasses, and associated equipment including automatic pilot.

4 Manoeuvre the Ship
(a) Conning the ship, effects of wind and current, effects of deadweight, draft, trim, speed and underkeel clearance on turning circles and stopping distances; interaction and squat.
(b) Berthing and unberthing at jetties, quays, mooring buoys and single-point moorings with/without tugs, with/without tidal stream, with/without wind.
(c) Manoeuvres in restricted waters and open ocean waters.
(d) Embarking and disembarking pilots.
(e) Limitations of remote control operation of marine power plant and auxiliary machinery.
(f) Anchors: different types of anchors and their advantages and disadvantages, preparation for anchoring, anchoring in a tideway and in confined water, operation of anchoring with a single anchor and use of a second anchor, dragging anchor, clearing a foul anchor and hawse, hanging off an anchor, breaking and slipping cables, getting under way.
(g) Navigation in the vicinity of ice, ice reporting and steps to be taken in the event of ice accretion.
(h) Manoeuvres to launch and recover rescue boats/survival craft.

TOPIC 2: CARGO HANDLING AND STOWAGE

1 Loading and Unloading of Cargoes
(a) Use, maintenance and testing of cargo handling equipment on board the vessel concerned.
(b) Application of the contents of relevant codes and guidelines concerning the safe handling of cargoes on board the vessel concerned.
(c) Knowledge of the effect on trim and stability, cargoes and cargo operations on board the vessel concerned.
(d) Use of stability and trim information, use of stress-calculating equipment, knowledge of loading cargoes and ballasting with respect to stability and hull stress.

2 Stowage, Securing and Care of Cargoes
(a) Application of the contents of relevant regulations, codes and guidelines concerning the safe stowage, securing and carriage of cargoes.

TOPIC 3: RESPONSE TO EMERGENCIES

1 Response to Navigational Emergencies
(a) Measures to be taken following: accidental damage including collision, grounding, flooding or major mechanical damage, including the possibility of beaching a ship; protection of the marine environment.
(b) Knowledge of the effect on trim and stability, and subsequent actions in the event of damage to and consequent flooding of a compartment.
(c) Preparations and precautions for towing and being towed.
(d) Use of the IAMSAR Manual (Volume III), distress and emergency signals, SAR around the UK and worldwide.
(e) SAR and rescue plans for passenger ships.
(f) Knowledge of the operation of emergency steering systems.

2 Respond to Other Emergencies
(a) The organisation and direction of fire-fighting and abandon ship parties.
(b) Methods of dealing with fire onboard ship, prevention of fire at sea and in port.
(c) Action to be taken to prevent the spread of fire.
(d) Operation, maintenance and testing of fire-fighting equipment, fire doors, dampers, screens and detection equipment.
(e) Operation, maintenance and testing of watertight doors, sidescuttles and scuppers.
(f) Launch, manage and ensure survival in survival craft, recover survival craft at sea and beach or land survival craft.
(g) Operation, maintenance and testing of life saving appliances.
(h) Knowledge of the contents of SOLAS training manuals.
(i) Action to be taken when disabled and in distress.
(j) Assisting a ship or aircraft in distress, rescuing the passengers and crew of a disabled ship or ditched aircraft.
(k) Safety during helicopter operations.

3 Communications
(a) Correct use of distress signals and awareness of penalties for misuse.
(b) Emergency communications within the GMDSS Regulations.
(c) Sources of radio medical advice.

TOPIC 4: ONBOARD SHIP OPERATIONS

1 Compliance with Pollution Prevention Requirements
(a) Measures to be taken to prevent pollution in port and at sea.
(b) Take appropriate action in response to pollution incidents on board and found at sea.
(c) Knowledge of the contents of the SOPEP Manual, Garbage Management Plan and use of provided anti-pollution equipment.
(d) Practical knowledge of the requirements of MARPOL Conventions.
(e) Knowledge of responsibilities, duties, obligations and liabilities in respect of pollution.

2 Seaworthiness of the Ship

(a) Preparations for sea prior to sailing with respect to watertight integrity and additional precautions to be taken before the onset of heavy weather.

(b) Practical knowledge of the particular load-line items affecting seaworthiness.

(c) Action in event of cargo shift, damage to hull or hatches, loss of cargo overboard or ingress of water into hull.

(d) Preparation for Dry Docking and Undocking with and without cargo/damage; general procedure and precautions to be observed.

(e) Use and care of deck machinery commonly fitted.

3 Crew Management

(a) Knowledge of personnel management, organisation and training including disciplinary procedures;

(b) Application of hours of work and rest legislation.

4 Maintain Safety of Ships Crew and Passengers

(a) Master's responsibility with respect to stowaways and prevention of smuggling.

(b) Precautions to safeguard against terrorism, piracy and armed robbery.

(c) Methods of pest control – fumigation of holds and living spaces, safeguards in applying various methods.

5 Legislative Requirements

(a) Knowledge of the application of current Merchant Shipping Health and Safety legislation including the Code of Safe Working Practices for Merchant Seamen and the main elements of risk assessment.

(b) Improvement and Prohibition Notices.

(c) Safe manning, crew agreements, conditions of employment, Official Log Book and the law relating to entries.

(d) Understanding of load-line marks, entries and reports in respect of freeboard, draft and allowances.

(e) Routine inspection of living quarters and storerooms and complaints procedure.

(f) Requirements for records including Oil Record Book.

(g) Requirements for drills and training.

(h) The requirements of the regulations concerning fire-fighting appliances.

(i) Knowledge of the requirements of the regulations concerning life saving appliances.

(j) Knowledge of the international conventions relevant to the operation of ships including certificates and other documents required to be carried onboard ships.

(k) Requirements for statutory and classification surveys.

(l) Reports required by the Marine Accident Investigation Branch (MAIB).

(m) Putting into port with damage to ship and/or cargo, both from business and technical points of view – safeguarding of cargo.

(n) Obligations with respect to pilotage.

(o) Towage and salvage agreements.

(p) Purpose of Flag State and Port State Control.

(q) Purpose and application of the International Safety Management (ISM) Code.

STCW REGULATION II/2: SYLLABUS DECK A (MASTER – UNLIMITED)

Candidates should demonstrate the ability to apply the knowledge outlined in this oral syllabus and oral examination syllabuses **Deck B** and **Deck C**, by the appropriate responses, anticipations and reactions to a range of routine, non-routine and contingency scenarios as presented by the examiner, from the perspective of **Master**.

TOPIC 1: NAVIGATION

1 Plan and Conduct Safe Navigation
(a) Voyage planning and navigation for all conditions including ships' routeing and reporting systems.
(b) IALA systems of maritime buoyage.
(c) Understand and interpret a synoptic chart and use of weather routeing services.
(d Knowledge of characteristics of various weather systems including tropical revolving storms, the avoidance of storm centres and dangerous quadrants.
(e) Practical measures to be taken when navigating in or near ice and dealing with ice accumulation on board.
(f) Danger messages and obligatory reporting requirements.

2 Establishing Safe Navigational Watchkeeping Arrangements and Procedures
(a) A thorough knowledge of the principles of navigational watchkeeping at sea, including under pilotage, watchkeeping at anchor and in port.
(b) A thorough knowledge of the content, application and intent of the international regulations for the prevention of collisions at sea.
(c) Knowledge and application of the ICS Bridge Procedures Guide.
(d) Limitations and risks involved with the use of ECDIS and RCDS; inter-relationship and optimum use of all navigational information available.
(e) A knowledge of principles of establishing a safe engineering watch at sea, anchor and in port.

3 Compasses
(a) The operation and care of various types of compasses.
(b) Care and maintenance of the magnetic compass and binnacle.
(c) Knowledge of the purpose and use of compass correctors (candidates will not be required to demonstrate a compass correction procedure).
(d) Knowledge of how to find the magnetic bearing of a distant object and subsequent construction of a deviation card.

4 Manoeuvre the Ship
(a) Knowledge of manoeuvring and propulsion characteristics of ships, with special reference to stopping distances and turning circles at various draughts and speeds, squat and interaction.

(b) Importance of navigating at reduced speed to avoid damage caused by own ship's bow wave and sternwave.

(c) Demonstrate an understanding of ship manoeuvres commonly undertaken under all weather conditions including berthing and unberthing, approaching pilot stations, restricted waters and shallow water.

(d) Management and handling of ships in heavy weather.

(e) Choice of anchorage and working anchors in all circumstances.

(f) Precautions when manoeuvring to launch rescue boats or survival craft in bad weather.

TOPIC 2: CARGO HANDLING AND STOWAGE

1 Plan and Ensure Safe Loading, Stowage, Securing, Care During Voyage and Unloading of Cargoes

(a) Knowledge and ability to apply relevant international regulations, codes and guidelines concerning the safe handling, stowage, securing and transport of cargoes.

TOPIC 3: RESPONSE TO EMERGENCIES

1 Response to Navigational Emergencies

(a) Precautions when beaching a ship.

(b) Grounding: action to be taken when imminent, after grounding and refloating and subsequent surveys.

(c) Measures to be taken following exceptional circumstances including loss of rudder and/or propeller and impairment of watertight integrity of the ship through any cause.

(d) Emergency towing arrangements and towing procedures.

(e) Plan and co-ordinate SAR operations including establishing and maintaining effective communications.

2 Response to Other Emergencies

(a) Preparation of contingency plans for response to emergencies.

(b) Actions to be taken when disabled and in distress.

(c) Organisation of fire and abandon ship exercises.

(d) Methods and aids for fire prevention, detection and extinction.

(e) Functions and use of life saving appliances.

(f) Abandoning ship and survival procedure.

(g) SAR plans for passenger ships.

(h) Maintenance of operational conditions of life saving appliances, fire-fighting appliances and other safety systems.

(i) Knowledge of the effect on trim and stability of a ship in the event of damage to and consequent flooding of a compartment and counter measures to be taken.

(j) Action to limit damage and salve the ship following a fire, explosion, collision or grounding including protection of the marine environment.

(k) Action to safe guard all persons on board in emergencies.
(l) Assisting a ship or aircraft in distress.

TOPIC 4: ONBOARD SHIP OPERATIONS

1 Compliance with Pollution Prevention Requirements

(a) Responsibilities under International Convention for Prevention of Pollution including Masters' duties, obligations and liabilities including the keeping of records.
(b) Methods and equipment to prevent pollution.

2 Seaworthiness of the Ship

(a) Effect of heavy weather on the ship's structure.
(b) Effect upon ship behaviour of lists, stiff and tender stability conditions, large angles of heel and associated righting precautions: the effect upon different cargoes.
(c) The importance of free surface effects and the identification and correction of an angle of loll.
(d) Specific effects on stability and stress caused by ship type or nature of trade.

3 Crew Management

(a) Knowledge of personnel management, organisation and training including disciplinary procedures.
(b) Application of hours of work and rest legislation.

4 Maintain Safety of Ships Crew and Passengers

(a) Master's responsibility with respect to stowaways and prevention of smuggling.
(b) Precautions to safeguard against terrorism, piracy and armed robbery.
(c) Methods of pest control, fumigation of holds and living spaces, safeguards in applying various methods.

5 Legislative Requirements

(a) Knowledge and application of current Merchant Shipping Health and Safety legislation including the Code of Safe Working Practices for Merchant Seamen and the main elements of risk assessment.
(b) Safe manning, crew agreements, conditions of employment, Official Log Book and the law relating to entries.
(c) Knowledge of international conventions relevant to the operation of ships including certificates and other documents required to be carried onboard ships.
(d) Requirements for statutory and classification surveys.
(e) Reports required by the Marine Accident Investigation Branch (MAIB).
(f) Putting into port with damage to ship and/or cargo, both from business and technical points of view, safeguarding of cargo.
(g) Towage and salvage agreements.
(h) Obligations with respect to pilotage.

(i) Maritime declarations of health and requirements of the international health regulations.

(j) Purpose and application of the International Safety Management (ISM) Code.

STCW REGULATIONS II/3 AND II/2: SYLLABUS DECK D (MASTER – NEAR-COASTAL – SHIPS UNDER 500 GT; CHIEF MATE – NEAR-COASTAL – SHIPS UNDER 3000 GT; CHIEF MATE – UNLIMITED – SHIPS UNDER 3000 GT)

Candidates should demonstrate the ability to apply the knowledge outlined in this oral examination syllabus and oral examination syllabus **Deck E**, by the appropriate responses, anticipations and reactions to a range of routine, non-routine and contingency scenarios as presented by the examiner, from the perspective of **Master – Near-Coastal – Ships under 500 GT or Chief Mate – Unlimited – Ships under 3000 GT (STCW Regulation II/2) or Chief Mate – Near-Coastal – Ships under 3000 GT as appropriate.**

TOPIC 1: NAVIGATION

1 Plan and Conduct Safe Navigation
(a) Demonstrate an ability to undertake voyage planning, taking into consideration:
    (i)   restricted waters;
    (ii) meteorological conditions, through the interpretation of a synoptic chart, and to forecast local area weather, the characteristics of various weather systems;
    (iii) restricted visibility;
    (iv) the requirements of ship routeing and mandatory reporting systems;
    (v) reporting in accordance with ship reporting systems.
(b) Limitations of electronic chart systems including ECDIS and RCDS navigational chart systems.
(c) Port radio information services: knowledge of the types of service available to aid vessels entering ports, berthing, VTIS and VTS services, as indicated in The Admiralty List of Radio Signals – VTS, Port Operations and Pilot Stations.
(d) Maritime Buoyage Systems – IALA region 'A'.

2 Establish and Maintain Safe Watchkeeping Arrangements and Procedures
(a) A thorough knowledge of the principles of navigational watchkeeping at sea, including under pilotage, and watchkeeping at anchor and in port.
(b) A thorough knowledge of the content, application and intent of the International Regulations for Preventing Collisions at Sea.

(c) Knowledge of principles of establishing a safe engineering watch at sea, anchor and in port.

3 Compasses

(a) Compasses commonly fitted on board the ships concerned – variation and deviation, causes and effects, siting of other equipment with reference to magnetic compasses.
(b) Knowledge of the purpose of correctors/corrections.

4 Manoeuvre the Ship and Operate Small Ship Power Plants

(a) Anchoring and working anchors and cables in all circumstances.
(b) Proper procedures for berthing and unberthing.
(c) Knowledge of factors affecting safe manoeuvring and handling.
(d) Knowledge of the operation of small ship power plants and auxiliaries.

TOPIC 2: CARGO HANDLING AND STOWAGE

1 Cargo Handling, Stowage, Securing and Care

(a) Knowledge of the regulations and recommendations affecting cargo handling, stowage, securing and carriage.
(b) Use of the IMDG Code.

TOPIC 3: RESPONSE TO EMERGENCIES

1 Response to Navigational Emergencies

(a) Action to be taken when disabled and in distress, abandoning ship, survival procedure, use of rockets and rocket apparatus.
(b) Measures to be taken following collision, grounding, heavy weather damage and leaks including the possibility of beaching a ship.
(c) Towing and being towed.
(d) Knowledge of emergency steering systems.
(e) Knowledge of search and rescue procedures, assisting a ship or aircraft in distress, rescuing the passengers and crew of a disabled ship or ditched aircraft.
(f) Use of the IAMSAR Manual (Volume III), distress and emergency signals.
(g) SAR plans for passenger ships.
(h) Emergency communications within the GMDSS Regulations.

2 Response to Other Emergencies

(a) Methods of dealing with fire onboard ship, prevention of fire at sea and in port.
(b) Use and maintenance of fire-fighting equipment, fire dampers, doors and screens and detection equipment.
(c) The organisation and direction of fire-fighting drill training.
(d) Launch and manage survival craft, recover rescue boats at sea.
(e) The organisation and direction of lifeboat and liferaft drill training.

(f) Understand the fundamental actions to be taken in the event of partial loss of intact buoyancy.
(g) Precautions for the protection and safety of passengers in emergencies.
(h) Appreciation of action to be taken when emergencies arise in port.
(i) Sources of medical information available.

TOPIC 4: ONBOARD SHIP OPERATIONS

1 Pollution Prevention Requirements

(a) Precautions to be taken to prevent pollution of the marine environment as required by the MARPOL Conventions including Restricted Areas.
(b) Take appropriate action in response to pollution incidents onboard and found at sea.
(c) Knowledge of the contents of the SOPEP Manual, Garbage Management Plans and anti-pollution equipment.
(d) Master's duties, obligations and liabilities including the keeping of records.

2 Seaworthiness of the Ship

(a) Precautions to be taken before the onset of heavy weather, management of small ships in heavy weather, handling a disabled ship.
(b) Understand the fundamentals of watertight integrity.
(c) Preparation for Dry Docking and Undocking, with and without cargo/damage – general procedure and precautions to be observed.
(d) Working knowledge of stability and trim information.

3 Legislative Requirements

(a) Contents and use of Merchant Shipping Notices, Marine Guidance Notes, Marine Information Notes and the Annual Summary of Admiralty Notices to Mariners.
(b) Knowledge of the application of current Merchant Shipping Health and Safety legislation, including the Code of Safe Working Practices for Merchant Seamen, and the main elements of risk assessment.
(c) Knowledge of the relevant IMO Conventions concerning SOLAS and protection of the marine environment.
(d) Crew agreements, the Official Log Book and the law relating to entries, inspection of living quarters and storerooms, complaints procedure.
(e) Reports required by the Marine Accident Investigation Branch (MAIB).
(f) Load-line marks – entries and reports in respect of freeboard, draft and allowances.
(g) The requirements of the regulations concerning life-saving and fire-fighting appliances.
(h) Application of hours of work and rest legislation.
(i) The law relating to the reporting of dangers to navigation.
(j) A knowledge of the Master's obligations with respect to pilotage.
(k) Purpose and application of the International Safety Management (ISM) Code.
(l) Purpose of Flag State and Port State Control.

Appendix B: The Merchant Shipping – Regulations for the Prevention of Collisions at Sea

(Distress Signals and Prevention of Collisions) Regulations 1996

(to include all amendments effective from November 2003)

TABLE OF CONTENTS OF THE INTERNATIONAL REGULATIONS

PART A: GENERAL

Rule 1: Application
(a) These Rules shall apply to all vessels upon the high seas and in all waters connected therewith navigable by seagoing vessels.
(b) Nothing in these Rules shall interfere with the operation of special rules made by an appropriate authority for roadstead, harbours, rivers, lakes or inland waterways connected with the high seas and navigable by seagoing vessels. Such special rules shall conform as closely as possible to these Rules.

(c) Nothing in these Rules shall interfere with the operation of any special rules
     made by the Government of any State with respect to additional station or
     signal lights, shapes or whistle signals for ships or war and vessels proceedings
     under convoy, or with respect to additional station or signal lights, shapes or
     whistle signals shall, so far as possible, be such that they cannot be mistaken
     for any light, shape or signal authorised elsewhere under these Rules.
(d) Traffic separation schemes may be adopted by the organisation for the
     purpose of these Rules.
(e) Whenever the Government concerned shall have determined that a vessel of
     any special construction or purpose cannot comply with the provision of any
     of these Rules with respect to the number, position, range or arc of visibility
     of lights or shapes, as well as to the disposition and characteristics of
     sound-signalling appliances, such vessel shall comply with such other
     provisions in regard to the number, position, range or arc of visibility of
     lights or shapes, as well as to the disposition and characteristics of sound-
     signalling appliances, as her Government shall have determined to be the
     closest possible compliance with the Rules in respect of that vessel.

Rule 2: Responsibility

(a) Nothing in these Rules shall exonerate any vessel, or the owner, master or
     crew thereof, from the consequences of any neglect to comply with these
     Rules or the neglect of any precaution which may be required by the ordin-
     ary practice of seamen, or by the special circumstances of the case.
(b) In construing and complying with these Rules due regard shall be had to all
     dangers of navigation and collision and to any special circumstances, includ-
     ing the limitations of the vessels involved which may make a departure from
     these Rules necessary to avoid immediate danger.

Rule 3: General Definitions

For the purpose of these Rules, except where the context otherwise requires:

(a) The word 'vessel' includes every description of water craft, including non-
     displacement craft and seaplanes, used or capable of being used as a means
     of transportation on water.
(b) The term 'power-driven vessel' means any vessel propelled by machinery.
(c) The term 'sailing vessel' means any vessel under sail provided that propelling
     machinery, if fitted, is not being used.
(d) The term 'vessel engaged in fishing' means any vessel fishing with nets, lines,
     trawls or the fishing apparatus which restrict manoeuvrability, but does not
     include a vessel fishing with trolling lines or other fishing apparatus which
     do not restrict manoeuvrability.
(e) The word 'seaplane' includes any aircraft designed to manoeuvre on the water.
(f) The term 'vessel not under command' means a vessel which through some
     exceptional circumstances is unable to manoeuvre as required by these Rules
     and is therefore unable to keep out of the way of another vessel.
(g) The term 'vessel restricted in her ability to manoeuvre' means a vessel which
     from the nature of the work is restricted in her ability to manoeuvre as
     required by these Rules and is therefore unable to keep out of the way of

another vessel. The term 'vessels restricted in their ability to manoeuvre' shall include but not be limited to:

(i)   a vessel engaged in laying, servicing or picking up a navigation mark, submarine cable or pipeline;
(ii) a vessel engaged in dredging, surveying or underwater operations;
(iii) a vessel engaged in replenishment or transferring persons, provisions or cargo while underway;
(iv) a vessel engaged in the launching or recovery of aircraft;
(v)   a vessel engaged in mine clearance operations;
(vi) a vessel engaged in towing operation such as severely restricts the towing vessel and her tow in their ability to deviate from their course.

(h) The term 'vessel constrained by her draught' means a power-driven vessel which, because of her draught in relation to the available depth and width of navigable water, is severely restricted in her ability to deviate from the course she is following.

(i) The word 'underway' means that a vessel is not at anchor, or made fast to the shore, or aground.

(j) The words 'length' and 'breadth' of a vessel mean her length overall and greater breadth.

(k) Vessels shall be deemed to be in sight of one another only when one can be observed visually from the other.

(l) The term 'restricted visibility' means any condition in which visibility is restricted by fog, mist, falling snow, heavy rainstorms, sandstorms or any other similar causes.

PART B: STEERING AND SAILING RULES

Section I: Conduct of Vessels in Any Conditions of Visibility
Rule 4: Application

Rules in this section apply in any conditions of visibility.

Rule 5: Lookout

Every vessel shall at all times maintain a proper lookout by sight and hearing as well as by all available means appropriate in the prevailing circumstances and condition so as to make a full appraisal of the situation and of the risk of collision.

Rule 6: Safe speed

Every vessel shall at all times proceed at a safe speed so that she can take proper and effective action to avoid collision and be stopped within a distance appropriate to the prevailing circumstances and conditions.

In determining a safe speed the following factors shall be among those taken into account:

(a) By all vessel:
   (i)   the state of visibility;
   (ii) the traffic density including concentrations of fishing vessels or any other vessels;

    (iii) the manoeuvrability of the vessel with special reference to stopping distance and turning ability in the prevailing conditions;

    (iv) at night the presence of background light such as from shore lights or from back scatter of her own lights;

    (v) the state of wind, sea and current, and the proximity of navigational hazards;

    (vi) the draught in relation to the available depth of water.

(b) Additionally, by vessels with operational radar:

    (i) the characteristics, efficiency and limitations of the radar equipment;

    (ii) any constraints imposed by the radar range scale in use;

    (iii) the effect on radar detection of the sea state, weather and other sources of interference;

    (iv) the possibility that small vessels, ice and other floating objects may not be detected by radar at an adequate range;

    (v) the number, location and movement of vessels detected by radar;

    (vi) the more exact assessment of the visibility that may be possible when radar is used to determine the range of vessels or other objects in the vicinity.

Rule 7: Risk of Collision

(a) Every vessel shall use all available means appropriate to the prevailing circumstances and conditions to determine if risk of collision exits. If there is any doubt such risk shall be deemed to exist.

(b) Proper use shall be made of radar equipment if fitted and operational, including long-range scanning to obtain early warning of risk collision exists. If there is any doubt such risk shall be deemed to exist.

(c) Assumptions shall not be made on the bases of scanty information, especially scanty radar information.

(d) In determining if risk collision exists the following considerations shall be among those taken into account:

    (i) such risk shall be deemed to exist if the compass bearing of an approaching vessel does not appreciably change;

    (ii) such risk may sometimes exist even when an appreciable bearing change is evident, particularly when approaching a very large or a tow or when approaching a vessel at close range.

Rule 8: Action to Avoid Collision

(a) Any action taken to avoid collision, shall if the circumstances of the case admit, be positive, made in ample time and with due regard to the observance of good seamanship.

(b) Any alteration of course and/or speed to avoid collision shall, if the circumstances of the case admit, be large enough to be readily apparent to another vessel observing visually or by radar; a succession of small alterations of course and/or speed should be avoided.

(c) If there is sufficient sea room, alteration of course alone may be the most effective action to avoid a close-quarters situation provided that it is made in good time, is substantial and does not result in another close-quarters situation.

(d) Action taken to avoid collision with another vessel shall be such as to result in passing at a safe distance. The effectiveness of the action shall be carefully checked until the other vessel is finally past and clear.

(e) If necessary to avoid collision or allow more time to assess the situation, a vessel shall slacken her speed or take all way off by stopping or reversing her means of propulsion.

(f) (i)   A vessel which, by any of these Rules, is required not to impede the passage or safe passage of another vessel shall, when required by the circumstances of the case, take early action to allow sufficient sea room for the safe passage of the other vessel.

(ii) A vessel required not to impede the passage or safe passage of another vessel is not relieved of this obligation if approaching the other vessel so as to involve risk of collision and shall, when taking action, have full regard to the action which may be required by the Rules of this Part.

(iii) A vessel the passage of which is not to be impeded remains fully obliged to comply with the Rules of this Part when the two vessel are approaching one another so as to involve risk of collision.

Rule 9: Narrow Channels

(a) A vessel proceeding along the course of a narrow channel or fairway shall keep as near to the other limit of the channel or fairway which lies on her starboard side as is safe and practicable.

(b) A vessel of less than 20 m in length or a sailing vessel shall not impede the passage of a vessel which can safely navigate only within a narrow channel or fairway.

(c) A vessel engaged in fishing shall not impede the passage of any other vessel navigating within a narrow channel or fairway.

(d) A vessel shall not cross a narrow channel or fairway if such crossing impedes the passage of a vessel which can safely navigate only within such channel or fairway. The latter vessel may use the sound signal prescribed in Rule 34(d) if in doubt as to the intention of the crossing vessel.

(e) (i)   In a narrow channel or fairway when overtaking can take place only if the vessel to be overtaken has to take action to permit safe passing, the vessel intending to overtake shall indicate her intention by sounding the appropriate signal prescribed by Rule 34(c)(i). The vessel to be overtaken shall, if in agreement, sound the appropriate signal prescribed in Rule 34(c)(ii) and take steps to permit safe passing. If in doubt she may sound the signals prescribed in Rule 34(d).

(ii) This rule does not relieve the overtaking of her obligation under Rule 13.

(f) A vessel nearing a bend or an area of a narrow channel or fairway where other vessel may be obscured by an intervening obstruction shall navigate with particular alertness and caution and shall sound the appropriate signal prescribed in Rule 34(e).

(g) Any vessel shall, if the circumstances of the case admit, avoid anchoring in a narrow channel.

Rule 10: Traffic Separation Schemes

(a) This Rule applies to traffic separation schemes adopted by the organisation and does not relieve any vessel of her obligation under any other Rule.

(b) A vessel using a traffic separation scheme shall:
  (i)   proceed in the appropriate traffic lane in the general direction of traffic flow for that lane;
  (ii)   so far as practicable keep clear of a traffic separation line or separation zone;
  (iii) normally join or leave a traffic lane at the termination of the lane, but when joining or leaving from either side shall do so at as small an angle to the general direction of traffic flow as practicable.

(c) A vessel shall, so far as practicable, avoid crossing traffic lanes but if obliged to do so shall cross on a heading as nearly as practicable at right angles to the general direction of traffic flow.

(d) (i)   A vessel shall not use an inshore traffic zone when she can safely use the appropriate traffic lane within the adjacent traffic separation scheme. However, vessels of less than 20 m in length, sailing vessels and vessels engaged in fishing may use the inshore traffic zone.
  (ii)   Notwithstanding sub-paragraph (d)(i), a vessel may use an inshore traffic zone when en route to or from a port, offshore installation or structure, pilot station or any other place situated within the inshore traffic zone, or to avoid immediate danger.

(e) A vessel other than a crossing vessel or a vessel joining or leaving a lane shall not normally enter a separation zone or cross a separation line except:
  (i)   in cases of emergency to avoid immediate danger;
  (ii) to engage in fishing within a separation zone.

(f) A vessel navigating in areas near the terminations of traffic separation schemes shall do so with particular caution.

(g) A vessel shall so far as practicable avoid anchoring in a traffic separation scheme or in areas near its terminations.

(h) A vessel not using a traffic separation scheme shall avoid it by as wide a margin as is practicable.

(i) A vessel engaged in fishing shall not impede the passage of any vessel following a traffic lane.

(j) A vessel of less than 20 m in length or a sailing vessel shall not impede the safe passage of a power-driven vessel following a traffic lane.

(k) A vessel restricted in her ability to manoeuvre when engaged in an operation for the maintenance of safety of navigation in a traffic separation scheme is exempted from complying with this Rule to the extend necessary to carry out the operation.

(l) A vessel restricted in her ability to manoeuvre when engaged in an operation for the laying, servicing or picking up of a submarine cable, within a traffic separation scheme, is exempted from complying with this Rule to the extent necessary to carry out the operation.

Section II: Conduct of Vessel in Sight of One Another
Rule 11: Application

Rules in this Section apply to vessels in sight of one another.

Rule 12: Sailing Vessels

(a) When two sailing vessels are approaching one another, so as to involve risk of collision, one of them shall keep out of the way of the other as follows:
   (i) when each has the wind on a different side, the vessel which has the wind on the port side shall keep out of the way of the other;
   (ii) when both have the wind on the same side, the vessel which is to windward shall keep out of the way of the vessel which is to leeward.
(b) For the purposes of this Rule the windward side shall be deemed to be the side opposite to that on which the mainsail is carried or, in the case of a square-rigged vessel, the side opposite to that on which the largest fore and aft sail is carried.

Rule 13: Overtaking

(a) Notwithstanding anything contained in the Rules of Part B, Sections I and II, any vessel overtaking any other shall keep out of the way of the vessel being overtaken.
(b) A vessel shall be deemed to be overtaking when coming up with another vessel from a direction more than 22.5° abaft her beam, i.e. in such a position with reference to the vessel she is overtaking, that at night she would be able to see only the sternlight of that vessel but neither of her sidelights.
(c) When a vessel is in any doubt as to whether she is overtaking another, she shall assume that this is the case and act accordingly.
(d) Any subsequent alteration of the bearing between the two vessels shall not make the overtaking vessel a crossing vessel within the meaning of these Rules or relieve her of the duty of keeping clear of the overtaken vessel until she is finally past and clear.

Rule 14: Head-On Situation

(a) When two power-driven vessels are meeting on reciprocal or nearly reciprocal courses so as to involve risk of collision each shall alter her course to starboard so that each shall pass on the port side of the other.
(b) Such a situation shall be deemed to exist when a vessel sees the other ahead or nearly ahead and by night she would see the mast head lights of the other in a line or nearly in a line and/or both sidelights and by day she observes the corresponding aspect of the other vessel.
(c) When a vessel is in any doubt as to whether such a situation exists she shall assume that is does exist and act accordingly.

Rule 15: Crossing Situation

When two power-driven vessels are crossing so as to involve risk of collision, the vessel which has the other on her own starboard side shall keep out of the way and shall, if the circumstances of the case admit, avoid crossing ahead of the other vessel.

Rule 16: Action by Give-Way Vessel

Every vessel which is directed to keep out of the way of another vessel shall, so far as possible, take early and substantial action to keep well clear.

Rule 17: Action by Stand-On Vessel

(a) (i)   Where one of two vessels is to keep out of the way the other shall keep her course and speed.
     (ii) The latter vessel may however take action to avoid collision by her manoeuvre alone, as soon as it becomes apparent to her that the vessel required to keep out of the way is not taking appropriate action in compliance with these Rules.
(b) When, from any cause, the vessel required to keep her course and speed finds herself so close that collision cannot be avoided by the action of the give-way vessel alone, she shall take such action as will best aid to avoid collision.
(c) A power-driven vessel which takes action in a crossing situation in accordance with sub-paragraph (a)(ii) of this Rule to avoid collision with another power-driven vessel shall, if the circumstances of the case admit, not alter course to port for a vessel on her own port side.
(d) This Rule does not relieve the give-way vessel of her obligation to keep out of the way.

Rule 18: Responsibilities between Vessels

Except where Rules 9, 10 and 13 otherwise require:

(a) A power-driven vessel underway shall keep out of the way of:
     (i)   a vessel not under command;
     (ii)   a vessel restricted in her ability to manoeuvre;
     (iii) a vessel engaged in fishing;
     (iv)   a sailing vessel.
(b) A sailing vessel underway shall keep out of the way of:
     (i)   a vessel not under command;
     (ii)   a vessel restricted in her ability to manoeuvre;
     (iii) a vessel engaged in fishing.
(c) A vessel engaged in fishing when underway shall, so far as possible, keep out of the way of:
     (i)   a vessel not under command;
     (ii)   a vessel restricted in her ability to manoeuvre.
(d) (i)   Any vessel other than a vessel not under command or a vessel restricted in her ability to manoeuvre shall, if the circumstances of the case admit, avoid impeding the safe passage of a vessel constrained by her draught, exhibiting the signals in Rule 28.
     (ii)   A vessel constrained by her draught shall navigate with particular caution having full regard to her special condition.
(e) A seaplane on the water shall, in general, keep well clear of all vessel and avoid impeding their navigation. In circumstances, however, where risk of collision exists, she shall comply with the Rules of this Part.

Section III: Conduct of Vessels in Restricted Visibility
Rule 19: Conduct of Vessels in Restricted Visibility

(a) This Rule applies to vessels not in sight of one another when navigating in or near an area of restricted visibility.

(b) Every vessel shall proceed at a safe speed adapted to the prevailing circumstances and condition of restricted visibility. A power-driven vessel shall have her engines ready for immediate manoeuvre.

(c) Every vessel shall have due regard to the prevailing circumstances and conditions of restricted visibility when complying with the Rules of Section I of this Part.

(d) A vessel which detects by radar alone, the presence of another vessel, shall determine if a close-quarters situation is developing and/or risk of collision exists. If so, she shall take avoiding action in ample time, provided that when such action consists of an alteration of course, so far as possible the following shall be avoided:

(i) an alteration of course to port for a vessel forward of the beam, other than for a vessel being overtaken;

(ii) an alteration of course towards a vessel abeam or abaft the beam.

(e) Except where it has been determined that a risk of collision does not exist, every vessel which hears apparently forward of her beam the fog signal of another vessel, or which cannot avoid a close-quarters situation with another vessel forward of her beam, shall reduce her speed to the minimum at which she can be kept on her course. She shall if necessary take all her way off and in any event navigate with extreme caution until danger of collision is over.

PART C: LIGHTS AND SHAPES

Rule 20: Application

(a) Rules in this Part shall be complied with in all weathers.

(b) The Rules concerning lights shall be complied with from sunset to sunrise and during such times no other lights shall be exhibited, except such lights as cannot be mistaken for the lights specified in these Rules or do not impair their visibility or distinctive character, or interfere with the keeping of a proper lookout.

(c) The lights prescribed by these Rules shall, if carried, also be exhibited from sunrise to sunset in restricted visibility and may be exhibited in all other circumstances when it is deemed necessary.

(d) The Rules concerning shapes shall be complied with by day.

(e) The lights and shapes specified in these Rules shall comply with the provisions of Annex I to these Regulations.

Rule 21: Definitions

(a) 'Masthead light' means a white light placed over the fore and aft centreline of the vessel showing an unbroken light over an arc of the horizon of $225°$ and so fixed as to show the light from right ahead to $22.5°$ abaft the beam on either side of the vessel.

(b) 'Sidelights' means a green light on the starboard side and a red light on the port side each showing an unbroken light over an arc of the horizon of 112.5° and so fixed as to show the light from the right ahead to 22.5° abaft the beam on its respective side. In a vessel of less than 20 m in length the sidelights may be combined in one lantern carried on the fore and aft centreline of the vessel.

(c) 'Sternlight' means a white light placed as nearly as practicable at the stern showing an unbroken light over an arc of the horizon of 135° and so fixed as to show the light 67.5° from right aft on each side of the vessel.

(d) 'Towing light' means a yellow light having the same characteristics as the 'sternlight' defined in paragraph (c) of this Rule.

(e) 'All-round light' means a light showing an unbroken light over an arc of the horizon of 360°.

(f) 'Flashing light' means a light flashing at regular intervals at a frequency of 120 flashes or more per minute.

Rule 22: Visibility of Lights

The lights prescribed in these Rules shall have an intensity as specified in Section 8 of Annex I to these Regulations so as to be visible at the following minimum ranges:

(a) In vessels of 50 m or more in length:
    (i)   a masthead light, 6 miles;
    (ii)   a sidelight, 3 miles;
    (iii) a sternlight, 3 miles;
    (iv) a towing light, 3 miles;
    (v)   a white, red, green or yellow all-round light, 3 miles.

(b) In vessels of 12 m or more in length but less than 50 m in length:
    (i)   a masthead light, 5 miles; except that where the length of the vessel is less than 20 m, 3 miles;
    (ii)   a sidelight, 2 miles;
    (iii) a sternlight, 2 miles;
    (iv) a towing light, 2 miles;
    (v)   a white, red, green or yellow all-round light, 2 miles.

(c) In vessels of less than 12 m in length:
    (i)   a masthead light, 2 miles;
    (ii)   a sidelight, 1 mile;
    (iii) a sternlight, 2 miles;
    (iv) a towing light, 2 miles;
    (v)   a white, red, green or yellow all-round light, 2 miles.

(d) In inconspicuous, partly submerged vessel or objects being towed:
    (i)   a white all-round light, 3 miles.

Rule 23: Power-Driven Vessels Underway

(a) A power-driven vessel underway shall exhibit:
    (i)   a masthead light forward;
    (ii)   a second masthead light abaft of and higher than the forward one; except that a vessel of less than 50 m in length shall not be obliged to exhibit such light by may do so;

(iii) sidelights;

(iv) a sternlight.

(b) An air-cushion vessel when operating in the non-displacement mode shall, in addition to the light prescribed in paragraph (a) of this Rule, exhibit an all-round flashing yellow light.

(c) (i) A power-driven vessel of less than 12 m in length may in lieu of the lights prescribed in paragraph (a) of this Rule exhibit an all-round white light and sidelights;

(ii) A power-driven vessel of less than 7 m in length whose maximum speed does not exceed 7 knots may in lieu of the lights prescribed in paragraph (a) of this Rule exhibit an all-round white light and shall, if practicable, also exhibit sidelights;

(iii) The masthead light or all-round white light on a power-driven vessel of less than 12 m in length may be displaced from the fore and aft centreline of the vessel if centreline fitting is not practicable, provided that the sidelights are combined in one lantern which shall be carried on the fore and aft centreline of the vessel or located as nearly as practicable in the same fore and aft line as the masthead light or the all-round white light.

Rule 24: Towing and Pushing

(a) A power-driven vessel when towing shall exhibit:

(i) instead of the light prescribed in Rule 23(a)(i) or (a)(ii) two masthead lights in a vertical line. When the length of the tow, measuring from the stern of the towing vessel to the aft end of the tow exceeds 200 m, three such lights in a vertical line;

(ii) sidelights;

(iii) a sternlight;

(iv) a towing light in a vertical line above the sternlight;

(v) when the length of the tow exceeds 200 m, a diamond shape where it can best be seen.

(b) When a pushing vessel and a vessel being pushed ahead are rigidly connected in a composite unit they shall be regarded as a power-driven vessel and exhibit the lights prescribed in Rules 23.

(c) A power-driven vessel when pushing ahead or towing alongside, except in the case of a composite unit, shall exhibit:

(i) instead of the light prescribed in Rule 23(a)(i) or (a)(ii), two masthead lights in a vertical line;

(ii) sidelights;

(iii) a sternlight.

(d) A power-driven vessel to which paragraph (a) or (c) of this Rule applies shall also comply with Rule 23(a)(ii).

(e) A vessel or object being towed, other than those mentioned in paragraph (g) of this Rule, shall exhibit:

(i) sidelights;

(ii) a sternlight;

(iii) when the length of the tow exceeds 200 m, a diamond shape where it can best be seen.

(f) Provided that any number of vessels being towed alongside or pushed in a group shall be lighted as one vessel,
  (i) a vessel being pushed ahead, not being part of a composite unit, shall exhibit at the forward end sidelights;
  (ii) a vessel being towed alongside shall exhibit a sternlight and at the forward end, sidelights.
(g) An inconspicuous, partly submerged vessel or object, or combination of such vessel or objects being towed, shall exhibit:
  (i) if it is less than 25 m in breadth, one all-round white light at or near the forward end and one at or near the after end except that dracones need not exhibit a light at or near the forward end;
  (ii) if it is 25 m or more in breadth, two additional all-round white lights at or near the extremities of its breadth;
  (iii) if it exceeds 100 m in length, additional all-round white lights between the lights prescribed in sub-paragraphs (i) and (ii) so that the distance between the lights shall not exceed 100 m;
  (iv) a diamond shape at or near the aftermost extremity of the last vessel or object being towed and if the length of the tow exceeds 200 m an additional diamond shape where it can best be seen and located as far forward as is practicable.
(h) Where from any sufficient cause it is impracticable for a vessel or object towed to exhibit the lights or shapes prescribed in paragraph (e) or (g) of this Rule, all possible measures shall be taken to light the vessel or object towed or at least to indicate the presence of such vessel or object.
(i) Where from any sufficient cause it is impracticable for a vessel not normally engaged in towing operations to display the lights prescribed in paragraph (a) or (c) of this Rule, such vessel shall not be required to exhibit those lights when engaged in towing another vessel in distress or otherwise in need of assistance. All possible measures shall be taken to indicate the nature of the relationship between the towing vessel and the vessel being towed as authorised by Rule 36; in particular by illuminating the towline.

Rule 25: Sailing Vessels Underway and Vessels Under Oars

(a) A sailing vessel underway shall exhibit:
  (i) sidelights;
  (ii) a sternlight.
(b) In a sailing vessel of less than 20 m in length the lights prescribed in paragraph (a) of this Rule may be combined in one lantern carried at or near the top of the mast where it can best be seen.
(c) A sailing vessel underway may, in addition to the lights prescribed in paragraph (a) of this Rule, exhibit at or near the top of the mast, where they can best be seen, two all-round lights in a vertical line, the upper being red and the lower green, but these lights shall not be exhibited in conjunction with the combined lantern permitted by paragraph (b) of this Rule.
(d) (i) A sailing vessel of less than 7 m in length shall, if practicable, exhibit the lights prescribed in paragraph (a) or (b) of this Rule, but if she does not, she shall have ready at hand an electric torch or lighted lantern

showing a white light which shall be exhibited in sufficient time to prevent collision.

(ii) A vessel under oars may exhibit the lights prescribed in this Rule for sailing vessels, but if she does not, she shall have ready at hand an electric torch or lighted lantern showing a white light which shall be exhibited in sufficient time to prevent collision.

(e) A vessel proceeding under sail when also being propelled by machinery shall exhibit forward where it can best be seen a conical shape, apex downwards.

Rule 26: Fishing Vessels

(a) A vessel engaged in fishing, whether underway or at anchor, shall exhibit only the lights and shapes prescribed in this Rule.

(b) A vessel when engaged in trawling, by which is meant the dragging through the water of a dredge net or other apparatus used as a fishing appliance, shall exhibit:

    (i) two all-round lights in a vertical line, the upper being green and the lower white, or a shape consisting of two cones with their apexes together in a vertical line one above the other;

    (ii) a masthead light abaft of and higher than the all-round green light; a vessel of less than 50 m in length shall not be obliged to exhibit such a light but may do so;

    (iii) when making way through the water, in addition to the lights prescribed in this paragraph, sidelights and a sternlight.

(c) A vessel engaged in fishing, other than trawling, shall exhibit:

    (i) two all-round lights in a vertical line, the upper being red and the lower white, or a shape consisting of two cones with apexes together in a vertical line one above the other;

    (ii) when there is outlying gear extending more than 150 m horizontally from the vessel, an all-round white light or a cone apex upwards in the direction of the gear;

    (iii) when making way through the water, in addition to the lights prescribed in this paragraph sidelights and a sternlight.

(d) The additional signals described in Annex II to these Regulations apply to a vessel engaged in fishing in close proximity to other vessel engaged in fishing.

(e) A vessel when not engaged in fishing shall not exhibit the lights or shapes prescribed in this Rule, but only those prescribed for a vessel of her length.

Rule 27: Vessels Not Under Command or Restricted in Their Ability to Manoeuvre

(a) A vessel not under command shall exhibit:

    (i) two all-round red lights in a vertical line where they can best be seen;

    (ii) two balls or similar shape in a vertical line where they can best be seen;

    (iii) when making way through the water, in addition to the lights prescribed in this paragraph sidelights and a starlight.

(b) A vessel restricted in her ability to manoeuvre, except a vessel engaged in mine-clearance operations, shall exhibit:

    (i)   three all-round lights in a vertical line where they can best be seen. The highest and lowest of these lights shall be red and the middle light shall be white;

    (ii) three shapes in a vertical line where they can best be seen. The highest and lowest of these shapes shall be balls and the middle one a diamond;

    (iii) when making way through the water, a masthead light or lights, side-lights and a sternlight, in addition to the lights prescribed in sub-paragraph (i);

    (iv) when at anchor, in addition to the lights or shapes prescribed in sub-paragraphs (i) and (ii), the light, lights or shape prescribed in Rule 30.

(c) A power-driven vessel engaged in a towing operation such as severely restricts the towing vessel and her tow in their ability to deviate from their course shall, in addition to the lights or shapes prescribed in Rule 24(a), exhibit the lights or shapes prescribed in sub-paragraphs (b)(i) and (ii) of this Rule.

(d) A vessel engaged in dredging or underwater operations, when restricted in her ability to manoeuvre, shall exhibit the lights and shapes prescribed in sub-paragraphs (b)(i), (ii) and (iii) of this Rule and shall in addition, when an obstruction exists, exhibit:

    (i)   two all-round red lights or two balls in a vertical line to indicate the side on which the obstruction exists;

    (ii) two all-round green lights or two diamonds in a vertical line to indicate the side on which another vessel may pass;

    (iii) when at anchor, the lights or shapes prescribed in this paragraph instead of the lights or shape prescribed in Rule 30.

(e) Whenever the size of a vessel engaged in diving operations makes it imprac-ticable to exhibit all lights and shapes prescribed in paragraph (d) of this Rule, the following shall be exhibited:

    (i)   three all-round lights in a vertical line where they can best be seen. The highest and lowest of these lights shall be red and the middle light shall be white;

    (ii) a rigid replica of the International Code flag 'A' not less than 1 m in height. Measures shall be taken to ensure its all-round visibility.

(f) A vessel engaged in mine-clearance operations shall in addition to the lights prescribed for a power-driven vessel in Rule 23 or the lights or shape pre-scribed for a vessel at anchor in Rule 30 as appropriate, exhibit three all-round green lights or three balls. One of these lights or shapes shall be exhibited near the foremast head and one at each end of the fore yard. These lights or shapes indicate that it is dangerous for another vessel to approach within 1000 m of the mine clearance vessel.

(g) Vessels of less than 12 m in length, except those engaged in diving opera-tions, shall not be required to exhibit the lights and shapes prescribed in this Rule.

(h) The signals prescribed in this Rule are not signals of vessels in distress and requiring assistance. Such signals are contained in Annex IV to these Regulations.

Rule 28: Vessels Constrained by Their Draught

A vessel constrained by her draught may, in addition to the lights prescribed for power-driven vessels in Rule 23, exhibit where they can best be seen three all-round red lights in a vertical line, or a cylinder.

Rule 29: Pilot Vessels

(a) A vessel engaged on pilotage duty shall exhibit:
- (i) At or near the masthead, two all-round lights in a vertical line, the upper being white and the lower red;
- (ii) when underway, in addition, sidelights and a starlight;
- (iii) when at anchor, in addition to the lights prescribed in sub-paragraph (i), the light, lights or shape prescribed in Rule 30 for vessels at anchor.

(b) A pilot vessel when not engaged in pilotage duty shall exhibit the lights or shapes prescribed for a similar vessel of her length.

Rule 30: Anchored Vessels and Vessels Aground

(a) A vessel at anchor shall exhibit where it can best be seen:
- (i) in the fore part, an all-round white light or one ball;
- (ii) at or near the stern and at a lower level than the light prescribed in sub-paragraph (i), an all-round white light.

(b) A vessel of less than 50 m in length may exhibit an all-round white light where it can best be seen instead of the lights prescribed in paragraph (a) of this Rule.

(c) A vessel at anchor may, and a vessel of 100 m and more in length shall, also use the available working or equivalent lights to illuminate her decks.

(d) A vessel aground shall exhibit the lights prescribed in paragraphs (a) or (b) of this Rule and in addition, where they can best be seen:
- (i) two all-round red lights in a vertical line;
- (ii) three balls in a vertical line.

(e) A vessel of less than 7 m in length, when at anchor, not in or near a narrow channel, fairway or anchorage, or where other vessel normally navigate, shall not be required to exhibit the lights or shape prescribed in paragraphs (a) and (b) of this Rule.

(f) A vessel of less than 12 m in length, when aground, shall not be required to exhibit the lights or shapes prescribed in sub-paragraphs (d)(i) and (ii) of this Rule.

Rule 31: Seaplanes

Where it is impracticable for a seaplane to exhibit lights and shapes of the characteristics or in the positions prescribed in the Rules of this Part she shall exhibit lights and shapes as closely similar in characteristics and position as is possible.

PART D: SOUND AND LIGHT SIGNALS

Rule 32: Definitions

(a) The word 'whistle' means any sound signalling appliance capable of produc-
     ing the prescribed blasts and which complies with the specifications in
     Annex III to these Regulations.
(b) The term 'short blast' means a blast of about 1 second's duration.
(c) The term 'prolonged blast' means a blast of from 4 to 6 second's duration.

Rule 33: Equipment for Sound Signals

(a) A vessel of 12 m or more in length shall be provided with a whistle and a
     bell and a vessel of 100 m or more in length shall, in addition, be provided
     with a gong, the tone and sound of which cannot be confused with that of
     the bell. The whistle, bell and gong shall comply with the specification in
     Annex III to these Regulations. The bell or gong or both may be replaced
     by other equipment having the same respective sound characteristics,
     provided that manual sounding of the prescribed signals shall always be
     possible.
(b) A vessel of less than 12 m in length shall not be obliged to carry the sound
     signalling appliances prescribed in paragraph (a) of this Rule but if she does
     not, she shall be provided with some other means of making an efficient
     sound signal.

Rule 34: Manoeuvring and Warning Signals

(a) When vessels are in sight of one another, a power-driven vessel underway,
     when manoeuvring as authorised or required by these Rules, shall indicate
     that manoeuvre by the following signals on her whistle:
     (i)   one short blast to mean 'I am altering my course to starboard';
     (ii)   two short blasts to mean 'I am altering my course to port';
     (iii) three short blasts to mean 'I am operating astern propulsion'.
(b) Any vessel may supplement the whistle signals prescribed in paragraph (a) of
     this Rule by light signals, repeated as appropriate, whilst the manoeuvre is
     being carried out:
     (i)   these light signals shall have the following significance:
            – one flash to mean 'I am altering my course to starboard';
            – two flashes to mean 'I am altering courts to port';
            – three flashes to mean 'I am operating astern propulsion';
     (ii)   the duration of each flash shall be about 1 second, the interval between
            flashes shall be about 1 second, and the interval between successive sig-
            nals shall be not less than 10 seconds;
     (iii) the light used for this signal shall, if fitted, be an all-round white light,
            visible at a minimum range of 5 miles, and shall comply with the provi-
            sions of Annex I to these Regulations.
(c) When in sight of one another in a narrow channel or fairway:
     (i) a vessel intending to overtake another shall in compliance with Rule 9(e)(i)
         indicate her intention by the following signals on her whistle.

- two prolonged blasts followed by one short blast to mean 'I intend to overtake you on your starboard side';
- two prolonged blasts followed by two short blasts to mean 'I intend to overtake you on your port side'.

(ii) the vessel about to be overtaken when acting in accordance with Rule 9(e)(i) shall indicate her agreement by the following signal on her whistle:
- one prolonged, one short, one prolonged and one short blast, in that order.

(d) When vessels in sight of one another are approaching each other and from any case either vessel fails to understand the intentions or actions of the other, or is in doubt whether sufficient action is being taken by the other to avoid collision, the vessel in doubt shall immediately indicate such doubt by giving at least five short and rapid blasts on the whistle. Such signals may be supplemented by a light signal of at least five short and rapid flashes.

(e) A vessel nearing a bend or an area of a channel or fairway where other vessel may be obscured by an intervening obstruction shall sound one prolonged blast. Such signal shall be answered with a prolonged blast by any approaching vessel that may be within hearing around the bend or behind the intervening obstruction.

(f) If whistles are fitted on a vessel at a distance apart of more than 100 m, one whistle only shall be used for giving manoeuvring and warning signals.

Rule 35: Sound Signals in Restricted Visibility

In or near an area of restricted visibility, whether by day or night, the signals prescribed in this Rule shall be used as follows:

(a) A power-driven vessel making way through the water shall sound at intervals of not more than 2 minutes on prolonged blast.

(b) A power-driven vessel underway but stopped and making no way through the water shall sound at intervals of not more than 2 minutes two prolonged blasts in succession with an interval of about 2 seconds between them.

(c) A vessel under command, a vessel restricted in her ability to manoeuvre, a vessel constrained by her draught, a sailing vessel, a vessel engaged in fishing and a vessel engaged in towing or pushing another vessel shall, instead of the signals prescribed in paragraph (a) or (b) of this Rule, sound at intervals of not more than 2 minutes three blasts in succession, namely one prolonged followed by two short blasts.

(d) A vessel engaged in fishing, when at anchor, and a vessel restricted in her ability to manoeuvre when carrying out her work at anchor, shall instead of the signals prescribed in paragraph (g) of this Rule sound the signal prescribed in paragraph (c) of this Rule.

(e) A vessel towed or if more than one vessel is towed the last vessel of the tow, if manned, shall at intervals of not more than 2 minutes sound four blasts in succession, namely one prolonged followed by three short blasts. When practicable, this signal shall be made immediately after the signal made by the towing vessel.

(f) When a pushing vessel and a vessel being pushed ahead are rigidly connected in a composite unit they shall be regarded as a power-driven vessel and shall give the signals prescribed in paragraph (a) or (b) of this Rule.

(g) A vessel at anchor shall at intervals of not more than one minute ring the bell rapidly for about 5 seconds. In a vessel of 100 m or more in length the bell shall be sounded in the forepart of the vessel and immediately after the ringing of the bell the gong shall be sounded rapidly for about 5 seconds in the after part of the vessel. A vessel at anchor may in addition sound three blasts in succession, namely one short, one prolonged and one short blast, to give warning of her position and of the possibility of collision to an approaching vessel.

(h) A vessel aground shall give the bell signal and if required the gong signal prescribed in paragraph (g) of this Rule and shall, in addition, give three separate distinct strokes on the bell immediately before and after the rapid ringing of the bell. A vessel aground may in addition sound an appropriate whistle signal.

(i) A vessel of less than 12 m in length shall not be obliged to give the above-mentioned signals but, if she does not, shall make some other efficient sound signal at intervals of not more than 2 minutes.

(j) A pilot vessel when engaged on pilotage duty may in addition to the signals prescribed in paragraph (a), (b) or (g) of this Rule sound an identity signal consisting of four short blasts.

Rule 36: Signals to Attract Attention

If necessary to attract the attention of another vessel any vessel may make light or sound signals that cannot be mistaken for any signal authorised elsewhere in these Rules, or may direct the beam of her searchlight in the direction of the danger, in such a way as not to embarrass any vessel. Any light to attract the attention of another vessel shall be such that it cannot be mistaken for any aid to navigation. For the purpose of this Rule the use of high-intensity intermittent or revolving lights, such as strobe lights, shall be avoided.

Rule 37: Distress Signals

When a vessel is in distress and requires assistance she shall use or exhibit the signals described in Annex IV to these Regulations.

PART E: EXEMPTIONS

Rule 38: Exemptions

Any vessel (or class of vessels) provided that she complies with the requirements of the International Regulations for Preventing Collisions at Sea, 1960 (a), the keel of which is laid or which is at a corresponding stage of construction before the entry into force of these Regulations may be exempted from compliance therewith as follows:

(a) The installation of lights with ranges prescribed in Rule 22, until 4 years after the date of entry into force of these Regulations.

(b) The installation of lights with colour specification as prescribed in Section 7 of Annex I to these Regulations, until 4 years after the date of entry into force of these Regulations.

(c) The repositioning of lights as a result of conversion from imperial to metric units and rounding off measurement figures, permanent exemption.

(d) (i) The repositioning of masthead lights on vessels of less than 150 m in length, resulting from the prescriptions of Section 3(a) of Annex I to these Regulations, permanent exemption.

   (ii) The repositioning of masthead lights on vessels of 150 m or more in length, resulting from the prescriptions of Section 3(a) of Annex I to these Regulations, until 9 years after the date of entry into force of these Regulations.

(e) The repositioning of masthead lights resulting from the prescriptions of Section 2(b) of Annex I to these Regulations, until 9 years after the date of entry into force of these Regulations.

(f) The repositioning of sidelights resulting from the prescriptions of Section 2(g) and 3(b) of Annex I to these Regulations, until 9 years after the date of entry into force of these Regulations.

(g) The requirements for sound signal appliances prescribed by Annex III to these Regulations, until 9 years after the date of entry into force of these Regulations.

(h) The repositioning of all-round lights resulting from the prescription of Section 9(b) of Annex I to these Regulations, permanent exemption.

ANNEX I: POSITIONING AND TECHNICAL DETAILS OF LIGHTS AND SHAPES

1 Definition
The term 'height above the hull' means height above the uppermost continuous deck. This height shall be measured from the position vertically beneath the location of the light.

2 Vertical Positioning and Spacing of Lights
(a) On a power-driven vessel of 20 m or more in length the masthead lights shall be placed as follows:
   (i) the forward masthead light, or if only one masthead light is carried, then the light, at a height above the hull of not less than 6 m, and, if the breadth of the vessel exceeds 6 m, then at a height above the hull not less than such breadth, so however that the light need not be placed at a greater height above the hull than 12 m;
   (ii) when two masthead lights are carried the after one shall be at least 4.5 m vertically higher than the forward one.

(b) The vertical separation of the masthead lights of power-driven vessels shall be such that in all normal conditions of trim after light will be seen over and separate from the forward light at a distance of 1000 m from the stern when viewed from sea-level.

(c) The masthead light of a power-driven vessel of 12 m but less than 20 m in length shall be placed at a height above the gunwale of not less than 2.5 m.

(d) A power-driven vessel of less than 12 m in length may carry the uppermost light at a height of less than 2.5 m above the gunwale. When however a masthead light is carried in addition to sidelights and a sternlight or the all-round light prescribed in Rule 23(c)(i) is carried in addition to sidelights, then such masthead light or all-round light shall be carried at least 1 m higher than the sidelights.

(e) One of the two or three masthead lights prescribed for a power-driven vessel when engaged in towing or pushing another vessel shall be placed in the same position as either the forward masthead light of the after masthead light; provided that, if carried on the after mast, the lowest after masthead light shall be at least 4.5 m vertically higher than the forward masthead light.

(f) (i) The masthead light or lights prescribed in Rule 23(a) shall be so placed as to be above and clear of all other lights and obstructions except as described in sub-paragraph (ii).

  (ii) When it is impracticable to carry the all-round lights prescribed by Rule 27(B)(i) or Rule 28 below the masthead lights, they may be carried above the after masthead light(s) or vertically in between the forward masthead light(s) and the after masthead light(s) provided that in the latter case the requirement of Section 3(c) of this annex shall be complied with.

(g) The sidelights of a power-driven vessel shall be placed at a height above the hull not greater than three quarters of that of the forward masthead light. They shall not be so low as to be interfered with by deck lights.

(h) The sidelights, if in a combined lantern and carried on a power-driven vessel of less than 20 m in length, shall be placed not less than 1 m below the masthead light.

(i) When the Rules prescribe two or three lights to be carried in a vertical line, they shall be spaced as follows:

  (i) on a vessel of 20 m in length or more such lights shall be spaced not less than 2 m apart, and the lowest of these lights shall, except where a towing light is required, be placed at a height of not less then 4 m above the hull;

  (ii) on a vessel of less than 20 m in length such lights shall be spaced not less than 1 m apart and the lowest of these lights shall, except where a towing light is required, be placed at a height of not less than 2 m above the gunwale;

  (iii) when the three lights are carried they shall be equally spaced.

(j) The lower of the two all-round lights prescribed for a vessel when engaged in fishing shall be at a height above the sidelights not less than twice the distance between the two vertical lines.

(k) The forward anchor light prescribed in Rule 30(a)(i), when two are carried, shall not be less than 4.5 m above the after one. On a vessel of 50 m or more in length this forward anchor light shall be placed at a height of not less than 6 m above the hull.

3 Horizontal Positioning and Spacing of Lights

(a) When two masthead lights are prescribed for a power-driven vessel, the horizontal distance between them shall not be less than one-half of the length but need not be more than 100 m. The forward light shall be placed not more than one-quarter of the length of the vessel from the stem.

(b) On a power-driven vessel of 20 m of more in length the sidelights shall not be placed in front of the forward masthead lights. They shall be placed at or near the side of the vessel.

(c) When the lights prescribed in Rule 27(b)(i) or Rule 28 are placed vertically between the forward masthead light(s) and the after masthead light(s) these all-round lights shall be placed at a horizontal distance of not less than 2 m from the fore and aft centreline of the vessel in the athwartship direction.

(d) When only one masthead light is prescribed for a power-driven vessel, this light shall be exhibited forward of amidships; except that a vessel of less than 20 m in length need not exhibit this light forward of amidships but shall exhibit it as far forward as is practicable.

4 Details of Location of Direction-Indicating Lights for Fishing Vessels, Dredgers and Vessels Engaged in Underwater Operations

(a) The light indicating the direction of the outlying gear from a vessel engaged in fishing as prescribed in Rule 26(c)(ii) shall be placed at a horizontal distance of not less than 2 m and not more than 6 m away from the two all-round red and white lights. This light shall be placed not higher than the all-round white light prescribed in Rule 26(c)(i) and not lower than the sidelights.

(b) The lights and shapes on a vessel engaged in dredging or underwater operations to indicate the obstructed side and/or the side on which it is safe to pass, as prescribed in Rule 27(d)(i) and (ii), shall be placed at the maximum practical horizontal distance, but in no case less than 2 m from the lights or shapes prescribed in Rule 27(b)(i) and (ii). In no case shall the upper of these lights or shapes be at a greater height than the lower of the three lights or shapes prescribed in Rule 27(b)(i) an d(ii).

5 Screens for Sidelights

The sidelights of vessels of 20 m or more in length shall be fitted with inboard screens painted matt black, and meeting the requirements of Section 9 of this annex. On vessels of less than 20 m in length the sidelights, if necessary to meet the requirements of Section 9 of this annex, shall be fitted with inboard matt black screens. With a combined lantern, using a single vertical filament and a very narrow division between the green and red sections, external screens need not be fitted.

6 Shapes

(a) Shapes shall be black and of the following sizes:
   (i)   a ball shall have a diameter of not less than 0.6 m;
   (ii)   a cone shall have a base diameter of not less than 0.6 m and a height equal to its diameter;
   (iii) a cylinder shall have a diameter of at least 0.6 m and a height of twice its diameter;
   (iv)   a diamond shape shall consist of two cones as defined in (ii) above having a common base.

(b) The vertical distance between shapes shall be at least 1.5 m.

(c) In a vessel of less than 20 m in length, shape of lesser dimensions but commensurate with the size of the vessel may be used and the distance apart may be correspondingly reduced.

7 Colour Specification of Lights

The chromaticity of all navigation lights shall conform to the following standards,
which lie within the boundaries of the area of the diagram specified for each
colour by the International Commission on Illumination (CIE). The boundaries of
the area for each colour are given by indicating the corner co-ordinates, which are
as follows:

(i)   White

| x | 0.525 | 0.525 | 0.452 | 0.310 | 0.310 | 0.443 |
| y | 0.382 | 0.440 | 0.440 | 0.348 | 0.283 | 0.382 |

(ii) Green

| x | 0.028 | 0.009 | 0.300 | 0.203 |
| y | 0.385 | 0.723 | 0.511 | 0.356 |

(iii) Red

| x | 0.680 | 0.660 | 0.735 | 0.721 |
| y | 0.320 | 0.320 | 0.265 | 0.259 |

(iv) Yellow

| x | 0.612 | 0.618 | 0.575 | 0.575 |
| y | 0.382 | 0.382 | 0.425 | 0.406 |

8 Intensity of Lights

(a)   The minimum luminous intensity of lights shall be calculated by using

$$I = 3.43 \times 10^6 \times T \times D^2 \times K^{-D}$$

where I is luminous intensity in candelas under service conditions, T is
threshold factor 2×10^{-7} lx, D is the range of visibility (luminous range) of
the light in nautical mile, K is the atmospheric transmissivity. For prescribed
lights the value of K shall be 0.8, corresponding to a meteorological visibility
of approximately 13 nautical miles.

(b)   A selection of figures derived from the formula is given in the following
table:

Range of visibility (luminous range) of light in nautical miles, D	Luminous intensity of light in candelas for $K = 0.8$, I
1	0.9
2	4.3
3	12
4	27
5	52
6	94

Note: The maximum luminous intensity of navigation lights should be
limited to avoid undue glare. This shall not be achieved by a variable
control of the luminous intensity

9 Horizontal Sectors

(a) (i)   In the forward direction, sidelights as fitted on the vessel shall show
the minimum required intensities. The intensities shall decrease to
reach practical cut-off between 1° and 3° outside the prescribed
sectors.

 (ii) For sternlights and masthead lights at 22.5° abaft the beam for sidelights, the minimum required intensities shall be maintained over the
arc of the horizon up to 5° within the limits of the sectors prescribed
in Rule 21. From 5° within the prescribed sectors the intensity may
decrease by 50 per cent up to the prescribed limits; it shall decrease
steadily to reach practical cut-off at nor more than 5° outside the prescribed sectors.

(b) (i)   All-round lights shall be so located as not to be obscured by masts, top-
masts or structures within angular sectors of more than 6°, except
anchor lights prescribed in Rule 30, which need not be place at an
impracticable height above the hull.

 (ii) If it is impracticable to comply with paragraph (b)(i) of this section by
exhibiting only one all-round light, two all-round lights shall be used
suitably positioned or screened so that they appear, as far as practicable,
as one light at a distance of 1 mile.

10 Vertical Sectors

(a) The vertical sectors of electric lights as fitted, with the exception of lights on
sailing vessel underway shall ensure that:

  (i)   least the required minimum intensity is maintained at all angles from 5°
above to 5° below the horizontal;

  (ii) at least 60 per cent of the required minimum intensity is maintained
from 7.5° above to 7.5° below the horizontal.

(b) In the case of sailing vessels underway the vertical sectors of electric lights as
fitted shall ensure that:

  (i)   least the minimum intensity is maintained at all angles from 5° above to
5° below the horizontal;

  (ii) at least 50 per cent of the required minimum intensity is maintained
from 25° above to 25° below the horizontal.

(c) In the case of lights other than electric these specifications shall be met as
closely as possible.

11 Intensity of Non-Electric Lights

Non-electric lights shall so far as practicable comply with the minimum intensities,
as specified in the table given in Section 8 of this annex.

12 Manoeuvring Light

Notwithstanding the provisions of paragraph 2(f) of this annex the manoeuvring light described in Rule 34(b) shall be placed in the same fore and aft vertical
plane as the masthead light or lights and, where practicable, at a minimum height
of 2 m vertically above the forward masthead light, provided that it shall be carried
not less than 2 m vertically above or below the after masthead light. On a vessel
where only one masthead light is carried the manoeuvring light, if fitted, shall be

carried where it can be seen, not less than 2 m vertically apart from the masthead light.

13 High Speed Craft

The masthead light of high speed craft with a length to breadth ratio of less than 3.0 may be placed at a height related to the breadth of the craft lower than that prescribed in paragraph 2(a)(i) of this annex, provided that the base angle of the isosceles triangles formed by the sidelights and masthead light, when seen in end elevation, is not less than 27°.

14 Approval

The construction of lights and shapes, and the installation of lights on board the vessel shall be to the satisfaction of the appropriate authority of the State whose flag the vessel is entitled to fly.

ANNEX II: ADDITIONAL SIGNALS FOR FISHING VESSELS FISHING IN CLOSE PROXIMITY

1 General

The lights mentioned herein shall, if exhibited in pursuance of Rule 26(d), be placed where they can best be seen. They shall be at least 0.9 m apart but at a lower level than lights prescribed in Rule 26(b)(i) and (c)(i). The lights shall be visible all round the horizon at a distance of at least 1 mile but at a lesser distance than the lights prescribed by these Rules for fishing vessels.

2 Signals for Trawlers

(a) Vessels of 20 m or more in length when engaged in trawling, whether using demersal or pelagic gear, shall exhibit:
  (i)   when shooting their nets, two white lights in a vertical line;
  (ii) when hauling their nets, one white light over one red light in a vertical line;
  (iii) when the net has come fast upon an obstruction, two red lights in a vertical line.
(b) Each vessel of 20 m or more in length engaged in pair trawling shall exhibit:
  (i)   by night, a searchlight directed forward and in the direction of the other vessel of the pair;
  (ii) when shooting or hauling their nets or when the nets have come fast upon an obstruction the lights prescribed in 2(a) above.
(c) A vessel of less than 20 m in length engaged in trawling, whether using demersal or pelagic gear or engaged in pair trawling, may exhibit the lights prescribed in paragraph (a) or (b) of this Section, as appropriate.

3 Signals for Purse Seiners

Vessels engaged in fishing with pursue seine gear may exhibit two yellow lights in a vertical line. These lights shall flash alternately every second and with equal light and occultation duration. These lights may be exhibited only when the vessel is hampered by its fishing gear.

ANNEX III: TECHNICAL DETAILS OF SOUND SIGNAL APPLIANCES

1 Whistles

(a) *Frequencies and range of audibility*: The fundamental frequency of the signal shall lie within the range 70–700 Hz.

The range of audibility of the signal from a whistle shall be determined by those frequencies which may include the fundamental and/or one or more higher frequencies, which lie within the range 180–700 Hz (+1 per cent) and which provide the sound pressure levels specified in paragraph 1(c) below.

(b) *Limits of fundamental frequencies*: To ensure a wide variety of whistle characteristics, the fundamental frequency of a whistle shall be between the following limits:

   (i)   70–200 Hz, for a vessel 200 m or more in length;

   (ii) 130–350 Hz, for a vessel 75 m but less than 200 m in length;

   (iii) 250–750 Hz, for a vessel less than 75 m in length.

(c) *Sound signal intensity and range of audibility*: A whistle fitted in a vessel shall provide, in the direction of maximum intensity of the whistle and at a distance of 1 m from it, a sound pressure level in at least one 1/3rd-octave band within the range of frequencies 180–700 Hz (+1 per cent) of not less than the appropriate figure given in the table below.

Length of vessel in metres	1/3rd-octave band level at 1 m in dB referred to $2 \times 10^{-5} N/m^2$	Audibility range in nautical miles
200 or more	143	2
75 but less than 200	138	1.5
20 but less than 75	130	1
Less than 20	120	0.5

The range of audibility in the table above is for information and is approximately the range at which a whistle may be heard on its forward axis with 90 per cent probability in conditions of still air on board a vessel having average background noise level at the listening posts (taken to be 68 dB in the octave centred on 250 Hz and 63 dB in the octave centred on 500 Hz).

In practice the range at which a whistle may be heard is extremely variable and depends critically on weather conditions; the values given can be regarded as typical but under conditions of strong wind or high ambient noise level at the listening post the range may be much reduced.

(d) *Directional properties*: The sound pressure level of a directional whistle shall be not more than 4 dB below the prescribed sound pressure level on the axis at any direction in the horizontal plane within +45° of the axis. The sound pressure level at any other direction in the horizontal plant shall be not more than 10 dB below the prescribed sound pressure level on the axis, to that the range in any direction will be at least half the range on the forward axis. The sound pressure level shall be measured in that 1/3rd-octave band which determines the audibility range.

(e) *Positioning of whistles*: When a directional whistle is to be used as the only whistle on a vessel, it shall be installed with its maximum intensity directed straight ahead. A whistle shall be placed as high as practicable on a vessel, in order to reduce interception of the emitted sound by obstructions and also to minimise hearing damage risk to personnel. The sound pressure level of the vessel's own signal at listening posts shall not exceed 110 dB (A) and so far as practicable should not exceed 100 dB (A).

(f) *Fitting of more than one whistle*: If whistles are fitted at a distance apart of more than 100 m, it shall be so arranged that they are not sounded simultaneously.

(g) *Combined whistle systems*: If due to the presence of obstructions the sound field of a single whistle or one of the whistles referred to in paragraph 1(f) above is likely to have a zone of greatly reduced signal level, it is recommend that a combined whistle system be fitted so as to overcome this reduction. For the purposes of the Rules a combined whistle system is to be regarded as a single whistle. The whistles of a combined system shall be located at a distance apart of not more than 100 m and arranged to be sounded simultaneously. The frequency of any one whistle shall differ from those of the others by at least 10 Hz.

2 Bell or Gong

(a) *Intensity of signal*: A bell or gong, or other device having smaller sound characteristics shall produce a sound pressure level of not less than 110 dB at a distance of 1 m from it.

(b) *Construction*: Bells and gongs shall be made of corrosion-resistant material and designed to give a clear tone. The diameter of the mouth of the bell shall be not less than 300 mm for vessels of 20 m or more in length, and shall be not less than 200 mm for vessel of 12 m or more, but of less than 20 m in length. Where practicable, a power-driven bell striker is recommended to ensure constant force but manual operation shall be possible. The mass of the striker shall be not less than 3 per cent of the mass of the bell.

3 Approval

The construction of sound signal appliances, their performance and their installation on board the vessel shall be to the satisfaction of the appropriate authority of the State whose flag the vessel is entitled to fly.

ANNEX IV: DISTRESS SIGNALS

(1) The following signals, used or exhibited either together or separately, indicate distress and need of assistance:

(a) a gun or other explosive signal fired at intervals of about a minute;

(b) a continuous sounding with any fog-signalling apparatus;

(c) rockets or shells, throwing red stars fired one at a time at short intervals;

(d) a signal made by radiotelegraphy or by any other signalling method consisting of the group $\cdots --- \cdots$ (SOS) in the Morse Code;

(e) a signal sent by radiotelephony consisting of the spoken word 'MAYDAY';

(f) the International Code Signal of distress by NC;

(g) a signal consisting of a square flag having above or below it a ball or anything resembling a ball;

(h) flames on a vessel (as from a burning tar barrel, oil barrel, etc.);

(i) a rocket parachute flare or a hand flare showing a red light;

(j) a smoke signal giving off orange-coloured smoke;

(k) slowly and repeatedly raising and lowering arms outstretched to each side;

(l) the radiotelegraph alarm signal;

(m) the radiotelephone alarm signal;

(n) signals transmitted by Emergency Position Indicating Radio Beacons;

(o) approved signals transmitted by radio-communication systems, including survival craft radar transponders.

(2) The use of exhibition of any of the foregoing signals except for the purpose of indicating distress and need of assistance and the use of other signals which may be confused with any of the above signals is prohibited.

(3) Attention is drawn to the relevant sections of the International Code of Signals, the *Merchant Ship Search and Rescue Manual* and the following signals:

(a) a piece of orange-coloured canvas with either a black square and circle or other appropriate symbol (for identification from the air);

(b) a dye marker.

Reference: M1642/COLREG 1.

Appendix C: Search and Rescue Helicopter Hi-Line Technique

Extracts from MGN 161 (M+F)

Notice to Owners and Masters of Merchant Vessels, Owners and Skippers of Fishing Vessels and Masters of Yachts and all other Sea-going Vessels

Summary

This notice draws attention to mariners of a technique employed by search and rescue helicopter crews to recover a casualty from a vessel under certain conditions.

HI-LINE TECHNIQUE

In certain weather conditions it may not be possible to winch the helicopter winchman or the strop (rescue harness) from a position directly above a vessel to the vessel's deck. Under such circumstances a weighted rope extension to the winch wire may be lowered to the vessel. This extension is known as a Hi-Line Heaving-in Line and is connected via a weak link to the aircraft's winch hook.

When the Hi-Line Technique is used, once the weighted line is placed on the deck, one crew member must handle the line. **He should take up the slack on the Hi-Line and haul in ONLY when instructed to do so by the helicopter crew by radio message or hand signal. The Hi-Line must NOT be secured to any part of the vessel.** A second crew member should coil the slack line into a bucket or similar container clear of obstructions. It is advisable for the handling crew to wear protective gloves to prevent rope burns. If the helicopter has to break away during the operation the line must be paid out or, if necessary, released completely ensuring that the line passes clear outboard.

As the Hi-Line is paid out, the helicopter will move to one side of the vessel and descend. Normally the winchman will be winched out; the ship's crew should continue to take in the slack. As the winchman or strop approach the vessel the earthing lead or hook must make contact with the vessel to discharge the static electricity before the vessel's crew make contact with the wire. Considerable effort may be needed when pulling the winchman onboard.

Once the casualty has been secured in the strop, the winchman, if he is present, or a member of the vessel's crew, should indicate that all is ready by making a hand signal. The helicopter will commence to winch in the wire. As this occurs a crew member should pay out the Hi-Line, maintaining sufficient firmness to prevent any swing. If the operation involves a single recovery the Hi-Line should be released once the end is reached. If further winching is required to take place then the crew member should maintain a hold on the Hi-Line and repeat the process for the next lift.

If multiple lifts are required two strops may be delivered with the hook and it is required that a casualty is placed into both strops in the normal manner.

Appendix D: Accidents when Using Power-Operated Watertight Doors

Extracts from MGN 35 (M+F) on Guidance to Shipowners, Masters, Safety Officers and Safety Representatives of Merchant Vessels and Owners and Skippers of Fishing Vessels

This Note supersedes Merchant Shipping Notice No. M.1326

Summary

This Note sets out guidance regarding the safe use of power-operated water-tight doors.

Key Points

- Procedure when passing through power-operated watertight doors.
- Procedures when carrying loads through power-operated watertight doors.
- Initial and continuation training in the safe use of power-operated water-tight doors.

1. BACKGROUND

1.1 A number of lives have been lost and serious injury caused by the incorrect operation of power-operated watertight doors.

1.2 In order to reduce the risk of injury to personnel passing through watertight doors some ships have central control units located on the navigating bridge which have two operating positions, one marked 'local control' and the other 'doors closed'. Under normal conditions and potentially hazardous situations the operating condition is set to 'local control'. The 'doors closed' position is only used in emergencies and for drill or testing periods.

1.3 When the bridge central control unit is set at 'local control', any watertight door can be locally opened and locally closed without automatic closure of the door. Since closure of the door requires deliberate action the risk of a person being trapped is very much reduced.

1.4 The 'doors closed' mode will also permit doors to be opened locally, but the doors automatically reclose upon release of the local control mechanism.

1.5 Accidents have occurred when crew members were using the controls provided at the doors to pass through watertight doors which had been closed from the navigating bridge. Under these circumstances if the control at the door is released the door closes automatically with a force sufficient to injure anyone caught in its path.

2. PROCEDURES

2.1 It is essential therefore that when using a watertight door which has been closed, irrespective of the mode of closure, that both the local controls – one on each side of the bulkhead – are held in the 'open' position while passing through the door. That can be done by first fully opening the door using the nearside control with one hand, reaching through the opening to the control on the far side and using the far side control to keep the door fully open until passage is complete.

2.2 A person, when unaccompanied, must have both hands free to operate the controls and should never attempt to carry any load through unassisted. Accordingly supervision should be exercised over any work requiring movement of tools, parts or materials through a door. This will effectively make it a two-man operation – one man to operate the door and another to carry the load.

2.3 To avoid potentially fatal slips, the accumulation of oil leakage in the vicinity of the watertight doors should not be permitted.

2.4 Written instructions need to be provided for the ship on the safe operation of the doors and it is essential that all crew members who may use the doors:
   (a) know what type of control system is fitted;
   (b) are well trained in the correct operating procedure for the system;
   (c) fully appreciate the crushing power of watertight doors.

This crushing power, together with expeditious closing, is necessary to ensure that watertight doors fulfil their primary purpose of ensuring maximum safety of the ship and its crew but if accidents to personnel are to be avoided it is essential that the operating instructions are strictly observed. Permanent notices clearly stating the correct operating procedure must be prominently displayed on both sides of every watertight door.

3. TRAINING

3.1 Under Health and Safety legislation it is required that on all seagoing vessels fitted with power-operated watertight doors there are procedures for training personnel in there use when joining a vessel. Also that training is repeated at regular intervals in order to remind personnel of the dangers of these doors.

3.2 For passenger ships attention is drawn to Merchant Shipping (Passenger Ship Construction: Ships of Classes I, II and II(A)) Regulations 1998 and Merchant Shipping (Passenger Ship Construction: Ships of Classes III to VI(A)) Regulations 1998.

3.3 Attention is also drawn to MGN 71 (M) section 8.

3.4 Records of training should be kept as part of the vessels Safety Management System for inspection at a later date.

3.5 Under the International Safety Management Code shipowners and managers are required to establish safeguards against all identified risks (paragraph 1.2.2.2) and to investigate and analyse non-conformities, accidents and hazardous situations (paragraph 9.1). Then to ensure that training is provided for all personnel concerned (paragraph 6.5). Documentation of such training is kept in accordance with section 11 of the Code. They should also take into account guidelines, etc. recommended by Administrations (paragraph 1.2.3.2).

MSPP1A
The Maritime and Coastguard Agency
Spring Place
Commercial Road
Southampton SO15 1EG
UK

Appendix E: Compliance with Mandatory Ship Reporting Systems

Extracts from MGN 153 (M+F)

Notice to Shipowners, Operators, Masters, Officers and Crew of Merchant Ships, Skippers of Fishing Vessels, Yachts and All Other Sea-going Craft

This note supersedes Marine Guidance Note MGN 24 (M+F)

Summary

Key Points

- UK ships must comply with IMO adopted mandatory ship reporting systems anywhere in the world.
- Mandatory schemes are detailed in the Admiralty List of Radio Signals.
- Non-compliance with mandatory reporting requirements may lead to prosecution.

(1) The Merchant Shipping (Mandatory Ship Reporting) Regulations 1996 came into force on 1 August 1996. The Regulations implement amendments to Chapter V of the Safety of Life at Sea (SOLAS) Convention allowing for the introduction of mandatory ship reporting systems adopted by the International Maritime Organisation (IMO).

(2) UK ships anywhere in the world must comply with any mandatory ship reporting system adopted by the IMO, which applies to them.

(3) The details of mandatory systems will be promulgated through the relevant parts of the Admiralty List of Radio Signals, including any amendments, corrections or replacements. Relevant entries will be annotated with the words: 'Mandatory system under SOLAS Regulation V/8-1'.

(4) Ships to which a mandatory ship reporting system applies should report to the shore-based authority without delay when entering and, if necessary,

when leaving the area covered by the system. A ship may be required to provide additional reports or information to update or modify an earlier report.

(5) Failure of a ship's radio communications equipment would not, in itself, be considered as a failure to comply with the rules of a mandatory ship reporting system. However, Masters should endeavour to restore communications as soon as practicable. If a technical failure prevents a ship from reporting, the Master should enter the fact and reasons for not reporting in the navigational log.

(6) Masters of ships which contravene mandatory ship reporting requirements may be liable to prosecution.

Maritime and Coastguard Agency
Navigation Safety Branch

Index

Instructions for use with Interactive Compact Disc

Welcome to the use of this interactive CD-Rom on the topics of the IALA buoyage system and the Rule of the Road. It should be realised from the onset that this CD is meant as a learning tool for the marine student and any relation to actual circumstances met at sea cannot be assumed to always suit the answer options presented within this compendium.

Once the student has accessed the CD, an introductory screen will be displayed automatically (in the event that the introductory screen does not appear, go to 'My computer' – press CD drive, and then double left click the mouse on the file named 'INDEX'). From the introductory page press 'enter'; initially a main menu will appear. Select either the ROR menu or Buoys menu on this page. Respective menus of exercises will now appear for your selection.

Once an exercise is selected, movement of the mouse to direct the indicator will generate a flow of 10, 15 or 20 questions on that subject. The questions (and answers) are addressed from the point of view of the Watch Officer. Each answer can be checked on screen with additional feedback to both right and wrong answers. However, it is pointed out to the marine student that some questions will have multiple answers and that questions should be read carefully before seeking to check the answer. This is especially important for students studying for Marine Examinations, as examiners would expect to take the first answer offered by a candidate.

NB. These answers are provided in the best of faith by the authors, and it is realised that any actions or options offered may differ from another's point of view. This is not to say that one opinion is right and another is wrong. In certain circumstances, both opinions may be right or both opinions may be equally wrong.

As a learning tool the presentations are made for a single ship in open water conditions (unless otherwise stated), of which the student is assumed to have the 'con'. As such, it should be realised that in real life the Watch Officer would benefit from being able to seek advice from the Master aboard a vessel at sea.

Do not lose sight of the fact that the CD is a learning tool, and circumstances in real life may make some of the options/answers offered here impractical. This CD-Rom is meant as an examination preparation exercise in conjunction with the Self-Examiner Book.

Be advised that:

1. All courses and bearing presented on the programmes are considered as being 'TRUE' (unless otherwise expressed).
2. Vessels fitted with AIS would expect to obtain additional target information, inclusive of the type of ship code. Actions with such information may differ. NB. Vessels under 300 grt would not be expected to have the AIS facility.
3. Candidates for Marine Examinations would be expected to attain 100% in the question areas of Rule of the Road and the Maritime Buoyage subjects, in order to pass the officer qualifications.

Abbreviations for use with Interactive Compact Disc

A/C	Alter Course	grt	Gross Registered Tons	Q	Quick flashing
AIS	Automatic Identification System	IALA	International Association of Lighthouse Authorities	R	Red
ALRS	Admiralty List of Radio Signals	Kts	Knots	Rel	Relative
Brg	Bearing	L.Fl.	Long Flash	Rg	Range
CD	Compact Disc	m	metres	ROR	Rule of the Road
CPA	Closest Point of Approach	Min	Minutes	s	Seconds
deg	Degrees	Misc	Miscellaneous	S	South
E	East	MMSI	Maritime Mobile Service Identity (number)	Spd	Speed
Exe.	Exercise			Stbd	Starboard
F	Fixed	nm	Nautical Miles	T	True
Fl.	Flashing	N	North	TSS	Traffic Separation Scheme
Fwd	Forward	NUC	Not Under Command	VHF	Very High Frequency (Radio)
G	Green	OOW	Officer of the Watch	V.Q.	Very Quick flashing
Gp	Group	Pt.	Port	W	West
				WIG	Wing in Ground (craft)